BLACK MONDAYS

Cover by Tony Greco.

Library of Congress Cataloging-in-Publication Data

Joseph, Joel D.
Black Mondays

1. United States-Constitutional law-Cases.
2. Civil Rights-United States-Cases
3. United States. Supreme Court.
1. Title
KF4549.J67 1987 347.73'26 87-14051
34730735

ISBN 979-8-89589-386-9

Sixth Edition

BLACK MONDAYS

Worst Decisions
Of the Supreme Court

Joel D. Joseph

Sixth Edition

Imprint Books
La Jolla, California

Dedication

This book is dedicated to my parents, Harold and Doris Joseph who inspired me always to seek justice.

Acknowledgments

The author thanks Alex Joseph for his assistance with the third edition of this book. He also thanks Ayfer Jafri for her outstanding editorial assistance and George E. Perryfor his in-depth research. The author also acknowledges the assistance of the following individuals and organizations: American Civil Liberties Union, Professor Chester Antieau, Scott Atlas, Bruce Boraas, Jack Breard, Jr., Carroll County Historical Society, Walter Chaplinski, Harold Chernock, Circuit Court of Carroll County, Maryland, Sarisse Creighton, Arthur Eisenberg, Irving Feiner, Ralph Ginzburg, William Gobitas, Michael Hardwick, Fred Korematsu, Richard Kupfer, Library of Congress, James McNamara, Justice Thurgood Marshall (for the foreword and for his other comments and criticisms), Ernest Mathews, Nat- ional Archives, Carl Neil, John Sheehy, Professor David Skover, James Stanley, Professor Clyde Summers, Su-preme Court Watch, Don Tamaki, United States SupremeCourt Library, Reason Warehime and Kathleen L. Wilde. Last, but not least, I would like to thank my wife, Marlene Joseph, for carefully reading and commenting on the Fourth and Fifth Editions of this book. I would also like to thank Judge Alex Kozinski for his suggestions and comments.

Preface to the Sixth Edition

The first edition of this book was published in 1987 on the 200th anniversary of the enactment of the Constitution of the United States. The second edition was published in1988. The third edition was published in 2008. Only four new decisions were added to the third edition. Five more cases were added to the fourth edition.

The Supreme Court has ventured more into politics in the past decade than at any time in its history. *Bush v. Gore* was added to the third edition. *Citizens United* has been added to the third edition as are two gun control decisions. In addition, a case about violent video games was added to the third edition. The Supreme Court, by failing to allow regulation of violent video games and firearms, has contributed to the violent cul-ture of the United States.

Further, when the Court refuses to consider a case because it finds there is no "standing," the nation is deprived of a ruling on the merits. The Supreme Court recently decided *Clapper v. Amnesty International.* Amnesty International was challenging the government's surveillance program that allowed eavesdropping on private citizens and organizations. The Court ruled, by a 5-4 majority that since Amnesty International could not prove that the government spied on it, that it was not injured, and
thus had no standing to sue.

That ruling came months before Edward Snowden exposed the extent of the National Security Agency's spying, eavesdropping, wiretapping and electronic surveillance. In addition to the Supreme Court ducking this considerable issue, the Foreign Intelligence Surveillance Court (FISC) provides no way for an individual or company to appeal an order allowing spying on it because the proceedings are in secret.

Many people consider the FISC to be a parallel Supreme Court that is taking away liberties from citizens and organizations in the United States. While that court will notbe discussed in this book, the Chief Justice of the Supreme Court appoints all eleven members of this secret court. Now ten of the eleven members of the FISC are Republicans, not subject to confirmation by the United States Senate. So, we may want to add John Robert's appointments to the FISC as some of the worst decisions of the Supreme Court or at least the worst decisions of the Chief Justice of the Supreme Court.

The Sixth Edition adds two cases: the case overturning the Chevron Deference Doctrine and the Presidential Immunity case, two cases that give the Supreme Court and the President new powers.

I am quite worried that the current Supreme Court is one of the worst in history. It is far too likely to rule for corporate rights against individual rights, to rule that the government can do no wrong and is immune when it errs, to substitute its opinions for those of legislators and, in general, be unaware of the real world beyond its ivory tower.

Table of Contents

Foreword

by Justice Thurgood Marshall

Nineteen-eighty-seven marked the 200th anniversary of the United States Constitution. The planned commemoration spanned three years, and I am told 1987 was "dedicated to the memory of the Founders and the document they drafted in Philadelphia."[1] We are to "recall the achievements of our Founders and the knowledge and experience that inspired them, the nature of the governmentthey established, its origins, its character, and its ends, and the rights and privileges of citizenship, as well as its attendant responsibilities."[2]

Like many anniversary celebrations, the plan for 1987 took particular events and held them up as the source of all the very best that has followed. Patriotic feelings surely swelled, prompting proud proclamations of the wisdom, foresight, and sense of justice shared by the Framers and reflected in a written document now yellowed with age. This is unfortunate—not that patriotism itself, but the tendency for the celebration to oversimplify, and overlook the many other events that have been instrumental to our achievements as a nation. The focus of this celebration invited a complacent belief that the vision of those who debated and compromised in Philadelphia yielded the "more perfect Union" it is said wenow enjoy.

I cannot accept this invitation, for I do not believe that the meaning of the Constitution was forever "fixed" at the Philadelphia Convention. Nor do I find the wisdom, foresight, and sense of justice exhibited by the Framers particularly profound. To the contrary, the government they devised was defective from the start, requiring several

amendments, a civil war, and momentous social transformation to attain the system of constitutionalgovernment,
and its respect for the individual freedoms andhuman rights,
we hold as fundamental today. When contemporary
Americans cite "The Constitution," they invoke a concept
that is vastly different from what the Framers barely began
to construct two centuries ago. For a sense of the evolving
nature of the Constitution we need look no further than the
first three words of the document's preamble: "We the
People." When the Founding Fathers used this phrase in
1787, they did not have in mind the majority of America's
citizens. "We the People" included, in the words of the
Framers, "the whole Number of free Persons."[3] On a matter
so basic as the right to vote, for example, Negro slaves were
excluded, although they were counted for representational
purposes at three-fifths each. Women did not gain the right
to vote for over a hundred and thirty years.[4]

These omissions were intentional. The record of the
Framers' debates on the slave question is especially clear.
The Southern States acceded to the demands of the New
England States for giving Congress broad power to regulate
commerce, in exchange for the right to continue the slave
trade. The economic interests of the regions coalesced:
New Englanders engaged in the "carrying trade" wouldprofit
from transporting slaves from Africa as well as goods
produced in America by slave labor. The perpetuation of
slavery ensured the primary source of wealth in the Southern
States.

Despite this clear understanding of the role slavery would
play in the new republic, use of the words "slaves" and
"slavery" was carefully avoided in the original document.

Political representation in the lower House of Congress was to be based on the population of "free Persons" in each State, plus three-fifths of all "other persons."[5] Moral principles against slavery, for those who had them, were compromised, with no explanation of the conflicting principles for which the American Revolutionary War has ostensibly been fought: the self-evident truths "that all men are created equal, that they are endowed by their Creator with certain unalienable Rights, that among these are Life, Liberty and the pursuit ofHappiness."[6]

It was not the first such compromise. Even these ringing phrases from the Declaration of Independence are filled with irony, for an early draft of what became that Declaration assailed the King of England for encouraging slave rebellions.[7] The final draft adopted in 1776 did not contain this criticism. And so again at theConstitutional Convention eloquent objections to the institution of slavery went unheeded, and its opponents eventually consented to a document which laid a foundation for the tragic events that were to follow.

Pennsylvania's Gouverneur Morris provides an example. He opposed slavery and the counting of slaves in determining the basis for representation in Congress. At the Convention he objected that: "the inhabitants of Georgia (or) South Carolina who goes to the coast of Africa, and in defiance of the most sacred laws of humanity tears away his fellow creatures from their dearest connections and damns them to the most cruel bondages, shall have more votes in a Government instituted for the protection of the rights of mankind, than the Citizen of Pennsylvania or New Jersey who views with a laudable horror, so nefariousa practice.[8]

And yet Gouverneur Morris eventually accepted the three-fifths accommodation. In fact, he wrote the final draft of the Constitution, the very document the bicentennial will commemorate. As a result of the compromise, the right ofthe Southern States to continue importing slaves was extended, officially, at least until 1808. We know that it actually lasted a good deal longer, as the Framers possessedno monopoly on the ability to trade moral principles for self-interest. But they nevertheless set an unfortunate example. Slaves could be imported, if the commercial interests of the North were protected. To make the compromise even more palatable, customs duties would be imposed at up to ten dollars per slave as a means of raising public revenues.[9]

No doubt it will be said, when the unpleasant truth of the history of slavery in America is mentioned during this bicentennial year, that the Constitution was a product of its times, and embodied a compromise which, under other circumstances, would not have been made. But the effects of the Framers' compromise have remained for generations. They arose from the contradiction between guaranteeing liberty and justice to all, and denying both to Negroes.

The original intent of the phrase, "We the People," was far too clear for any ameliorating construction. Writing for the Supreme Court in 1857, Chief Justice Taney penned the following passage in the *Dred Scott* case,[10] on the issue whether, in the eyes of the Framers, slaves were"constituent members of the sovereignty," and were to beincluded among "We the People":

> We think they are not, and that they are not included, and were not intended to be included.... They had for more than a century before been regarded as beings of an inferior order, and altogether unfit to associate with the white race . . .; and so far inferior, that they had no

rights which the white manwas bound to respect;
and that the negro mightjustly and lawfully be
reduced to slavery for his benefit . . . .
(A)ccordingly, a negro of the African race was
regarded ... as an article ofproperty, and held, and
bought and sold as such. (N)o one seems to have
doubted the correctness of the prevailing opinion of
the time.

And so, nearly seven decades after the Constitutional
Convention, the Supreme Court reaffirmed the prevailing
opinion of the Framers regarding the rights of Negroes in
America. It took a bloody civil war before the 13th
Amendment would be adopted to abolish slavery, though not
the consequences slavery would have for future Americans.

While the Union survived the civil war, the Constitution
didnot. In its place arose a new, more promising basis for
justice and equality, the 14th Amendment, ensuring
protection of the life, liberty, and property of all persons
against deprivations without due process, and guaranteeing
equal protection of the laws. And yet almost another century
would pass before any significant recognition was obtained
of the rights of black Americans to share equally even in
such basic opportunities as education, housing, and employment, and to have their votes counted, and counted
equally. In the meantime, blacks joined America's military
to fight its wars and invested untold hours working in its
factories and on its farms, contributing to the development
of this country's magnificent wealth and waiting to share in
its prosperity.

What is striking is the role legal principles have played throughout America's history in determining the conditions of Negroes. They were enslaved by law, emancipated by law, disenfranchised by law and segregated by law; and finally they have begun to win equality by law. Along the way, new constitutional principles have emerged to meet the challenges of a changing society. The progress has been dramatic, and it will continue.

The men who gathered in Philadelphia in 1787 could not have envisioned these changes. They could not have imagined, nor would they have accepted, that the document they were drafting would one day be construed by a Supreme Court to which had been appointed a woman and the descendent of an African slave. "We the People" no longer enslave, but the credit does not belong to the Framers. It belongs to those who refused to acquiesce in the outdated notions of "liberty," "justice," and "equality," and who strived to better them.

And so we must be careful, when focusing on the events which took place in Philadelphia two centuries ago, that we not overlook the momentous events which fol- lowed, and thereby lose our proper sense of perspective. Otherwise, the odds are that for many Americans the bicentennial celebration will be little more than a blindpilgrimage to the shrine of the original document now storedin a vault in the National Archives. If we seek, instead, a sensitive understanding of the Constitution's inherent defects, and its promising evolution through 200 yearsof history, the celebration of the "Miracle at Phila- delphia"[11] will, in my view, be a far more meaningful and humbling experience. We will see that the true miracle was not the birth of the Constitution but its life nurtured through two turbulent centuries of our own making, and a life embodying much good fortune that was not.

Thus, in this bicentennial year, we may not all participate in the festivities with flag-waving fervor. Somemay more quietly commemorate the suffering, struggle, and sacrifice that has triumphed over much of what waswrong with the original document, and observe the anniversary with hopes not realized and promises notfulfilled. I plan to celebrate the bicentennial of the Constitution as a living document, including the Bill of Rights and the other amendments protecting individual freedoms and human rights.

Endnotes

1. Commission on the Bicentennial of the United States Constitution, First Full Year's Report, at 7 (September 1986).

2. *Ibid,* at 6.

3. *United States Constitution,* Art. 1, Section 2 (September 17, 1787).

4. The 19th Amendment (ratified in 1920).

5 *United States Constitution,* Art. 1, Section 2 (September 17, 1787)

6. *Declaration of Independence (July 4, 1776).*

7. *See Becker, The Declaration of Independence: A Study in the History of Political Ideas* 147 (1942).

8. Farrant, ed., *The Records of the Federal Convention of 1787, vol. 11,* 222 (New Haven, Conn., *1911).*

9. *United States Constitution,* Art. 1, Section *9* (September 17, 1787).

10. 19 How. (60 U.S.) 393, 405, 407-408 (1857).

11. Bowen, *Miracle at Philadelphia: The Story of the Constitutional Convention May to September* 1787 (Boston, 1966).

Chapter One

Introduction

*"We have long suffered under base prostitution of
law to party passions in one judge,
and the imbecility of another."*
—Thomas Jefferson

The Constitution of the United States was, and as amended is, an excellent document. It is the oldest written constitution still in force in the world and has been used asa model for the constitutions of many other nations.

Although I generally agree with the views of Justice Marshall, expressed in his opinions and expressed in the foreword to this book, I disagree with his view that the Constitution was defective from the start. Of course it had defects. Some of the major defects were quickly corrected by passing the first ten amendments known as the Bill of Rights in 1791, just two years after the Constitution went into effect. The First Amendment, which includes the right to free speech and the right to freedom of religion, was light years ahead of the standards of other nations at the time, and is still far ahead of the standards of human rights throughout most of the world today.

Most of the problems cited by Justice Marshall stem from those whose duty it is to interpret the Constitution:

the nine justices of the Supreme Court, and not from the document itself.

For example, Justice Marshall cites *Dred Scott v. Sandford* in his foreword. In that case, the Supreme Court ruled that slaves and former slaves were not citizens of the United States. Justice Marshall blames the Framers of the Constitution for the *Dred Scott* decision (see Chapter Fourteen).

However, nowhere in the Constitution does it state that Americans of African descent are not citizens of the United States. The Constitution defines "We the People" of the United States as the number of "free Persons" residing in the States. Slavery was recognized in theConstitution as part of a compromise to form this nation.In the document, slaves were to be counted as three-fifthsof a free person for the purposes of representation inCongress. However, at the time the Constitution waswritten there were a significant number of Negro free Persons. These citizens were allowed to vote.

The Supreme Court should have recognized freeAfrican-Americans as citizens. The majority of the justicesof the Supreme Court who ruled in the *Dred Scott* casewere from the slave states, and their biases and prejudicesshaped the opinions that they wrote. I blame the membersof the Supreme Court for the *Dred Scott* decision, not the Constitution. Although we are a nation of laws, notmen, it takes men (and women) to interpret those laws. The Supreme Court's erroneous decision in the *Dred Scott*case, not the Constitution, led to the War Between the States. Concerning women's rights, Justice Marshall implied that the Constitution was defective in that it deniedwomen the right to vote. Nowhere in the Constitution does it state that only men had the right to vote.

As with the rights of Negroes, the Supreme Court, with

no constitutional basis, the rights of Negroes, the Supreme Court, with noconstitutional basis, unanimously ruled in 1875 that women did not have the right to vote (see Chapter Eighteen). And that was *after* the Fourteenth Amendment, with its equal protection clause was enacted. It took the Nineteenth Amendment, which overturned that decision of the Supreme Court to clarify the Constitution and to man- date that women had the right to vote.

I agree with Justice Marshall that too much effort is now being spent waving the flag and printing the Constitution on fast food placemats. The major thrust of this book book is to examine the worst twenty or so decisionsof the Supreme Court, out of thousands of cases, so that we can avoid making similar mistakes in the future.

Black Mondays

The title to this book was selected because most of the Supreme Court's decisions are announced on Monday. This has been so for most of the court's history. In recentyears, however, the court's backlog has made it necessary to issue some decisions on other days of the week.

Criteria for Selection of Cases

Numerous associations and law professors were asked for nominations of the Supreme Court's "worst decisions." In order to qualify for inclusion in this book, a case had to have been poorly reasoned as well as had a major impacton the freedoms of American citizens. In a few cases the Supreme Court admitted that it had erred in its decision in an earlier case. In others, such as the *Japanese Internment* case (see Chapter Seventeen), later actions of Congress and overseas reactions made it clear that the decision was overruled by the "court of history."

Most cases never reach the Supreme Court. Many of the worst decisions of courts come at the lowest levels. Many of those cases are not appealed. In addition, the Supreme Court declines to review thousands of cases every year. Although a denial of review can be a horrendous decision, I only considered cases when the Supreme Court granted review and issued an opinion in a case. Hundreds of cases were considered and the list was narrowed to twenty-four.

Most of the cases selected for inclusion in this book had strong dissenting opinions. Some were close cases (five to four) and very few were unanimous. The unanimous decisions tended to rely on a series of earlier cases where the court tended not to focus on the express language of the Constitution.

What Potter Stewart said of pornography-he could not define it but "knew it when he saw it"—applies to an attempt to define the worst decisions. Both are in the minds of the readers. One man's pornography is another man's art. What is a bad decision for one person might be a good decision for another.

Concerning the pornography decisions of the court, unlike other areas of law, it was very difficult to single out one case that was especially loathsome. For much of the twentieth century, the Supreme Court has struggled without success to define pornography and to exclude it from First Amendment protection. Every decade theCourt tinkers with its definition, as it has done again thisyear. Justice Douglas opposed all of these definitions andfelt that until there was a constitutional amendment concerning the regulation of pornography, the courtshould not become the censor of last resort. Justice Stewart, although opposing "hardcore pornography," felt that the worst Supreme Court decision during his tenure was the *Ginz-*

burg censorship case. Many other "obscenity" cases could have also been included.

Research Techniques

In addition to the traditional sources for legal research, I interviewed the parties and attorneys involved in most of the cases cited in this book. This was done in an attempt to add flesh to the bare facts of the cases and to bring them to life. These interviews filled in missing facts unavailable elsewhere, including what had happened to the parties after the decisions were rendered by the Supreme Court. Concerning the older cases, where all of the parties and attorneys were deceased, old newspapers, magazines, archives and other sources were used.

Organization

The cases in the book are divided into seven parts. Freedom of Religion is the first, and although none of the cases in that part involve anyone going to jail or sufferingan atrocious injustice, nevertheless the fundamental principle of religious tolerance was violated. Freedomof religion is one fundamental right which sets the United States apart from many other nations, including England. This is one reason that many sought refuge in this country.

The second part includes two cases involving freedom of association and the right to privacy. These cases involve the right to choose your roommates, and the right to privacy in your bedroom. The third part includes seven freedom of speech cases. The cases are quite varied, involving disputes concerning "fighting words," "dirty words," unpopular speakers, going door-to-door, freedom of speech in shopping malls and the right to protest against the Soviet Union. The first three parts of the book stem from rights enumerated in the First Amendment, which, to a large extent, separates free countries from totalitarian regimes.

Part Four covers equal protection of the law. It includes the landmark civil rights cases as well as some lesser-known discrimination decisions. Few Americans are aware that the Supreme Court, not the Constitution, denied women the right to vote over a hundred years ago. The Japanese Internment case is also included in this part.

Part Five involves property rights. The two cases in this part involve the government taking property from private individuals and the right of citizens to own guns.

The sixth part, concerned with criminal rights, includes five cases. These cases involved the right to counsel, cruel and unusual punishment and the presumption of innocence. The court held that it was not cruel or unusual to sentence a man to life imprisonment for stealing $229.11 in three non-violent crimes. Newly added are cases concerning strip searches and the rights of foreign defendants under international law.

The last part of this book deals with access to justice. Four cases are included, two concerning the rights of veterans. The court denied plaintiffs in these cases the right to sue or granted defendant immunity from suit. Immunity from suit was granted to the Army, the FBI and judges, even though the constitutional rights of   the plaintiffs were violated.

This book does not have to be read in order. If women's rights, or civil rights, or free speech interest you most, read those cases first. The last part of the book containssome of the most compelling cases, so it should not be missed.

Why Good Courts Make Bad Decisions

Even the best courts occasionally make bad decisions. Many bad decisions are made during national emergencies, especially during war time. It was during the chaos of World War II that the court approved the internment of American citizens of Japanese descent. Ironically, one of the advocates of the Japanese-American internment, Earl Warren, became, in my opinion, one of the best chief justices of the Supreme Court.

Another reason for poor decisions is that the courts sometimes rely on history to make decisions for them. For example, the court will say, "this practice has gone unchallenged for 150 years."

Or the court will rely on early decisions which rely on an earlier decision. So what! One early case can breed hundreds of clones all resting on one lousy, albeit early, decision. The separate but equal cases were built up this way.

In a related manner, the court will often get wound up in its own line of cases on a particular subject. For example, in the *Soviet Boycott* case (see Chapter Eleven) the court followed its line of labor law cases on secondary boycotts and lost sight of the constitutional rights of citizens. In that case, the court unanimously ruled that American longshoremen could not boycott Soviet ships in protest against the Russian invasion of Afghanistan. That isthe only case in this book where I parted company with Justice Marshall. The next time the court examines a clash between our labor laws and the right to free speech and association, perhaps the First Amendment will prevail.

Amending the Constitution

Because the Framers knew that the Constitution was not perfect, they built in an amendment process. The Framers recognized that the compromises which were struck in 1787 would not last forever. The amendment process was made to be intentionally difficult. After the Bill of Rights was enacted we have had less than one amendment per decade.

If the Constitution is to be perfected, it has to be carefully amended. One major problem with the document that no judge will point out is that the Constitution gives federal judges life tenure. In theory, this makes judges independent. In reality it keeps inept judges on the bench. Currently, the only way to remove a federal judge is by Congressional impeachment.

Life expectancy has increased dramatically since the Constitution was enacted. A life appointment made then might have meant a fifteen-year judgeship. Now it can be a forty-year appointment, or more. A Constitutionalamendment providing for judicial terms of ten years (withfive years of additional salary for retirement or for a buffer period) would give judges independence while instituting new energy into the judiciary. An excellent judge could serve ten years at the district court level, ten at the appellate level, and ten at the Supreme Court. No judgewould be allowed to be reappointed at the lower twolevels. At the Supreme Court reappointment would be reasonable because the Senate exercises careful monitoring of the highest court.

Most observers agree that the electoral college needs amending. The two-year term of members of Congress is also the target of many who want to amend the document. The principle of "one person, one vote" is violated by an early constitutional compromise: the United States Senate. It is undemocratic that New York State should get only two senators while Wyoming and Hawaii (not admitted to the Union until relatively recently and not parties to the original compromise) and other sparsely populated states should get the same number of senators. I propose that the Senate be kept to one hundred members, and that each state get at least one. However, the other fifty Senate seats should be appointed by population. New York may get eight, Illinois five and Delaware one. The senators would still represent their states at large, but larger states would get a new senator more often. There is no longer any justification for this oddity in our Constitution.

Conclusion

I hope that this book will cause citizens, students, lawyers and judges to think about our Constitution. Since the amendment process was built into it, it is not made out of stone. I also hope that this book will cause the nation to turn its attention to the quality of our judges at all levels.

PART 1
Freedom of Religion

Chapter Two

The Day of Rest

"Congress shall make no law respecting an establishment of religion, or prohibiting the free exercise thereof"

—First Amendment

Springfield, Massachusetts has only a small Jewish population. However, beginning in 1953 it supported the Crown Kosher Super Market at 57 Sumner Avenue. Orthodox Jews from as far away as Vermont and Connecticut shopped in Harold Chernock's market because their small towns did not have a purveyor of kosher foods. The closest kosher supermarket was twenty-six miles away in Hartford, Connecticut.

Because Mr. Chernock and other owners of the store were Orthodox Jews, the Crown market closed at sundown on Friday night and did not reopen until Sunday morning. Observance of the Jewish sabbath required this practice. More than one-third of Crown's business took place on Sundays.

Crown Kosher Super Market during the 1960s, courtesy of Harold Chernock.

The Lord's Day

Massachusetts had a Sunday closing law called the "Lord's Day Statute" which required most stores to be closed on Sunday. The Massachusetts law was originally enacted in 1653, more than one hundred years before the U.S. Constitution was ratified The early law undeniablyhad a religious purpose, to compel observance of the Christian sabbath. Although the law had been amendedover the 300-year period, it remained in effect in the twentieth century.

The Law provided:

> Whoever on the Lord's day keeps open his shop, warehouse or workhouse, or does any manner of labor, business or work, except Works of necessity and charity, shall be punished by a fine of fifty dollars.

On May 2nd, May 30th and June 6th, 1954 (all Sundays), members of the Springfield Police Department went to the Crown Market and made purchases of food items. Based on those "illegal" sales three criminal complaints were filed against Mr. Chernock. He was tried and convicted of violating the "Lord's Day Statute" on June 15, 1954 and was fined forty-five dollars.

Raymond P. Gallagher, the Chief of Police of Springfield, threatened to continue to enforce the "Lord's Day" law. To prevent this harassment, the Crown Kosher Super Market and three of its customers sued Mr. Gallagher in Federal Court in Boston. The Chief Rabbi of Massachusettsjoined them in the case. They argued that the Sunday closing law violated the First Amendment's principles of separation of church and state. The Supreme Court hadearlier ruled that the First Amendment applied to the states as well as to the Federal Government.

In Federal Court

The federal court sitting in Boston ruled that the Lord's Day Statute was unconstitutional and enjoined the Chief of Police from enforcing it. The panel of three judgesruled against the validity of the law by a two to one vote with Judge McCarthy dissenting. The Commonwealth of Massachusetts appealed to the United States Supreme Court. While the appeal progressed, Crown continued to open on Sundays.

The Supreme Court

On Monday, May 29th, 1961, the Supreme Court ruled six to three that the Massachusetts law did not violate the constitutional provision which separates church and state.[1] The court found that, although the origins of the law were undoubtedly religious, its purpose had become secular. A day of rest, claimed the court, is good for people, and the idea of a day of rest need not have religious implications. Further, the court argued, the day of rest should be uniform for all members of the society.

The Supreme Court's decision was wrongly decided because a trulysecular law could have exempted stores like Crown. The law had seventy exceptions, allowing stores to selltobacco, ice cream, milk, bread, live bait for fishing andnewspapers. With all of these exceptions, why not haveone more for kosher food stores? Or, why not allow stores to close on one day other than Sunday?

Even if it is granted that a day of rest is a good thing, why must everyone rest on the same day? The "Lord'sDay Statute" allowed the Boston Celticsto playbasketball, the Bruins to play hockey and the Red Soxbaseball. Don't professional athletes need a day of restalso? Why should a law permit Larry Bird of the Celticsto shoot a basketball while forbidding a kosher butcher from chopping meat? What great harm would have cometo Springfield had Crown been allowed to open on Sunday? Consid-erable harm could come, however, to a small grocery store forced to stay closed on Sunday, theonly day Orthodox Jewish customers who work on weekdays are able to do their shopping.

Freedom of religion is one of the fundamental rights provided in the Constitution. Religious persecution forced many people to seek asylum in the United States. Yet the

Supreme Court turned a deaf ear to religious tolerance and showed its insensitivity to the concept of separation of church and state. Three justices dissented. One of them, Justice William O. Douglas, said:

> The question is whether a State can impose criminal sanctions on those who, unlike the Christian majority that makes up our society, worship on a different day or do not share the religious scruples of the majority.
>
> If the 'free exercise' of religion were subject to reasonable regulation, as it is under some constitutions, or if all laws "respecting establishment of religion" were not proscribed, I could understand how rational men, representing a predominantly Christian civilization, might think that Sunday laws did not unreasonably interfere with anyone's free exercise of religion.
>
> I dissent from applying criminal sanctions against any of the complainants since to do so implicates the state in religious matters contrary to the constitutional mandate.

Justice Stewart joined Justice Douglas in dissent. He remarked,

> Massachusetts has passed a law which compels an Orthodox Jew to choose between his religious faith and his economic survival. That is a cruel choice. It is a choice which I think no State can constitutionally demand.

> For me this is notsomething that can be
> swept under the rugand forgotten in the
> interest of Sundaytogetherness. I think the
> impact of this law on these "religious men"
> grossly violatestheir constitutional right to
> free exercise of their religion.

A majority of the court forgot a warning issued during the Congressional discussion of the First Amendment:[2]

> The rights of conscience are, in their nature, of particular delicacy, and will bear the gentlest touch of governmental hand.
>
> Freedom of thought and religion are fundamental freedoms. It can be argued that they are even more fundamental than free speech, because the free exercise of these rights has virtually no impact on others. Thought and religion are most often in the mind of the believer, while speech by its very nature thrusts itself at others.

Epilogue

The year after the Supreme Court's decision the Commonwealth of Massachusetts changed its "Lord's Day Statute" to allow the Crown Market to open for business on Sundays.

Crown Kosher Super Market stayed in business for twenty-four years, from 1953 until 1979. In 1979 Harold Chernock sold the building that housed the market to the Friendly Ice Cream Company, and retired.

Friendly's Ice Cream tore down the market and built one of its restaurants on the site.

Endnotes

1   *1. Gallagher v. Crown Kosher Super Market,* 366 U.S. 617 (1961).

2. 1: Annals of Congress, 730 (remarks of Rep. Daniel Carroll of Maryland, August 15th, 1789).

Chapter Three

Freedom of Thought

"If there is any principle of the Constitution that more imperatively calls for attachment than any other it is the principle of free thought-not free thought for those whoagree with us but freedom for the thought that we hate"

—Oliver Wendell Holmes

The Flag Salute Case

Founded in 1831, Minersville, Pennsylvania, is a small town of some 10,000 souls in eastern Pennsylvania midway between Harrisburg and Wilkes-Barre. True to its name, coal mining is the principal industry in this town.

One afternoon, in the Depression year of 1936, Lillian Gobitas and her brother William, ages twelve and ten

respectively, were sent home from school. The principal of
the school had told the Gobitas children that they could no
longer attend the Minersville schools unless they agreed to
salute the American flag at the opening exercises each
morning.

Other children, along with their teachers, repeated the
Pledge of Allegiance without objection. The Gobitas
children refused to salute the flag because of theirreligious
upbringing. The Gobitas family belonged to the Jehovah's
Witnesses faith. They took the Ten Commandments liter-
ally and believed that when a personsalutes a flag, any
flag, he was bowing down before agraven image. Walter
and Ruth Gobitas told their childrenthat their religion
prohibited them from saying the Pledge of Allegiance and
saluting the flag at school or anywhere else.

The Minersville Board of Education placed the Pledge
of Allegiance and the flag salute in the daily publicschool
program as they felt this would promote patriotismand
good citizenship. The Gobitas family did not ask thatthe
ceremony be abolished, only that their children be excused
from the ceremony if they had an objection to it.

The members of the Minersville Board of Education
discussed the issue and were unable to understand how
saluting the flag could hurt any American child. The board
consisted of the town's leading citizens, doctors, and
businessmen. The board declined to make an exceptionfor
the Gobitas children and directed the Superintendentof
Schools, Charles Roudabush, to expel the children.

Roudabush followed the board's directive. Rather than
having his children violate their religious faith, Walter
Gobitas took Lillian and William out of the public school
system and enrolled them in the Jones Kingdom School,

a private school located in the nearby town of Andreas, Pennsylvania. The Gobitas family was not poor but could not really afford the expenses of a private school.

Reluctant Plaintiff

Mr. Gobitas discussed his dilemma with members of his church. They advised him to discuss the situation with the American Civil Liberties Union. Walter Gobitas regretted that he had to file suit against the school board, but believed it was the right thing to do. He sued on behalf of his children, and on his own behalf, to be relieved of the financial burden of sending his children to private school. He emphasized that the laws of Pennsylvania madeattendance at school compulsory. At the same timethe local schoolboard had expelled his children for practicing their religion.

The school board, on the other hand, argued simply that it is proper to instill patriotism and a sense of country in schoolchildren and that the right of the Minersville schools to do so should override the children's religious rights.

William and Lillian Gobitas with their father.

The case was assigned to Judge Albert Maris in thefederal court in Philadelphia. Maris was a new judge, having just been appointed to the court by President Franklin D. Roosevelt. Judge Maris ruled in favor of the Gobitas family:

> The refusal of Lillian and William to salute the flag in the Minersville Public School was based solely upon their sincerely held religious convictions that the act was forbidden by the express command of God as set forth in the Bible.
>
> * * *
>
> The enforcement of defendants' regulation requiring the flag salute by children whoare sincerely opposed to it upon con-scientious religious grounds is not a reasonable method of teaching civics, including loyalty to the State and FederalGovernment, but tends to have the contrary effect upon such children.

Judge Maris ordered the school board to pay $3,200 to the Gobitas family to reimburse them for the expense of private schooling. In addition, he issued a restraining order requiring the school to reinstate the Gobitas children and prohibited the school from requiring them to salute theflag and say the Pledge of Allegiance.

The School Board's Appeal

The Board of Education couldn't accept Judge Maris' order. They voted to appeal the decision to the Court of Appeals. Apparently, the board had to justify its earlier decisions which had cost the community a tidy sum for attorneys' fees, in addition to the award against it.

In 1939 the Third Circuit Court of Appeals in Philadelphia issued its decision. The three-judge panel was unanimous in its decision against the school board. Judge Clark wrote the opinion of the court, castigating Pennsylvania and seventeen other large states with flag salute policies. According to the court, some 120 students had been victimized by their policies.

Judge Clark compared the policy of these large states to those of Adolf Hitler, who during the same decade had declared that Jehovah's Witnesses were quacks and that all of their literature should be confiscated. The court concluded that the Board of Education of Minersville violated the basic principles upon which the Commonwealth of Pennsylvania was founded. Judge Clark said:

> The state was colonized by William Penn. He came to the new country because hisrefusal to subordinate religious scruples to educational coercion led to his expulsion from Oxford University in the old.

The Supreme Court

The Board of Education appealed Judge Clark's ruling to the United States Supreme Court. The highest court agreed to hear the case. On behalf of the school board, Joseph W. Henderson, a Philadelphia lawyer, argued the case before the Supreme Court. George K. Gardner of Boston, a Harvard Law School professor, argued on behalf of Mr. Gobitas and his children. A team of ACLU lawyers joined Professor Gardner in handling the case. The American Bar Association, which ordinarily avoids taking a position on pending cases, submitted a brief on behalf of the Gobitis family.

The brief stated: "We suggest that no American court should presume to tell any person that he is wrong in his opinion as to how he may best serve the God in which he believes." The Bar Association added that there is no public need for a compulsory flag salute.

Despite all of the legal talent and arguments made for the Gobitas family, on Monday, June 3rd, 1940, the Su-preme Court ruled eight to one against them.[1] Justice Felix Frankfurter, a Jewish immigrant from Vienna, Austria, wrote the opinion for the court. The court decided that it should not interfere with the authority of the local school board, and that, indeed, schoolchildren should be instilled with a sense of patriotism. Justice Stone wrote the lone dissenting opinion. On the day the decision was announced, Justice Frankfurter, although expected to read his opinion, merely stated the result. Justice Stone was so agitated by the case that he read his dissent in full. He said "the mandatory flag salute, does more than suppress freedom of speech and more than prohibit the free exercise of religion . . . . For by this law the state seeks to coerce these children to express a sentiment which, as they interpret it, they do not entertain, and which violates their deepest religious convictions."

Public Reaction

The large-scale reaction of the media and the American people was an unusual response to a Supreme Court decision. More than 170 leading newspapers strongly crit-icized the decision while only a handful supported it. The *St. Louis Post-Dispatch* said: "Wethink its decision is a vio-lation of American principle. We think it is a surrender to popular hysteria. If patriotism depends upon such things as this—upon a violation of a fundamental right of religious freedom, then it becomes not a noble emotion of love for country, but something to be rammed down our throats by the law."

Soon after the decision was handed down, a rash of violent episodes victimized Jehovah's Witnesses around the country. A Jehovah's Witnesses Kingdom Hall was burned in Kennebunkport, Maine. A meeting of Witnesses in Rockville, Maryland was attacked. The lawyer for a group of Jehovah's Witnesses in Connorsville, Indiana was beaten and driven from town. In Litchfield, Illinois a caravan of Witnesses' cars was overturned.

In Minersville, the Gobitas family received threatening phone calls telling them to get out of town. Citizens boycotted Mr. Gobitas' grocery store. The boycott, in addition to private school expenses, put a tremendous financial strain on the Gobitas family. In many states flag salute regulations were strictly enforced, many Jehovah's Witnesses were expelled, and some were sent to reform school.

In 1941 West Virginia passed a compulsory flag salute law. Three Jehovah's Witnesses students who were expelled from school filed suit in Charleston, West Virginia. Their case worked its way to the Supreme Court rapidly. By 1943 the court was ready to make its decision.

During the three years between the Gobitis[1] case and *West Virginia State Board of Education v. Barnette,* the composition of the Supreme Court had changed dramatically. Justices McReynolds and Hughes had retired. Justice Stone was elevated to Chief Justice and Robert Jackson and James Byrnes were appointed to the bench. In the meantime, Justices Black, Douglas and Murphy distanced themselves from the *Gobitis* decision.

The Supreme Court handed down its ruling on Flag Day, Monday, June 14th, 1943. In three years, the Supreme Court made its quickest and most complete reversal in its history. The court ruled six to three, directly overruling the *Gobitis* decision. Justice Jackson wrote a virulent majority opinion; Justice Frankfurter wrote a bitter dissenting opinion.

Epilogue

The Gobitas children graduated from private schools and then moved to Brooklyn, New York to work at Watchtower, the national headquarters of the Jehovah's Witnesses. William Gobitas worked there for ten years. He met his future wife and moved to her hometown near Mil-waukee, Wisconsin, where he now resides. His three daughters attended the Waubeka-Freedonia schools and were not required to pledge allegiance to the flag. After working for an insurance company for twenty years, Mr. Gobitas took early retirement in 1976.

Lillian Gobitas met her future husband, Irwin Klose, while working at the Watchtower. Mr. Klose, also a Jehovah's Witness, escaped from Nazi Germany, where Witnesses had been put into concentration camps alongwith Jews and other "misfits" of society. The Kloses now reside in a suburb of Atlanta, Georgia.

Issues concerning the American flag continue to grab the attention of politicians and the American people. During the 1988 presidential campaign, Vice President Bush attacked Governor Michael Dukakis' position in a Massachusetts controversy in which the governor sided with teachers who did not want to lead students in reciting the pledge of allegiance.

During the 1984 Republican convention, Gregory Johnson burned an American flag in protest against the Reagan administration. Johnson was arrested and charged with desecration of the American flag. In 1989 the Supreme Court, in a five-to-four decision, ruled that Johnson had a constitutional right to burn the American flag as political protest protected by the First Amendment. President Bush and many others pushed for a constitutional amendment to "protect" the flag. Congress would not support a constitutional amendment and passed a federal statute as a compromise. On June 11, 1990 in *United States v. Eichman,* the Supreme Court ruled this new statute uncon- stitutional. Once again the President raised the specter of a constitutional amendment, but at this time it lookslike a lot of flag-waiving for political gain.

An Officer and a Gentleman

Clyde Summers was born on a farm in Grass Range, Montana in 1918. His family moved to Tecumseh,Nebraska and then settled in Winchester, Illinois whenClyde was eleven. It was 1929, the year of the stock marketcrash and the year that his mother had died. The Summersfamily remained in Illinois where Clyde Summers went tohigh school and then to college. He earned a bachelor of science degree in accounting at the University of Illinois and then graduated from the University's law school in 1942 with honors. It was war time and Summers' brother was in the Army. Clyde Summers was a religious man. He regularly attended services at the Methodist Church and led worship services at school. He worked his way through college doing kitchen work, washing windows, and running elevators.

The university hired him to work in the accounting office. He didn't have any dates with girls during the first three years at college because he didn't havemuch money and he was too busy studying and working. Because of deeply held religious beliefs Clyde Summers was opposed to war. Summers did not drink or smoke. He didn't even dance because he did not believe in it. He believed in non-violent resistance like that of MahatmaGandhi. He registered as a conscientious objector and the Illinois Draft Board accepted his beliefs as genuine, classifying him as a 4-E, a conscientious objector, not to bedrafted for the armed forces. Ironically, he failed his physical examination, so he would not have been draftedfor this reason as well.

Character and Fitness

Mr. Summers took the Illinois bar exam in June of 1942. He passed and applied for admission to practice law. Walter Bellatti, a member of the committee on character and fitness, questioned Clyde's fitness to practice law. On November 27th, 1942, Summers appeared before the full committee on character and fitness and was questioned at length.

Q. Mr. Summers, is there any question in your mind as to whether you were cut out for a preacher or a music teacher rather than a lawyer?

A: Sometimes I very seriously consider going into the ministry. The fact is I considered it through most of the two years of my schooling.

Q: Why did you change your mind?

A: Because I felt that there were enough religious people in the churches—I mean the ministry. I hink there is a lot of work to be done in the law.

Q: Do you expect to use the law as a vehicle for the extension of your ideas?

Clyde Wilson Summers while his case was pending before The United States Supreme Court, courtesy of Professor Summers.

A: That is not my purpose in law, just a means of getting at these things, but when the situation has come up in law that my principles guide me, I will follow them, whether it is in relation to non-violence or not. There is a lot of religion other than non-violence. I think there is work that needs tobe done. A lot of prison reform that needs to be done. I think it is un-Christian the kind of prisons we have. I think there are a lot of other things that perhaps the law has a place to do.

I think that the law has a place to see to it that every man has a chance to eat and a chance to live equally. I think the law has a place where people can go and get justice done for themselves without paying too much, for the bulk of the people that are too poor. I have been particularly interested in the legal clinics that have been set up in different places. It is in the right direction.

Q: And is it in your opinion that an oath to support the Constitution of the United States would not oblige you to use force at any time?

A: Military violent force.

Q: Or police force or individual physical force?

A: Yes.

Q: I cannot understand the distinction between military force and other force.

A: In the military you kill innocent people and in the other case you get the criminal.

On January 5th, 1943 Summers was advised that a majority of the committee on character and fitness declined to sign a favorable certificate as to his character and fitness. He was advised that the board of bar examiners would not certify him for admission to the bar without the certificate. No statement of the committee was supplied to him.

One member of the committee expressed his personal opinion:

> You eschew the use of force regardless of Circumstances .... Your conduct is governed by a higher law which we all hope may someday prevail.
>
> *   *   *
>
> What protection can the law be to the weak if lawyers do not consider its mandate to be entitled to obedience by force if necessary[?] . . . [Y]our position seems inconsistent with the obligations of an attorney.

Appealing to the Supreme Court

Admission to the practice of law in Illinois is granted or denied by the Supreme Court of Illinois. Because admission was denied, Mr. Summers filed a petition with the United States Supreme Court seeking the review of the denial of his admission to practice. While his petition was pending before the Supreme Court, Clyde Summers could not practice law. He was hired by the University of Toledo Law School as an instructor in law. Admission to a bar is not required for law professors or instructors.

The Highest Court Hands Down Its Decision

On June 11th, 1945, during the final chapter of World War II, the Supreme Court issued its ruling.[2] By the slimmest margin, five to four, the court ruled against Clyde Summers.

It affirmed the right of the State of Illinois to decide what constituted fitness to practice law. It ruled that Illinois could deny Summers' admission to the bar because of his deeply held belief that violence is contrary to the Bible. Illinois has a requirement that males between the ages of eighteen and forty-five serve in the militia in time of war, and because of this law, Clyde Summers was declared unfit to practice law.

Justice Black dissented:

> The State of Illinois has denied the pet- itioner the right to practice his profession and to earn a living as a lawyer. It has denied him a license on the ground that his present religious beliefs disqualify him from membership in the legal profession. The question is, therefore, whether a state which requires a license as a prerequisite to practicing law can deny an applicant a license solely because of his deeply rooted religious convictions. The fact that the petitioner measures up to every other requirement for admission to the Bar by the State demonstrates beyond doubt that the only reason for his rejection was his religious beliefs.

The conclusion seems to me inescapable. If Illinois can bar this petitioner from the practice of law, it can bar every person from every public occupation solely because he believes in non-resistance rather than in force. For a lawyer is not more subject to call for military duty than a plumber, a highway worker, a Secretary of State, or a prison chaplain.

Justice Holmes said that " 'if there is any principle of the Constitution that more imperatively calls for attachment than any other it is the principle of free thought-not free thought for those who agree with us but freedom for the thought that we hate.' Under our Constitution men are published for what they do or fail to do and not for what they think and believe." Justice Black was joined in dissent by Justices Douglas, Murphy, and Rutledge.

Epilogue

Clyde Wilson Summers had a distinguished career in law. After earning a masters degree in law and a doctorate in law from Columbia University, he was admitted to practice law in New York in 1951. He continued to teach at the University of Toledo Law School until 1949, when he moved to the University of Buffalo to teach law until 1957. In 1957, Harvard Law School professor Archibald Cox was asked by then-Senator John F. Kennedy to put together a panel of experts to draft labor law reform legislation that would address the issues raised by the Select Committee. The draft legislation which Summers helped write was the foundation of the 1958 Kennedy-Ives Bill, which itself was incorporated into the Landrum-Griffin Act.

After teaching at the University of Buffalo, Summers taught at Yale University until 1975. Professor Summers then taught at the University of Pennsylvania Law School until he retired in 2005. Professor Summers died in 2010 at age 91.

Professor Summers was the author of five books on labor law. He said the decision denying him admission to the bar directed him toward teaching, which he loved. His only practice of law concerned civil liberties cases and draft cases. Professor Summers was highly influential in the field of labor law, authoring more than 150 publications on the issue of union democracy alone. He was considered one of the nation's leading expert on union democracy.

Endnotes

1. *Minersville School District v. Gobitis,* 310 U.S. 589 (1940); the courts misspelled the name Gobitas.

2. *In Re Summers,* 326 U.S. 561 (1945).

Chapter Four

The Last Supper

"My last meal? The food would be much less significant than the company"

— Mario Batali, Chef and restauranteur

"Eat every meal as if it's your last; when the last one comes, you probably won't be very hungry."

— Nora Ephron, writer

On November 6, 2018, the Alabama prison system scheduled Domineque Ray's execution date for February 7, 2019 at the Holman Correctional Facility, in Atmore, Alabama in Escambia County, a few miles from Interstate 65. Holman lies fifteen miles north of Mobile. This prison had the reputation of being the most violent in the country, due to overcrowding and understaffing. Prisoners refer to the facility as a "slaughterhouse," as stabbings are a routine occurrence.

Holman regularly allowed a Christian chaplain to be present in the execution chamber. But Ray was devout Muslim. The prison refused his request to have an imam attend him in the last moments of his life.

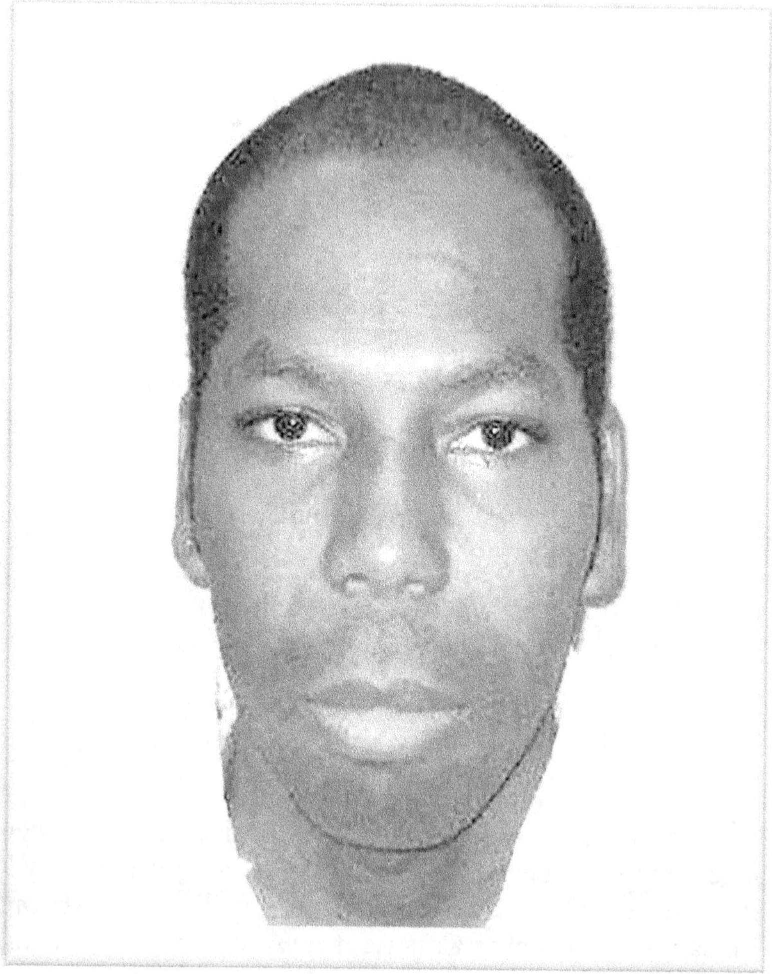

Domineque Hakim Ray

The federal court for the Middle District of Alabama denied Ray's request for a stay of execution and also denied his request to have his Muslim spiritual adviser, or imam, in the execution chamber during the lethal injection procedure. The court did order the Alabama Department of Corrections to remove the Christian chaplain, who was typically in the execution chamber, from the room andensure Ray could not see the chaplain.

Bob Horton, spokesperson for the ADOC, said that the department followed protocol "regardless of the chaplain's spiritual belief or that of the inmate." Horton said the ADOC protocol "only allows approved correctional officials, that includes the prison's chaplain, to be insidethe chamber where executions are lawfully carried out. The inmate's spiritual advisor may visit the inmate beforehand and witness the execution from a designated witness room that has a two-way window."

At the Court of Appeals

A unanimous three-judge panel of the United States Court of Appeals for the 11th Circuit, in Atlanta, stayed the execution, saying Mr. Ray had presented "a powerful Establishment Clause claim." The Eleventh Circuit concluded that there was a substantial likelihood that the prison's policy violated the First Amendment's Establishment Clause, and stayed Ray's execution so it could consider his claim on its merits.

The appeals court ruling continued, "Nevertheless, in the face of this limited record, it looks substantially likely to us that Alabama has run afoul of the Establishment Clause of the First Amendment." "What is central to Establishment Clause jurisprudence is the fundamental principle that at a minimum neither the states nor the federal government may pass laws or adopt policies that aid one religion or prefer one religion over another. And that, it appears to us, is what the Alabama Department of Corrections has done here. Alabama's policy facially furthers a denominational preference."

The appeals court's ruling stated, "We do not doubt that Alabama has a powerful interest in the secure and orderly administration of the death penalty.... And the prison's concerns may be at their apex during the most consequential act of carrying out an execution. As a general matter and at least at first blush, this seems asobvious to us as it did to the district court. Moreover, we can imagine many practical reasons as well why Alabama may wish to provide religious support and pastoral comfort of this kind to a condemned prisoner."

The appeals court said, "Notably, Alabama did not provide the Court with any affidavit from the Warden or from any other prison official addressing in any way why there were not lesser measures available to protect its interests and provide the same faith-based benefits to Christians and non-Christians alike. Nor did Alabama offer anything from its Chaplain or from anyone else about the perceived risks or the things that a cleric might need to learn in order to undertake this solemn and sensitive task. Alabama has presented us with nothing in support of its claims."

At the U.S. Supreme Court

Alabama appealed to the U.S. Supreme Court. Alabama wanted to conduct the execution of Dominique Ray in a hurry. And the U.S. Supreme Court, in an exceptional and unprecedented ruling, overturned the 11th Circuit and allowed Alabama to execute Mr. Ray without his religious advisor present.

Justice Kagan, joined by Justices Breyer, Ginsburg and Sotomayor, dissented:

The five justices who allowed the Alabama execution to proceed—Chief Justice John G. Roberts Jr. and Justices Clarence Thomas, Samuel A. Alito Jr., Neil M. Gorsuch and Brett M. Kavanaugh— lifted a stay imposed unanimously by a panelof the U.S. Court of Appeals for the 11th Circuit.That court said Ray had raised a "powerful" argument that prison protocol favored one religion over another: "it looks substantially likely to us that Alabama has run afoul of the Establishment Clause of the First Amendment."

It called for additional briefing in the case, but called for quick resolution to keep Ray's execution on track.

Instead, Alabama filed an emergency request to the Supreme Court, saying it should be allowed to go ahead with the procedure it had put in place to conduct executions in an "orderly and secure fashion." That meant having only correctional officials, which included the prison chaplain but not the imam who had been attending Ray, in the death chamber.

*   *   *

This Court is ordinarily reluctant to interfere with the substantial discretion Courts of Appeals have to issue stays when needed. See, e.g., *Dugger v. Johnson*, 485 U. S. 945, 947 (1988) (O'Connor, J., joined by Rehnquist, C. J., dissenting). Here, Ray has put forward a powerful claim that his religious rights will be violated at the moment the State puts him to death. The Eleventh Circuit wanted to hear that claim in full. Instead, this Court short-circuits that ordinary process— and itself rejects the claim with little briefing and no argument—just so the State can meet its preferred execution date.

Criticism

"I can't recall the last time that I was as shocked by a Supreme Court decision," said Deepak Gupta, a Washington lawyer who often argues before the justices. "This decision is indefensible on the merits, and the court doesn't even bother to try."

Criticism from the right was strong as well. "The Supreme Court Upholds a Grave Violation of the First Amendment," was the headline above conservative commentator David French's article in the *National Review*.

"Any policy that by law or practice provided death-row inmates with access only to Christian chaplains would likely fail 9-0 if addressed on the merits," French wrote. "In this case, however, the Supreme Court didn't decide the merits. It determined that Ray's request for an imam was made too late."

Amir H. Ali, Supreme Court and appellate counsel at the MacArthur Justice Center and a lecturer at Harvard Law School, said the court's order was in contrast with recent decisions that have protected religious rights. "Consider the opposite circumstance—a Christian person who is told that, during the final moments of his life, he can have only the services of an imam," Ali wrote in an email. "It is hard to imagine the court reaching the same result as it did here. And that's a real problem because the very purpose of the Establishment Clause is to prevent this sort of religious preference."

Ilya Somin, a libertarian professor at the Antonin Scalia Law School at George Mason University, posted on the Volohk Conspiracy website that the decision was a "grave injustice" but was probably motivated by the justices' impatience with last-minute death penalty appeals. But "to say that this factor likely explains the ruling is not to say that it excuses it," Somin wrote. "The fact that activist lawyers sometimes abuse the process does not relieve the justices of their obligation to carefully consider the facts of each case on their own merits." Ali said the court's 5-to-4 approval last term of President Trump's ban on travel for some from Muslim-majority countries stung Muslim lawyers. He pointed to language in Roberts's majority opinion. "The court went the extra step of saying that there was 'persuasive evidence' for banning people from several majority-Muslim countries," Ali said. "If that was a gut punch to the Muslim community, this will be seen as a follow-up kidney shot."

On March 28, 2019, less than two months after Ray's execution, the Supreme Court stayed the execution of Patrick Murphy in Texas over concerns that not allowinghim to have a Buddhist spiritual advisor instead of the mandated Christian chaplain would violate his Consti- tutional rights. The ruling in the *Murphy* case renewed attention to Ray's case due to the similarity and proximity ofthe cases and the lack of explanation from jus-ices Alito, Kavanaugh and Roberts for their latest positions.

PART 2

Freedom of Association and the Right to Privacy

Chapter Five

Roommates

"Individuality is the salt of common life. You may have to live in a crowd but you do not have to live like it."
—Henry Van Dyke

Parish, Michael Bruce Boraas, Anne Truman and three other students at the State University of New York at Stony Brook together rented a six- bedroom house in the Village of Belle Terre. Dr. Edwin and Judith Dickmanowned the home that the group rented and approved of the students' living arrangements.

Michael Truman signed a lease with the Dickmans beginning December 31, 1971 and ending the following May at $500 per month. At the end of the lease term, the students could elect to keep renting the property on a month-to-month basis. Bruce Boraas later co-signed thelease. None of the six students were related to each other. Each occupied one of the bedrooms and each paid a portion of the rent and other expenses. The group shared common kitchen facilities, dined together and paid common household expenses out of a "house" checking account. Four of the students were pursuing graduate studies in sociology at Stony Brook.

The group living arrangement was advantageous to the students because it kept their expenses down. Theyen-joyed living together and it helped their studies as theycould discuss sociology and other topics with their roommates.

The Village of Belle Terre

The Village of Belle Terre, which means "beautiful land" in French, consists of about 200 single-familyhomes, mostly built in the 1920s and 1930s, on large,wooded lots. Belle Terre has a town beach on Long IslandSound. Bruce Boraas and Michael Truman applied for village beach permits so that they could use the townbeach during the summer. On June 8, 1972, the Villagedenied them permits because it considered the students to be illegal residents.

The Village is zoned exclusively for single-family houses. The zoning law limits the number of unrelated persons who can live together to two. People related by blood or marriage are not limited in a similar manner. A family with fourteen children could live together in one house, but three nuns could not legally live together in Belle Terre.

On July 19, 1972, the Village, after learning of the living arrangements of Boraas and Truman, served the Dickmans with a summons. On July 31st, the Dickmans were served with an "Order to Remedy Violations" concerning the living arrangements at their Belle Terre home. The order required the Dickmans to evict at leastfour of the students so that only two unrelated personswould be left in the home.

A Federal Case

On, August 2nd, the New York Civil Liberties Union filed suit on behalf of the Dickmans and three of the students seeking to have the Belle Terre zoning law declared unconstitutional because it interfered with their freedom of association. The lawsuit was filed in federal court because it was based on federal civil rights laws and on the Constitution. The case was assigned to Judge Dooling, who promptly issued a temporary restraining order (TRO) against the village. This order restrained the village for ten days from enforcing the zoning ordinance against the group house.

Judge Dooling kept the TRO in force until he could hold a hearing on the matter. Following a hearing, on September 20, 1972, Judge Dooling issued a forty-page decision denying a permanent injunction. He ruled that the zoning ordinance was a valid exercise of the village's authority to control population density. However, he granted a five-day stay to allow the plaintiffs to file an appeal.

Lawyers for the students and the Dickmans filed anappeal with the Second Circuit Court of Appeals. The federal appeals court, by a vote of two to one, reversed the lower court ruling and reinstated the injunction against Belle Terre. Judge Mansfield ruled:

> The effect of the Belle Terre ordinance would be to exclude from the community, without any rational basis, unmarried groups seeking to live together, whether they be three college students, three single nurses, three priests, or three single judges.[1]

Before the Supreme Court

The Village of Belle Terre took the appeals court ruling to the Supreme Court. The Supreme Court agreed to review the case.

On April 1, 1974, the court issued its ruling. Justice Douglas, usually the court's dissenting liberal, deliveredthe opinion for the court:

> The ordinance places no ban on other forms of association, for a "family" may, so far as the ordinance is concerned, entertain whomever it likes.

* * *

> A quiet place where yards are wide, people few, and motor vehicles restricted.Are legitimate guidelines in a land-use project addressed to family needs.[2]

Rarely did Justice William O. Douglas brush aside freedom of association, but in this one case he sided with the authority of towns to zone out certain types of individuals. Douglas was a strong environmentalist and his bias in favor of environmental regulations must have contaminated his reasoning. His concern about controlling population density could have been dealt with by a village zoning ordinance which limited the number of persons living in a home to one person per bedroom, or to a certain number per house. The village could have also limited the number of automobiles per house in order to reduce traffic.

Justice Douglas said that the zoning ordinance "involves no 'fundamental' right guaranteed by the Constitution, such as voting, the right of association or any rights of privacy." What more fundamental right of association is there than determining whom you choose to live with? Isn't the right to privacy violated when a town can inquire into who is living with whom? If two un-married housemates have a friend stay with them for a week are they in violation of the zoning ordinance? What if the guest stays for two weeks, or a month, or six months? Do we want our city officials peeping into windows, or barging into our bedrooms to take notes as to whom is living with us? If this isn't part of our right to privacy then our right to privacy is meaningless.

Justices Brennan and Marshall dissented. Justice Marshall stated:

> In my view, the disputed classification burdens the students' fundamental rights of association and privacy guaranteed by the First and Fourteenth Amendments.

> *   *   *

> Our decisions established that the First and Fourteenth Amendments protect the freedom to choose one's associates The selection of one's living companions involves similar choices as to the emotional, social, or economic benefits to be derived from alternative living arrangements.

> *   *   *

The choice of household companions of whether a person's "intellectual and emotional" needs are best met by living with family, friends, professional associates or others-involves deeply personal considerations as to the kind and quality of intimate relationships within the home.

*   *   *

I would find the challenged ordinance unconstitutional. But I would not ask the village to abandon its goals of providing quiet streets, little traffic, and a pleasant and reasonably priced environment in which families might raise their children. Rather, I would commend the town to continue to pursue those purposes but bymeans of more carefully drawn andevenhanded legislation.

Endnotes

1. 476 F.2 808 (1973).

2. 416 U.S. 1 (April 1, 1974).

Chapter Six

In the Privacy of Your Bedroom

"While I nodded, nearly napping, suddenly there came a tapping, as of someone gently rapping, rapping at my chamber door."

—Edgar Allen Poe, *The Raven*

On a hot Atlanta day in 1982, the day after Independence Day, Michael Hardwick had just finished setting up a lighting system in a gay bar. He had a beer in his hand as he left for the day. When he was about ten feet out the door and into the parking lot, he remembered that the "drinking in public" law was being strictly enforced. He emptied the bottle and threw it into an empty trashcan on the bar's property.

It was then that he saw an officer making a U-turn on Monroe Street. The police car pulled up to Hardwick and the officer got out of the car. He searched Hardwick, asked for identification and asked where the beer bottle was. Michael Hardwick identified himself and said that the beer bottle was in the trashcan in the parking lot. The officer accused Hardwick of lying, but did not look for the bottle.

The officer, K.R. Torick, who had been harassing pa-trons of gay bars, issued Mr. Hardwick a complaint. Much like a minor traffic ticket, this was for drinking in public. The complaint had two different days written at the top left corner: "Wed Thurs," and commanded Hardwick to appear in court on July 13th, 1982, or suffer a fine. July 13th, 1982 was a Tuesday.

Because he thought that his court date was on a Wednesday or a Thursday, Hardwick failed to appear in court on July 13th, 1982.

Barging and Entering

On July 13th, at 2:30 in the afternoon, Officer Torick showed up at Hardwick's house. He entered the residence without permission. Questioning a guest, Kirk Slusser, the officer demanded identification and requested toknow of Hardwick's whereabouts. Slusser told the policeman that Hardwick had left earlier and would return about 5:00 p.m. Officer Torick proceeded down the apartment's hallway to the back bedroom where he barged in. He found another friend there, Bob Cheeks, and demanded identification of him. Officer Torick announced, "Tell him I will be back," as he left.

At about 4:00 that afternoon Hardwick arrived home to find his guests somewhat shaken. He then realized that he had been required to appear in court that morning. Hardwick called the courthouse and was advised to reportto the clerk of the court, Jerry Coote, first thing the next morning. He was told not to worry because it takes forty-eight hours to process an arrest warrant. Michael Hardwick was concerned because Officer Torick, without awarrant, had entered his home and upset his guests.

Citation given to Michael Hardwick on July 5, 1982.

Paying the Fine

Hardwick awoke early the next morning, arrived at the courthouse at 8:30, and promptly reported to the clerk. The clerk left for a few minutes and returned stating that because Hardwick had missed his court date, he had to pay the maximum fine of fifty dollars. Again he was advised not to worry because no warrant would be issued. After paying his fine, Hardwick received a receipt from the clerk as shown below:

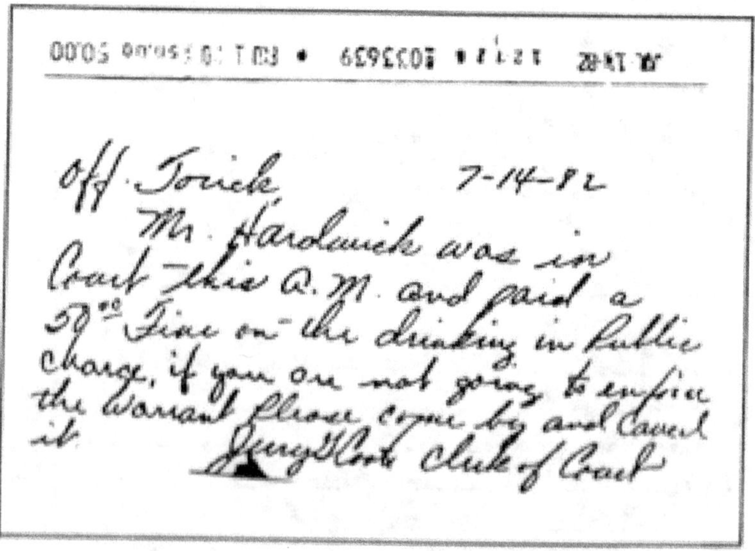

Peeping Police

Three weeks later, on the morning of August 3rd, Officer Torick again appeared at Hardwick's home. Torick had an arrest warrant with him concerning Hardwick's failure to appear in court on July 13th. The arrest warrant was invalid because the fine had been paid in full.

Torick entered the apartment, awakened a houseguest and asked for Michael Hardwick. Mr. Slusser, the houseguest, answered that he wasn't sure where Hardwick was. Officer Torick then entered Hardwick's bedroom without knocking and observed Hardwick involved in a sexual act with another man. Torick told the two men to get up and get dressed. He did not advise them of their rights.

Torick discovered a bowl with a small amount of marijuana in it and stated that both men were under arrest for sodomy and for possession of marijuana. He ordered them into his car and still did not read them their rights.

Hardwick told the officer that he had paid his fine for drinking in public and that if he would call in to verify it, or go with him to his place of employment, he could show him the receipt. Officer Torick said that he would not call in or go with Hardwick to find proof of payment because he "did not run a goddamned taxi service."

In Atlanta City Jail

Upon arriving at the Atlanta City Jail, Torick informed the processing officers that the two men were being charged with sodomy and possession of marijuana. They were placed in a holding cell with ten to twelve other men and were held for ten hours, six hours after bond was ready to be set. During incarceration some policemen taunted Hardwick and Dewitt, referring to them as "fags" and saying that they should enjoy being in the bullpen with other men. The processing officer had made a similar comment to the two men.

At 10:00 p.m. that night Hardwick and Dewitt were bonded out. Each was required to pay $275 for bond. Hardwick paid an additional fifty dollars for the earlier offense, even though he had paid this fine once already.

Sodomy in Georgia

The Georgia sodomy statute provides

> (a)   A person commits the offense of sodomy when he performs or submits to any sexual act involving the sex organs of one person and the mouth or anus of another.
> (b) A person convicted of the offense of sodomy shall be punished by imprisonment for not less than one nor more than 20 years . . . .

The statute clearly applies to heterosexual relations as well as to homosexual relations. However, the statute is vague: it fails to define "a sexual act" and "a sexualorgan." Is a female breast a sexual organ? Is kissing asexual act? If so, a man kissing his wife's breast could be in violation of the Georgia sodomy law.

On the Offensive

The district attorney decided not to prosecute Hard-wick. He stated that the state had already spent too muchmoney on the case. A group called Georgians Opposed toArchaic Laws (GOAL) was looking for a test case tochallenge the sodomy laws. When the criminal caseagainst Michael Hardwick was dropped, GOAL asked him if he would be a plaintiff in a test case against the law.

Kathleen Wilde, a civil liberties lawyer in Atlanta, was hired to prepare the case against the sodomy law. In addition to representing Hardwick, Ms. Wilde found a married couple who was opposed to the law. In the lawsuit that she prepared, the couple, referred to as John and Mary Doe, "wished to engage in sexual activity proscribed by" the Georgia sodomy law.

On Valentine's Day in 1983, Hardwick, John and Mary Doe filed suit in the federal court in Atlanta challenging the constitutionality of the Georgia sodomy law. The suit contended that the law violated the privacy rights of citizens who desired to practice sodomy in their homes. Hardwick asserted that he was a practicing homosexualand that he was in imminent danger of arrest. The district court dismissed the case, finding that the plaintiffs had put forward no claim that entitled them to a decision in their favor.

Hardwick and the Does appealed. The court of appeals ruled in favor of Mr. Hardwick:[1]

> The Georgia sodomy statute infringes upon the fundamental constitutional rights of Michael Hardwick. The Constitution prevents the States from unduly interfering in certain individual decisions critical to personal autonomy because those decisions are essentially private and beyond the legitimate reach of civilized society. Hardwick desires to engage privately in sexual activity with another consenting adult Although his behavior is not procreative, it does not involve important as associational interests.

Before the High Court

Michael I. Bowers, the Attorney General of the State of Georgia, appealed the decision to the Supreme Court. The

Supreme Court agreed to hear the case and set oral argument for March 31st, 1986. Several days after the oral argument, the justices met in conference to vote on the case. The justices voted five to four to rule in favor of Hardwick. A few days later, however, Justice Lewis F. Powell, Jr, of Virginia, sent a memo to the other justices saying that he had changed his mind. Now the vote was five to four against Hardwick and in favor of upholding the Georiga sodomy law. Justice Byron White wrote the majority opinion upholding the law.[2] The Court's opinion only discusses homosexual activities and completely ignores the fact that the law applies equally to heterosexual conduct.

Justice Powell cast the deciding vote and wrote a separate opinion. He said, "I cannot say the conduct condemned for hundreds of years has now become a fundamental right."

Justice Harry Blackmun took the unusual step of reading major portions of a harsh dissent from the bench on the day the decision was announced (Monday, June 30th, 1986) He said that despite "almost obsessive focus on homosexual activity" by a "bare majority" of the court, the Georgia law covers heterosexual activity as well. Blackmun said the case is not about whether there is a fundamental right to engage in homosexual acts but about "the most comprehensive of rights and the right most valued by civilized men, namely, the right to be let alone." Justice Blackmun was joined in his decision by Justices Brennan, Marshall, and Stevens.

Epilogue

Michael Hardwick was a twenty-nine-year-old bartender when he was arrested in 1982. He moved from

Atlanta to Miami, Florida, where he studied botany and horticulture. Mr. Hardwick is a talented interior designer as well as a sculptor.

His case brought him out into the open. He learned how politics, not law, decided his case, and how thehighest court of the land twisted the case into an"anti-homosexual" one.

After he retired, Justice Powell acknowledged in 1990 when he told students at New York University Law School that he had taken a second look at the *Bowers* case and regretted his vote. "I think I probably made a mistake in that one," he said. Justice Powell, who was 79 when *Bowers v. Hardwick* reached the court, had no personal experience with gay rights and found the issues raised by the case confusing and somewhat threatening. "I don't believe I've ever met a homosexual," he told one of his law clerks while the case was pending. The law clerk, who in fact was gay, told the justice, "Certainly you have, but you just don't know that they are."

The United States Supreme Court overturned *Hardwick v. Bowers* in 2003 in *Lawrence v. Texas*, 539 U.S. 558 (2003).

Michael Hardwick photographed by David Vance, courtesy of Mr. Hardwick.

Endnotes

1. 760 F.2d 1202 (1985).
2. 106 S.Ct. 2841 (1986).

Chapter Seven
Roe, Roe, Roe Your Boat: Abortion in America

"No matter what men think, abortion is a fact of life. Women have always had them; they always have and they always will. Are they going to have good ones or bad ones? Will the good ones be reserved for the rich, while the poor women go to quacks?"

— Shirley Chisholm, *Unbought and Unbossed*

"Governments who manipulate population growth have two choices: making maternity pleasant, or making it inescapable."

— Kate Millett, *Sexual Politics*

"No woman can call herself free who does not control her own body."

— Margaret Sanger, opened the first birth control clinic in the U.S., and established organizations that evolved into Planned Parenthood.

Roe v. Wade was the law of the land for 49 years, giving women the right to get an abortion during the first trimester of their pregnancy. Then came three Trump appointees, Justices Amy Coney Barrett, Bret Kavanaugh and Neil Gorsuch. They joined with old-line Republican appointees Clarence Thomas and Samuel Alito to overturn *Roe v. Wade*. Chief Justice John Roberts, no liberal, tried to hold the court, and the boat, together and keep *Roe v. Wade* afloat, but he failed. *Roe* had overturned and sunk into the deep morass of the new Supreme Court, possibly the worst court in 150 years.

Mississippi Law

In 2018, Mississippi passed the Gestational Age Act that provides that, "[e]xcept in a medical emergency or in the case of a severe fetal abnormality, a person shall not intentionally or knowingly perform . . . or induce an abortion of an unborn human being if the probable gestational age of the unborn human being has been determined to be greater than fifteen (15) weeks." *Roe v. Wade* allowed the states to restrict abortions after the first trimester. Each trimester is twelve weeks. So, the court could have easily held that the Mississippi law was valid under *Roe*.

But the five activist anti-abortionist jurists were hungry to overturn *Roe*.

Brief History of Abortion

The earliest known records of abortion techniques date as far back as 2700 BC in China and 1550 BC in Egypt. Religious texts often contained severe condemnations of abortion, recommending penance, but seldom enforcing secular punishment. As a matter of common law in England and the United States, abortion was illegal anytime after quickening—when the movements of the fetus could first be felt by the woman. Under the born alive rule, the fetus was not considered a "reasonable being" *in rerum natura* and abortion was not treated as murder under English law.

In the 20th century, many Western countries began to codify abortion laws or place further restrictions on the practice. Anti-abortion movements, also referred to as "pro-life" movements, were led by a combination of groups opposed to abortion on moral grounds.

By the first half of the 20th century, many countries had begun to liberalize abortion laws, at least when performed to protect the woman's life and in some cases on the woman's request. Under Vladimir Lenin, the Soviet Union becamethe first modern state in legalizing abortions on request—thelaw was first introduced in the Russian Republic in 1920, inthe Ukrainian SSR in July 1921, and then in the wholeSoviet Union.

In the 1930s, several countries, including Poland, Turkey, Denmark, Sweden, Iceland and Mexico legalized abortion in some special cases (pregnancy from rape, threat to mother's health, fetal malformation). In Japan, abortion was legalized in 1948 by the Eugenic Protection Law, amended in May 1949 to allow abortions for economic reasons. Abortion was legalized in 1952 in Yugoslavia (on a limited basis), and again in 1955 in the Soviet Union on request.

In the late 1950s, under pressure from the Soviet Union, some eastern European countries, including Poland, Hungary, Bulgaria, Czechoslovakia and Romania, legalized abortions.

The United Kingdom passed the Abortion Act of 1967 that clarified and allowed abortions as legal up to 28 weeks (later reduced to 24 weeks). Other countries soon followed, Canada (1969), the United States (1973), Austria (1974), France and Sweden (1975), New Zealand (1977), Italy (1978), the Netherlands (1984) and Belgium (1990).

In 2021 the Mexican Supreme Court, in a country that is 83% Catholic, unanimously struck down a law from the State of Coahuila which penalized doctors and pregnant women for having or performing an abortion with one to three years of prison time. Mexico's highest court declared the criminalization of abortion in general to be unconstitutional. "Never again must a woman or a person capable of gestating be criminally judged," said Justice Luís María Aguilar, who wrote the decision. "Today the threat of prison and the stigma that weighs on people who freely decide to interrupt their pregnancy are removed."

Reasoning Behind Overturning Roe v. Wade

The U.S Supreme Court reviewed the standard that the Court's cases have used to determine whether the Fourteenth Amendment's reference to "liberty" protects a particular right. The court found that the Constitution makes no express reference to a right to obtain an abortion, but several constitutional provisions have been offered as potential homes for an implicit constitutional right. *Roe* held that the abortion right is part of a right to privacy that springs from the First, Fourth, Fifth, Ninth and Fourteenth Amendments.

See 410 U. S., at 152–153. The *Casey* Court grounded its decision solely on the theory that the right to obtain an abortion is part of the "liberty" protected by the Fourteenth Amendment's Due Process Clause.

By overturning *Roe v. Wade*, the Supreme Court overruled nearly 50 years of precedents. The three Trump-appointed justices, who all promised in their confirmation hearings, to respect *stare decisis,* reneged on their promises. They lied. Under oath. *Stare decisis* is a legal principle by which judges are bound by precedents. In Latin *stare decisis* means "to stand with the-things-that-have-been-decided."

Justice Samuel Alito wrote the majority opinion:

> Abortion presents a profound moral issue on which Americans hold sharply conflicting views. Some believe fervently that a human person comes into being at conception and that abortion ends an innocent life. Others feel just as strongly that any regulation of abortion invades a woman's right to control her own body and prevents women from achieving full equality. Still others in a third group think that abortion should be allowed under some but not all circumstances, and those within this group hold a variety of views about the particular restrictions that should be imposed.
>
> For the first 185 years after the adoption of the Constitution, each State was permitted to address this issue in accordance with the views of its citizens. Then, in 1973, this Court decided *Roe v. Wade*, 410 U. S. 113. Even

though the Constitution makes no mention of abortion, the Court held that it confers a broad right to obtain one.

Justice Alito stated: "*Stare decisis* plays an important role in our case law, and we have explained that it serves many valuable ends. It protects the interests of those who have taken action in reliance on a past decision."

But he found that *Roe* was also "egregiously wrong" and deeply damaging and that *Roe's* constitutional analysis was far outside the bounds of any reasonable interpretation of the various constitutional provisions to which it vaguelypointed. It is difficult to understand how conservative justices, such as Warren Burger, Sandra Day O'Connor and Anthony Kennedy, all appointed by Republican presidents, could have been so egregiously wrong in affirming *Roe v. Wade* over the years.

Understanding Roe

Roe was a 7-2 decision. Chief Justice Warren Burger, appointed by President Richard Nixon, was in the majority. Burger was a very conservative jurist. He concurred in the decision:

> I do not read the Court's holdings today as having the sweeping consequences attributed to them by the dissenting Justices; the dissenting views discount the reality that the vast majority of physicians observe the standards of their profession, and act only on the basis of carefully deliberated medical judgments relating to life and health. Plainly,

the Court today rejects any claim that the Constitution requires abortions on demand.

Justice Sandra Day O'Connor, a Ronald Reagan appointee, and the first women on the court, wrote the decision in *Planned Parenthood v. Casey* upholding *Roe:* "Liberty finds no refuge in a jurisprudence of doubt. Yet 19 years after our holding that the Constitution protects a woman's right to terminate her pregnancy in its early stages, *Roe* v. *Wade,* 410 U.S. 113 (1973), that definition of liberty is still questioned." O'Connor wrote:

> Constitutional protection of the woman's decision to terminate her pregnancy derives from the Due Process Clause of the Fourteenth Amendment. It declares that no State shall "deprive any person of life, liberty, or property, without due process of law." The controlling word in the case before us is "liberty."

> Men and women of good conscience can disagree, and we suppose some always shall disagree, about the profound moral and spiritual implications of terminating a pregnancy, even in its earliest stage. Some of us as individuals find abortion offensive to our most basic principles of morality, but that cannot control our decision. Our obligation is to define the liberty of all, not to mandate our own moral code.

The Chief Justice usually tries to hold the court together. Justice Roberts failed to do that. He wrote is a separate opinion that the Court could have upheld Mississippi's 15-week abortion rule without overturning *Roe*. *Dobbs v. Jackson Women's Health Organization*, 597 U.S. ___ (2022).

Justice Roberts said, "out of adherence to a simple yet fundamental principle of judicial restraint: If it is not necessary to decide more to dispose of a case, then it is necessary not to decide more. Perhaps we are not always perfect in following that command, and certainly there are cases that warrant an exception. But this is not one of them. Surely, we should adhere closely to principles of judicial restraint here, where the broader path the Court chooses entails repudiating a constitutional right we have not only previously recognized, but also expressly reaffirmed aplying the doctrine of stare decisis."

Justice Roberts continued, "None of this, however, requires that we also take the dramatic step of altogether eliminating the abortion right first recognized in Roe. Mississippi itself previously argued as much to this Court in this litigation." Roberts said,

> When the State petitioned for our review, its basic request was straightforward: "clarify whether abortion prohibitions before viability are always unconstitutional." Pet. for Cert. 14. The State made a number of strong arguments that the answer is no, id., at 15–26—arguments that, as discussed, I find persuasive. And it went out of its way to make clear that it was not asking the Court to repudiate entirely the right to choose whether to terminate a pregnancy: "To be clear, the questions presented in this petition do not require the Court to overturn *Roe* or *Casey*."

Roberts concluded, "The Court's decision to overrule *Roe* and *Casey* is a serious jolt to the legal system—regardless of how you view those cases. A narrower decision rejecting the misguided viability line would be markedly less unsettling, and nothing more is needed to decide this case."

The Dissenters

Justice Stephen Breyer, in one of his last decisions, joined with Justices Sonya Sotomayor and Elena Kagan, dissenting vigorously. They wrote,

> Whatever the exact scope of the coming laws, one result of today's decision is certain: the curtailment of women's rights, and of their status as free and equal citizens. Yesterday, the Constitution guaranteed that a woman confronted with an unplanned pregnancy could (within reasonable limits) make her own decision about whether to bear a child, with all the life-transforming consequences that act involves. And in thus safeguarding each woman's reproductive freedom, the Constitution also protected "[t]he ability of women to participate equally in [this Nation's] economic and social life." *Casey,* 505 U. S., at 856. But no longer. As of today, this Court holds, a State can always force a woman to give birth, prohibiting even the earliest abortions. A State can thus transform what, when freely undertaken, is a wonder into what, when forced, may be a nightmare. Some women, especially women of means, will find ways around the State's assertion of

power. Others—those without money or childcare or the ability to take time off from work—will not be so fortunate. Maybe they will try an unsafe method of abortion, and come to physical harm, or even die. Maybe they will undergo pregnancy and have a child, but at significant personal or familial cost. At the least, they will incur the cost of losing control of their lives. The Constitution will, today's majority holds, provide no shield, despite its guarantees of liberty and equality for all.

PART 3

Freedom of Speech

Chapter Eight

Fighting Words

*"Sticks and stones will break my bones, but words
will never hurt me"*

—Children's taunt

On Saturday afternoon, April 6th, 1940, Walter Chaplinski, twenty-six, a Jehovah's Witness, was distributing the literature of his sect on the public sidewalks of Rochester, New Hampshire, a town of about 15,000 people. Chaplinski had come with several other Jehovah's Witnesses from Shenandoah, Pennsylvania and relocated in Dover, New Hampshire, not far from Rochester. Chaplinski condemned all other religions as a racket.

Members of the local citizenry complained to the city marshall, James Bowering, Jr., that Chaplinski was denouncing all religions. Bowering told them that Chaplinski was conducting himself lawfully, and then warned Chaplinski that the crowd was getting restless.

Four school-aged children, also Jehovah's Witnesses, were carrying placards around the town square while Chaplinski continued handing out leaflets, ballyhooing his religion and denouncing other religions. He said that his leaflets contained the truth about President Roosevelt's envoy to Europe. "Religion is a racket. Read the uncensored news," he said. The city marshall stated that he had warned Chaplinski to leave the city, that Chaplinski was inciting the people, and that he had received many complaints and requests to stop him. He told Chaplinskithat if a riot started Chaplinski would be responsible for it.

According to witnesses, Chaplinski made several derogatory remarks about this country. Several men brought an American flag and ordered Chaplinski to salute it He refused to salute the flag. As a Jehovah's Witness he believed that saluting any flag is contrary to God's commandment, "Thou shalt have no other gods before me." One man asked Chaplinski to take off his glasses and he refused. The man then took them off, another man knocked Chaplinski down, and several others joined in the attack.

A Fascist and a Racketeer

Marshall Bowering had just returned to City Hall when a car drove up and notified him that there was a riot on the square. He rushed back and found Chaplinski on the ground with his papers scattered about. Bowering escorted Chaplinski to the station. While he was being escorted to the station, Chaplinski called Bowering a Fascist and a racketeer and said that the whole government of Rochester were Fascists or agents of Fascists

Walter Chaplinski, circa 1942, courtesy of Mr. Chaplinski.

Chaplinski was charged with unlawfully using the words "Fascist" and "racketeer" under a New Hampshire law which prohibited using offensive, derisive and annoying words and names. He was taken to the Strafford County Farm to await a hearing that was to be held five days later. He told Judge Gardner S. Hall that he would not furnish twenty-five-dollar bail bond because he did notbelieve in bail.

Chaplinski was tried by Judge Hall and found guilty of the charge. He was sentenced to twelve days at the House of Corrections and was ordered to pay costs of $24.78.

He appealed to the Superior Court, but the court upheld the New Hampshire law and he was again found guilty and sentenced to serve six months at the House of Corrections. He served two weeks of the sentence before being released on bail. In March 1941, the New Hampshire Supreme Court ruled against Chaplinski, affirming his conviction. Chaplinski then filed the necessary papers with the Supreme Court of the United States, which agreed to hear his appeal.

In the United States Supreme Court

In 1942, while the United States was fighting Germany and Japan with more than fighting words, the United States Supreme Court ruled that "fighting words," which would be those words likely to cause an average person to fight, are not protected by the First Amendment.[1] Remarkably, the decision was unanimous.

Constitutional law professor Chester Antieau believes that the decision was wrongly decided[2]:

Fighting words have been used not only by American presidents but by many other citizens, and they are a traditional aspect of our communicated freedom. Further-more, the concept is so vague that no lawyer can adequately guide his client contemplating a public speech. Additionally, the assumption that the use of 'fighting words' generally leads to breaches of the peace must be seriously questioned. Even if fisticuffs follow at times, the interests of society can better be served by chastising the violentand not the verbal.

If we allow police to arrest speakers because of the content of their speeches then the First Amendment is meaningless. "Fighting words" to one person are dinner table conversation to another. Because of this it isimpossible to define them; the average person has no ideaof where free speech stops and fighting words begin.

Epilogue

Even in the 1980s, the Supreme Court often refers to the *Chaplinsky* case as an exception to free speech. Because of this, the fighting words exception lives on.

Years later at his retirement home in St. Petersburg, Florida, Walter Chaplinski stated that the case enrichedhis life. He stated that his imprisonment for eight months taught him about justice in this country, and that he experienced religious persecution that Christians experi- enced a thousand years ago. After the Supreme Court'sruling, he was a special pioneer Witness, spreading the gospel for the Jehovah's Witnesses.

Mr. Chaplinski worked as a stone mason for most of his life. He passed away in Florida at age 84 in 1998.

Endnotes

1. 315 US. 568 (1942). The Supreme Court misspelled Mr. Chaplinski's name.

2. I. Modern Constitutional Law, New York: Lawyers Co-operative Publishing Company.

Chapter Nine

Dirty Words

"I could never succeed in 'defining it' intelligibly, but I know it when I see it"

—Justice Potter Stewart on pornography

"Pornography is whatever gives a judge an erection."

—Anonymous lawyer

In 1962, Ralph Ginzburg published sexually oriented mag-azines and books, including *Eros, Liaison* and *The House-wife's Handbook on Selective Promiscuity. Eros* was ahardcover magazine, *The Housewife's Handbook* a short book and *Liaison* a bi-weekly newsletter.

Eros

Eros contained a wide variety of articles, including "The Short Story" by Ray Bradbury, "President Harding's Second Lady," "Was Shakespeare a Homosexual?" "Memoirs of a Male Chaperone," "Bawdy Limericks,"

"The Sexual Side of Anti-Semitism," "Natural Superiority of Women as Eroticists," "Sex and the Bible," "Lysistrata," and six other articles. A photo-essay was included, entitled "Black and White in Color," which portrayed a black man and a white woman in the nude.

Eros also included a lengthy excerpt from My *Life and Loves,* by Frank Harris. *Eros* was a hardcover magazine which cost twenty-five dollars per year. This work received extensive literary commentary in other publications, including *The New Yorker, New York Review of Books, Library Journal, Newsweek, New York Times Book Review* and *New Republic. Eros* won numerous awardsincluding the prestigious award from the Society of Publication Designers and a Gold Medal from the Art
Directors Club of New York.

Liaison

Liaison was a newsletter. Volume One, Issue One included articles entitled "Slaying the Sex Dragon," "Semen in the Diet" and "Sing a Song of Sex Life." This issue also included digests of two articles concerning sex and sexual relations which had earlier appeared in professional journals and a report of an interview with a psychotherapist.

The Housewife's Handbook on Selective Promiscuity

The *Handbook* is a sexual autobiography of Rey Anthony (Mrs. Lillian Maxine Serett) detailing the author's sexual experiences from age three to age thirty-six. The book include's the author's views on sex education, laws regulating private consentual adult sexual practices and the equality of women in sexual relationships. Before selling the rights of her book to Mr. Ginzburg, the author printed it privately. She sold some 12,000 copies of the book to medical and psychiatric professionals.

Advertising

The *Handbook* was advertised by mail. The advertisement included most of the introduction of the book, written by Dr. Albert Ellis. Dr. Ellis considered the book to be informational and to have therapeutic value. His introduction included a description of the book's sexual imagery. The advertisement included a guarantee that if the book was censored by the post office, a full refund would be made. One *Eros* advertisement claimed:

> *Eros* is a child of its times . . . . It is the result of recent court decisions that have realistically interpreted America's obscenity laws and that have given to this a country a new breadth of freedom of expression . . . . *Eros* takes advantage of this new freedom of expression. It is *the* magazine of sexual candor.

A mailing piece promoting *Liaison* appealed to its readers: "Though *Liaison* handles the subjects of love and sex with complete candor, I wish to make it clear that it is not a scandal sheet and it is not written for the man in the street. Liaison is aimed at intelligent, educated adults who can accept love and sex as a part of life."

The Statute

Congress passed the federal obscenity statute in 1865. This law declares that "obscene, lewd, lascivious, indecent, filthy or vile matter and devices" (and advertisements for them) are "nonmailable matter." This federal law punishes persons who attempt to mail or actually mail "nonmailable matter" by a fine of up to $5,000 and/or imprisonment of up to five years.

The Grand Jury and the Grand Judge

On March 15th, 1963, the Grand Jury sitting in Philadelphia returned a twenty-eight-count indictment charging that Ralph Ginzburg and his corporations violated the federal obscenity law. The case was assigned to Judge Body. Mr. Ginzburg wanted the case disposed of quickly so that he could continue publishing his books and magazines without the charges pending. His attorneys filed a motion to dismiss the charges, but the court denied the motion. Ginzburg made the fatal mistake of waiving his right to a jury trial and submitted to a trial before the judge.

The trial took five days. Experts were called to show the value of the publications in question. The author of the *Handbook* was called as a witness. The chairman of the Fine Arts Department of New York University testified that the photographs were outstanding, beautiful and artistic.

The judge found that only four of the fifteen articles in *Eros* were obscene. He found, however, that *"Eros* has no saving grace. The items of possible merit might be considered innocuous and a mere guise to avoid the law and in large measure enhance the pruriency of the entire work."

The court disregarded testimony concerning the value of the *Handbook* to sexual therapists. Judge Body said, "Any testimony to this effect is expressly disbelieved."

The judge similarly found that *Liaison* included "jokes and rhymes which clearly go beyond contemporary community standards of humor, even in applying liberal nightclub standards."

Judge Body found all three publications to be obscene and sentenced Ralph Ginzburg to five years in federal prison.

The Appeals

The federal court of appeals affirmed the lower court's ruling. Ginzburg's lawyers sought review in the United States Supreme Court and the highest court agreed to hear the case.

In 1957, the Supreme Court had decided that obscene literature was not protected by the First Amendment.[1] Justice William Brennan wrote the *Roth* opinion, which stated that books and magazines were obscene when, to the average person, applying contemporary community standards, the dominant theme of the material, taken as a whole, appeals to prurient interest. In a later opinion, the court added that the material could not be obscene unless it "was utterly without redeeming social value."[2]

Relying on this earlier decision, Justice Brennan wrote the opinion for the court in the *Ginzburg* case. He found that the "leer of the sensualist" permeated the advertising for the three publications and cited the advertisements quoted above. He remarked that Dr. Ellis is heavily quoted in one brochure but that the solicitation was "indiscriminate" because it was not limited to physicians or psychiatrists.

The Supreme Court ruled that because Ginzburg "pandered" (appealed to the sexual interests of the readers), the material in question would be considered obscene, even though the same materials would not be considered obscene if sold to a sex therapist. Brennan stated that Ginzburg and his companies, did not sell the book to such a limited audience, or focus . . . on its supposed therapeutic or educational value. Rather they deliberately emphasized the sexually provocative aspects of the work in order to catch the salaciously disposed.

The vote of the court was five to four. Justice Hugo Black, in dissent, wrote that Ginzburg was condemned by the court to serve five years in prison for distributing printed matter about sex, an offense which no one could possibly have known to be criminal. He stated that he was opposed to government censorship of any kind since the First Amendment forbids it.

Justice William O. Douglas also dissented:

> The advertisements in our best magazines are chock-full of thighs, ankles, calfs, bosoms, eyes and hair, to draw the potential buyer's attention to lotions, tires, food,

liquor, clothing autos and even insurance policies. The sexy advertisement neither adds to nor detracts from the quality of the merchandise being offered for sale. And I do not see how it adds to or detracts one whit from the legality of the book being distributed. A book should stand on its own, irrespective of the reasons why it was written or the wiles used in selling it.

Justice Douglas also said that,

Liaison's appeal is to the ribald sense of humor which is—for better or worse—a part of our culture. A mature society would not suppress this newsletter as obscene but would simply ignore it.

Douglas concluded:

I think that this is the ideal of the Free Society written into our Constitution. We have no business acting as censors or endowing any group with censorship powers. It is shocking to me for us to send to prison anyone for publishing anything, especially tracts so distant from any incitement to action as the ones before us.

Justices John Harlan and Potter Stewart also wrote separate dissenting opinions. Justice Stewart, who is quoted at the beginning of this chapter, wrote a brilliant dissent:

There was testimony at his trial that these publications possess artistic and social merit. Personally, I have a hard time discerning any. Most of the material strikes me as both vulgar and unedifying. But if the First Amendment means anything, it means that aman cannot be sent to prison merely for distributing publications which offend ajudge's aesthetic sensibilities, mine or any others.

Censorship reflects a society's lack of confidence in itself. It is a hallmark of an authoritarian regime. Long ago those who wrote our First Amendment charted a different course. They believed a society can betruly strong only when it is truly free.

Epilogue

Years after the decision was handed down Justice Stewart remarked at Columbia University that the two worst Supreme Court decisions were the *Dred Scott* and *Ginzburg* decisions. Justice Brennan, who authored the *Ginzburg* decision, changed his mind, and believed that *Roth* and *Ginzburg* and a slew of other obscenity decisions were mistakes.[3] In the intervening years, however, the composition of the court grew more conservative and Justice Brennan found himself in the liberal minority.

Censorship is alive and well in the United States. The Federal Communications Commission has recently warned radio stations to avoid obscenities by threatening to challenge license renewals. It is necessary for Congress to repeal the federal obscenities statute and to direct that the FCC and other government agencies abandon their attempts to serve as national censors.

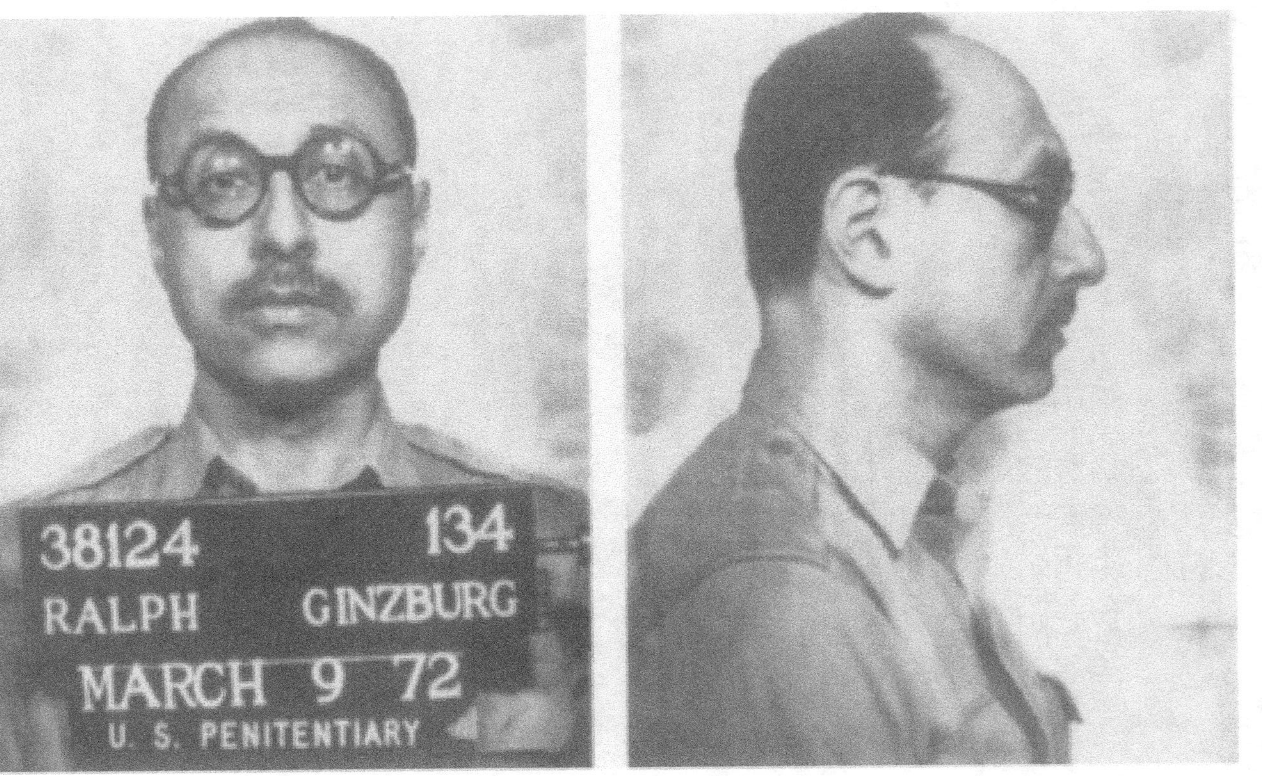

Mug shot of Ralph Ginzburg courtesy of Mr. Ginzburg.

Ralph Ginzburg served eight long months at Allenwood Federal Prison Camp in Pennsylvania. Ginzburg was the successful publisher of *Moneysworth, American Business* and *Better Living*. He felt that his trial, coviction and appeal ruined his career and deprived society of the first and only psychology magazine concerned with sex. He was fined $42,000 and paid his lawyers nearly a quarter of a million dollars for their representation. Ginzburg passed away in 2006 at the age of 76.

Endnotes

1. *Roth v. United States*, 354 U.S. 476.
2. *Memoirs v. Massachusetts*, 383 *U.S.* 413.
3. *Paris Adult Theatre I v. Slaton*, 413 *U.S.* 49 (1973).

Chapter Ten

Unpopular Speakers

"I disapprove of what you say,
but I will defend to the death your right to say it."

—Voltaire

Syracuse city officials granted a permit for John Rogge, a former U.S. assistant attorney general, to speak at a public school building on March 8, 1949. The subject of his speech was to highlight racial discrimination and civil liberties. He was coming to Syracuse to talk about a New Jersey case in which three blacks had been sentenced to theelectric chair for killing a storekeeper. Mr. Rogge and others believed that the sentences were unjust

On the day that the speech was to be given, authorities cancelled the permit. The Young Progressives, who sponsored the speech, arranged for Mr. Rogge to speak at the Hotel Syracuse instead of the public school.

***Irving Feiner at Syracuse University in 1949,
courtesy of Mr. Feiner.***

Irving Feiner

Irving Feiner was a member of the YoungProgressives. Feiner, who grew up in the Bronx, was theson of an immigrant Polish Jew. Once, while riding a train from New York to the South, he saw a black family behind a set of curtains in a segregated dining car. They were roped off from everyone else. Feiner said, "I'll never forgetthat. It made a tremendous impression on me." It was experiences like this one that made Feiner, while a student at Syracuse University, join the Young Progressives. The Young Progressives was a group that advocated equal rights for Negroes, a precursorof the civil rights movement.

Feiner entered the university in 1947 on the GI Bill after serving in the Army during World War II. To publicize the new meeting place, Feiner stood on a wooden box on the sidewalk near the hotel and addressed a group of people. Feiner was speaking into a microphone which was attached to speakers on an automobile parked onMcBride Street. Between five and ten other Young Progressives were distributing leaflets to the crowd andhelping with the sound system. Feiner began to spread the news about the last-minute change, informing the crowdthat city officials were responsible. In the course of his remarks, he called Syracuse Mayor Costello a "champagne-sipping bum." He also called President Truman a "bum" and compared the American Legion to Nazi Gestapo agents.

A Gathering Crowd

A complaint concerning the gathering was made by telephone to the police department, and, at about 6:30 p.m. two officers, Flynn and Cook, were dispatched to the scene to investigate.

As Officer Cook approached the scene in his police car, he had to slow down and almost stop because the crowd was bulging into the street. Officer Flynn, an acting sergeant, arrived in a police car a few minutes later and found that Officer Cook had already arrived. They noted that a crowd of seventy-five or eighty people, both black and white, had gathered around Feiner.

Some of the crowd spread out into the street. Pedestrians trying to use the sidewalk had to walk in the street to get around the crowd. As the officers attempted to maintain the crowd on the sidewalk, Officer Flynn thought he heard "angry muttering." He had trouble getting through the crowd and felt that people were getting "restless."

As Feiner continued, Flynn believed he saw some pushing and shoving. "Some were calm and some were not; they were discussing the speech, pro and con." There was no disorder, however, as Officer Flynn testified. After telephoning the police station from a nearby store, Flynn and Cook returned to the scene to mingle with the crowd and observe.

Feiner began to appeal to the black people, inparticular. He said that in current society, Negroes did not have equal rights. He wanted the crowd to "rise up and fight for their rights and go arm in arm, black and white alike, to the Hotel Syracuse to hear John Rogge." Although this appeal seems to suggest that blacks and whites unite, Officer Flynn got the impression that Feiner was trying to arouse the blacks against the whites. He noted that people were stirred by the remarks.

The Threat of Violence

Then, a man approached the officers and said, "If you don't get that son-of-a-bitch off, I will go over and get him off there myself." This was the only threat of violence that Flynn had heard up to that point. He testified that some other people did comment that the police force seemed unable to handle the situation, and "they did not see why they had to put up with that kind of stuff in the neighborhood."

At this point, Officer Flynn concluded that Feiner's speech had gone far enough. In his opinion, the crowd was getting to the point where they might become unruly. True, there was no actual disturbance, but Flynn claimed that "we stepped in to prevent it from resulting in a fight." He approached Irving Feiner, not to arrest him, but to get him to break up the congregation. Flynn asked Feiner to get off the box, but Feiner kept on talking. Officer Flynn waited a minute, then demanded that he get down, but Feiner refused. Neither Flynn nor officer Cook tried to do anything to the man who made the threat against Feiner. While Flynn was talking to Feiner the crowd was quiet.

Flynn told Feiner that he was under arrest and reached up to take hold of him. Feiner stepped down off the box and announced into the microphone that "the law has arrived, and I suppose they will take over now." He was then arrested and told that he was being charged with "unlawful assembly." Later, because the officers believed that there was not enough evidence to convict Feiner of thischarge, they changed it to "disorderly conduct."

But the new charge seemed no more compelling. Feiner had a legal right to give his speech and had the right to use loud-speaking equipment. The law for disorderly conduct requires citizens to obey "reasonable policeorders." Police often use disorderly conduct charges as a catch-all charge when they cannot find another law that applies to someone's "offending" conduct. A police order to "be quiet" when someone is interfering with an arrest is onething; an order when a public speaker is addressing a crowd is quite different. However, the "disorderly conduct" offense can be applied in both situations.

The Conviction

In May of that year, the case was tried before Judge William Bamerick in the Special Sessions court, and Irving Feiner was found guilty and sentenced to thirty days in the county jail. He served five days before being released on bail because he had decided to appeal the case.

The American Civil Liberties Union supported Feiner's appeal after the county court, and then the New York Court of Appeals, the state's highest court, affirmed Feiner's conviction.

Meanwhile, Feiner was expelled from Syracuse University because he had been convicted of disorderly conduct, disrupting his plans to go to law school. Two law schools that had accepted him withdrew their approvals, as he had not received his undergraduate degree.

At the Nation's Highest Tribunal

In the McCarthy days of 1951, Feiner's case made its way to the United States Supreme Court where its decision was handed down on Monday, January 15th. The Supreme Court, in a six to three decision, ruled that Feiner waslegally arrested, because he passed the bounds of argument or persuasion and undertook "incitement to riot." Chief Justice Vinson wrote:

> We are well aware that the ordinary murmuring and objections of a hostile audience cannot be allowed to silence a speaker, and are also mindful of the possible danger of giving overzealous police officials complete discretion to break up otherwise lawful public meeting.[1]

Justice Vinson gave lip service to free speech, while giving the local gendarmes complete discretion to stop unpopular speakers. The crowd was not violent and did no more than mutter. The threat to the peace came from one person in the crowd, not from the speaker.

Justice Black wrote a blistering dissent:

I think this conviction makes a mockery out of Free Speech guarantees of the First and Fourteenth Amendments. The end result of the affirmance here is to approve a simple and readily available technique by which cities and states can with impunity subject all speeches, political or otherwise, on streets or elsewhere, to the supervision and censorship of the local police. I will have no part or parcel in this holding which I view as a long step toward totalitarian authority.

I reject the implication of the Court's opinion that the police had no obligation to protect petitioner's constitutional right to talk. The police of course have power to prevent breaches of the peace. But if, in the name of preserving order, they ever can interfere with a lawful public speaker, they must first make all reasonable efforts to protect him. Here the policemen did not even pretend to protect petitioner.

Justices Douglas and Minton also dissented.

Epilogue

While his case was pending, Feiner went back to New York and found a job in the printing business. In February, Irving Feiner came back to Onondaga County and served the remaining twenty-five days of his sentence at the Jamesville Penitentiary. He then went back to his job in New York, started his own print shop, got married and moved to the suburbs where he raised two daughters. Years later, he set up "Fish, Fish, Fish" in Nyack, New York where he sold exotic and rare tropical fish. But because of his arrest and conviction, and the Supreme Court affirmance, he never became a lawyer.

Thirty-five years after being expelled from Syracuse University, Feiner was readmitted under a special program to complete his college degree. He completed the credits he was lacking when expelled, and in 1984, he was awarded his Bachelor of Arts degree. Although Feiner never did make it to law school, he occasionally lectured to constitutional law students regarding his case. Mr. Feiner died in 2009 at the age of 84.

Endnotes

1. 340 U.S. 315 (1951).

Chapter Eleven

Going Door-to-Door

"Behold, I stand at the door and knock."

—Revelations 3:20

Knocking on doors to support political causes or to sell Girl Scout cookies or wares has been an American institution since before the Constitution was enacted. This chapter includes two cases that severely undercut the right to go door-to-door for commercial or political reasons.

The Postal Monopoly

Did you know that despite the fact that you pay for your own mailbox, the government regulates what can be put into it? Have you ever put a note in your neighbor's mailbox without putting a postage stamp on it? If so, then you, like most Americans, have broken a federal law.

In May, 1976, in New York State, volunteers for the Hilltop Farms Civic Association (part of the Saw Mill Valley Civic Association) hand-delivered notices to the homes in their area. The notice told of a town meeting to be held on June 3rd. As usual, the notices were put in mailboxes, and no postage was put on them. The civic association did not have much money so it relied on volunteer labor rather than the U.S. Post Office to deliver its notices.

About the same time, political materials for Jimmy Carter, Walter Mondale, Senator Patrick Moynihan, Congressman J. Edward Meyer and various candidates for state offices were put into mailboxes in the same manner.

On June 2, 1976, Walter Rostenberg, the postmaster for White Plains, New York, learned that the notices were being put into mailboxes without postage. He wrote a letter to the leader of the civic association, enclosing acopy of the postal regulations. Rostenberg warned that thepractice was illegal and that failure to comply with the law would result in a fine of up to $300.

In 1934, Congress passed a law that provided:

> Whoever knowingly and willfully deposits any mailable matter such as statements of accounts, circulars, sale bills, or other like matter, **_on which no postage has been paid_**, in any letter box established, approved, or accepted by the Postal Service for the receipt or delivery of mail matteron any mail route with intent to avoid payment of lawful postage thereon, shall For each offense be fined no more than $300.[1]

In February, 1977, the Saw Mill Valley Civic Association, with other civic organizations, filed suit seeking relief from the Postal Service's threatened enforcement of the 1934 law. The plaintiffs argued that enforcement of the law would inhibit their ability to communicate with residents in their towns and would, thus, deny them freedom of speech and press secured by the First Amend- ment.

The case was assigned to federal Judge William Connor. Attorneys for the Post Office moved to have the case dismissed without trial because they contended that the statute was constitutional. Judge Connor granted the government's motion and dismissed the case. He ruled:

> [T]he Constitution does not guarantee plaintiffs an absolute right to the most efficient or effective means of communication.[2]

The civic associations appealed Judge Connor's ruling. The three-judge panel of the Second Circuit Court of Appeals in New York City agreed with the citizens groups. They ruled that the case should not have been dismissed without a trial. Quoting an earlier Supreme Court case, Judge Irving Kaufman wrote:

> Freedom of press necessarily embraces pamphlets and leaflets. These indeed have been historic weapons in the defense of liberty, as the pamphlets of Thomas Paine and others in our history abundantly attest! And probably the most effective way of ensuring that such literature reaches its intended audience is house-to-house distribution.

> Moreover, the individual householder's
> Right to receive information cannot be
> ignored.[3]

The Court of Appeals reversed the dismissal and sent the case back to Judge Connor, of the district court, for a trial. At the trial, the Post Office introduced evidence that the purpose of the statute was to protect mail revenues and to prevent overcrowding of mailboxes. The citizens group argued that they could not afford to pay for postage and, furthermore, that the Post Office was slow and that its volunteers delivered notices much more quickly. The district court found the Postal Service's reasons to be Insufficient and ruled that the statute was unconstitutional:

> Plaintiffs have shown that the burden on
> their ability to communicate ideas, pos-
> itions on local issues and civic information
> to their constituents is substantial.

> The court concludes that the cost to free
> expression of imposing this burden out-
> weighs the showing made by the Postal
> Service of its need to enforce the statute to
> promote effective delivery and protection of
> the mails.

Before the U.S. Supreme Court

The Post Office appealed the lower court's ruling directly to the U.S. Supreme Court. This is allowed when a court rules that a federal statute is unconstitutional. The court reversed Judge Connor's decision by a seven to two vote.[4] Only Justices Marshall and Stevens dissented.

Justice Marshall wrote that "door to door distribution of circulars is essential to the poorly financed causes of little people."[5]

Justice Stevens wrote a thoughtful dissent:

> The mailbox is private property. If a private party—by using volunteer workers or by operating more efficiently—can deliver written communications for less than the cost of postage, then public interest would be well served by transferring that portion of the mail delivery business out of the public domain. I see no reason to prohibit com-petition simply to prevent reduction in the size of a subsidized monopoly.
>
> I have the impression that the general public is at best only dimly aware of the law and that numerous otherwise law-abiding citizens regularly violate it with impunity.

Epilogue

Congress should amend the Postal law to allow non-profit organizations and individuals to put notices and leaflets in mailboxes. When the law makes criminals of us all, we lose respect for it. Since many of us leave notes for neighbors or leave flyers for political candidates or for the Red Cross or Girl Scouts in mailboxes, and still more of us indirectly endorse such actions by responding to flyers others leave, we are all federal criminals.

Selling Magazines Door-to-Door

Jack Breard was a regional representative, based in Dallas, Texas, for the Keystone Readers Service, a company that sold magazine subscriptions by door-to-door solicitations. The magazines they sold included the *Saturday Evening Post, Ladies' Home Journal, Country Gentleman, Holiday, Newsweek, American Home, Cosmopolitan, Esquire, Parents, Today's Woman* and *True* magazines. At the time, the early 1950s, annual subscriptions to these magazines were about two dollars.

Breard would send a team of solicitors, often college students, to canvass a town for a few days and then move on to another town. They would stay in inexpensive hotels, with two or three salesmen to a room. Pay was solely on a commission basis.

Green River Ordinances

Green River Ordinances got their name from the town of Green River, Wyoming, where they originated. With the exception of dairy and grocery products, these ordinances prohibited the practice of selling anything door-to-door, unless the homeowner or resident of the property requested the item. Dairy and grocery products were excluded because in the early 1950s, when most Green River Ordinances were passed, it was common practice to sell these itemsdoor-to-door, and it was convenient for the consumer. But all other solicitation—even by Girl Scouts, Little Leaguers or Red Cross volunteers, whether they were selling cookies, candles or magazines-was strictly prohibited.

Alexandria, Louisiana was one of over 400 towns and cities to pass a Green River Ordinance. Their ordinance declared violations to be a misdemeanor and provided for a fine of twenty-five dollars or a sentence of thirty days in jail.

Jack Breard photographed in 1950s, courtesy Jack Breard, Jr.

On June 28, 1949, Jack Breard andhis crew were workingon the streets of Alexandria, Louisiana when he was arrestedfor violating the law, regarding door-to-door solicitation.

In the Halls of Justice

Gus Voltz was the judge assigned to hear Mr. Breard's case in the City Court of Alexandria, Parish of Rapides. Attorneys for Breard argued that the First Amendment right of free speech and press allowed him to solicit subscriptions for magazines by knocking on doors. They argued that the magazines certainly enjoyed protection under the amendment, and that more than half of the subscribers to magazines at that time were signed up by neighborhood solicitors.

Jack Breard was tried for his offense before JudgeVoltz without a jury. Judge Voltz found him guilty and im- posed a fine of twenty-five dollars or thirty days in jail. Breard posted an appeal bond of a hundred dollars.

Mr. Breard's case came before Louisiana's highest court within one year. The courts of Louisiana were not sympathetic to out-of-towner Breard and his band of young solicitors. The Louisiana Supreme Court, while affirming Jack Breard's conviction, stated,

> A man's home is his castle. No one has any vested prerogative to invade another's privacy. Each community knows its own problems best.[6]

The United States Supreme Court

The Supreme Court agreed to hear Mr. Breard's case and set oral argument for March, 1951. Breard's attorneys were optimistic because eight years earlier the court had ruled that cities and states could not enforce lawsthat taxed door-to-door sales of religious literature.

On June 4, 1951, by a vote of six to three, the court issued its decision.[7] The court ruled that the ordinance was valid and that it did not impose any improper restraint on free speech or on freedom of the press.

The court held that because the solicitations were for profit, they could be prohibited. The opinion distinguished between free distributions and commercial solicitations. The court still affirmed the right to go door-to-door to hand out free publications.

Chief Justice Vinson, who rarely dissents, and who wrote the majority opinion for the court in the *Feiner* case, decided just five months earlier (see previous chapter), wrote a strong dissenting opinion. Joining the Chief Justice in dissent were Justices Hugo Black and William O. Douglas. In Justice Vinson's opinion, the Alexandria ordinance was a regulation of interstate commerce, which was a function of Congress, not of local city councils.

Justice Black wrote a separate dissent, resting on the First Amendment:

> The constitutional sanctuary for the press Must necessarily include liberty to publish And to circulate. In view of our economic system, it must also include freedom to solicit paying subscribers. Of course homeowners can if they wish forbid newsboys, reporters or magazine solicitors to ring their doorbells. But when the homeowner himself has not done this, I believe that the First Amendment, interpreted with due regard for

the freedoms it guarantees, bars laws like the present ordinance which punish persons who peacefully go from door to door as agents of the press.

Epilogue

Jack Breard's case did not cause the end of the *Saturday Evening Post* or *Ladies' Home Journal,* or make itimpossible for customers to renew their subscriptions. But because of the decision, many college students lost a sourceof income and magazine publishers had to look for other ways to sell subscriptions.

Jack Breard died in 1959 at the age of 49. Magazine subscriptions are now sold by television advertising, telephone solicitation and by direct mail. Jack Breard, Jr. adopted his father's career and sold magazine subscriptions. He said that magazines are still sold door-to-door, but not like they were in the 1940s.

Conclusions

While each of   these two cases, on its own, might be consideredminor, each represents a significant deterioration of our right to free speech. Cities and states have the power to prohibit the door-to-door solicitation of businesses. The Post Office and Congress have put up a barrier to the use of mailboxes. In the next chapter, another mode of communication is eliminated; the handing out of leaflets in shopping malls. If citizens cannot reach people attheir homes and cannot reach them where they shop, what First Amendment freedoms are left?

Concerning the concept that "a man's home is his castle," the Supreme Court uses this argument only when a minor intrusion is made into the home by private citizens.

See Chapter Twenty-Seven on how the court deals with government intrusion into the home.

Of course, some citizens do not want to be bothered by having people knock on their doors or by having leaflets left in their mailboxes. These people have the right to put out a small sign saying either "No solicitors" or "U.S. mail only." I believe that a law protecting the right of citizens to limit receipt of messages would be constitutional. Citizens have a right to be let alone, as well as to receive information. But unless a citizen asserts his right to be let alone, the right of others to communicate their ideas should prevail.

Endnotes

1. 18 U.S.C. Section 1725.
2. 448 F. Supp. 159 (March 29, 1978).
3. 586 F.2d 935 (October 30, 1978).
4. 490 F. Supp. 157 (April 24, 1980).
5. 453 U.S. 11 (June 21, 1981), quoting *Martin v. City of*

    Struthers, 319 U.S. 141, 146.
6. 47 So. 2nd 553, 556 (June 30, 1950).
7. 341 U.S. 622 (1951).

Chapter Twelve

The Malling of America

"We've got it all at Springfield Mall."

—Advertising slogan

In November of 1968, a week after Richard Nixon won the November 5th election, Lyndon Baines Johnson was still President of the United States. The Vietnam War and the protest movement were both being waged at full tilt. More than 500,000 American soldiers were in Vietnam at the time.

On Thursday, November 14, 1968, Donald Tanner, Susan Roberts, Betsy Wheeler and one or two others handed out leaflets inviting the public to a meeting to protest the draft and the Vietnam War. The leafleteers weremembers of "The Resistance Community," and their handouts invited people to talks about the draft board, a potluck dinner, a communion and a dance at Reed College. Copies of the actual leaflets handed out that day are reproduced on the next two pages.

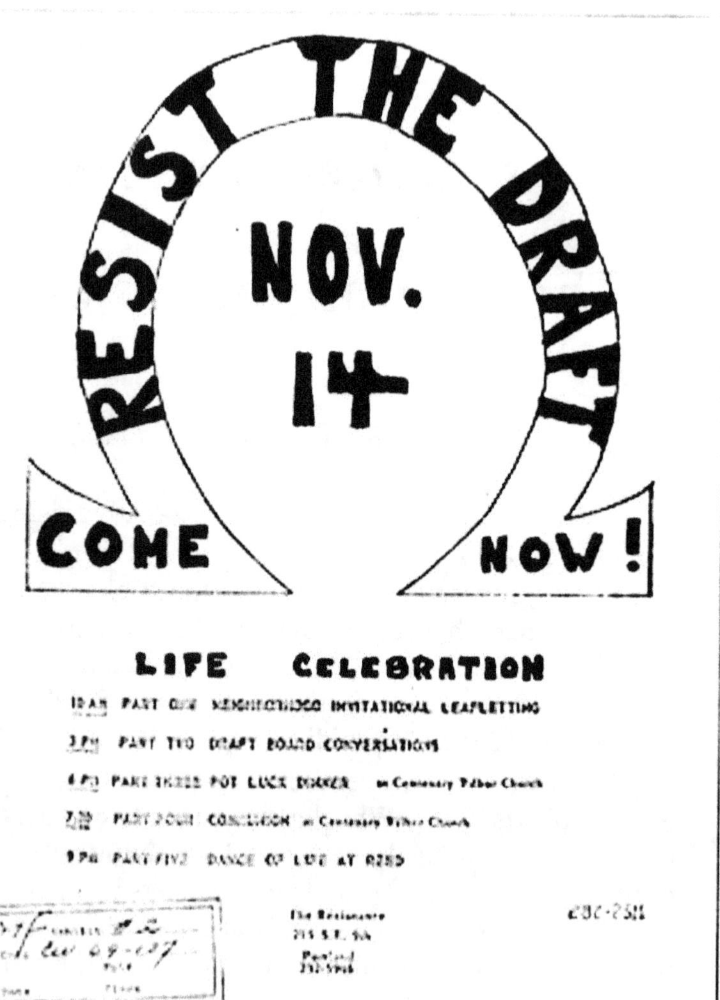

**Leaflet handed out by Resistance Community
at Lloyd Center Mall.**

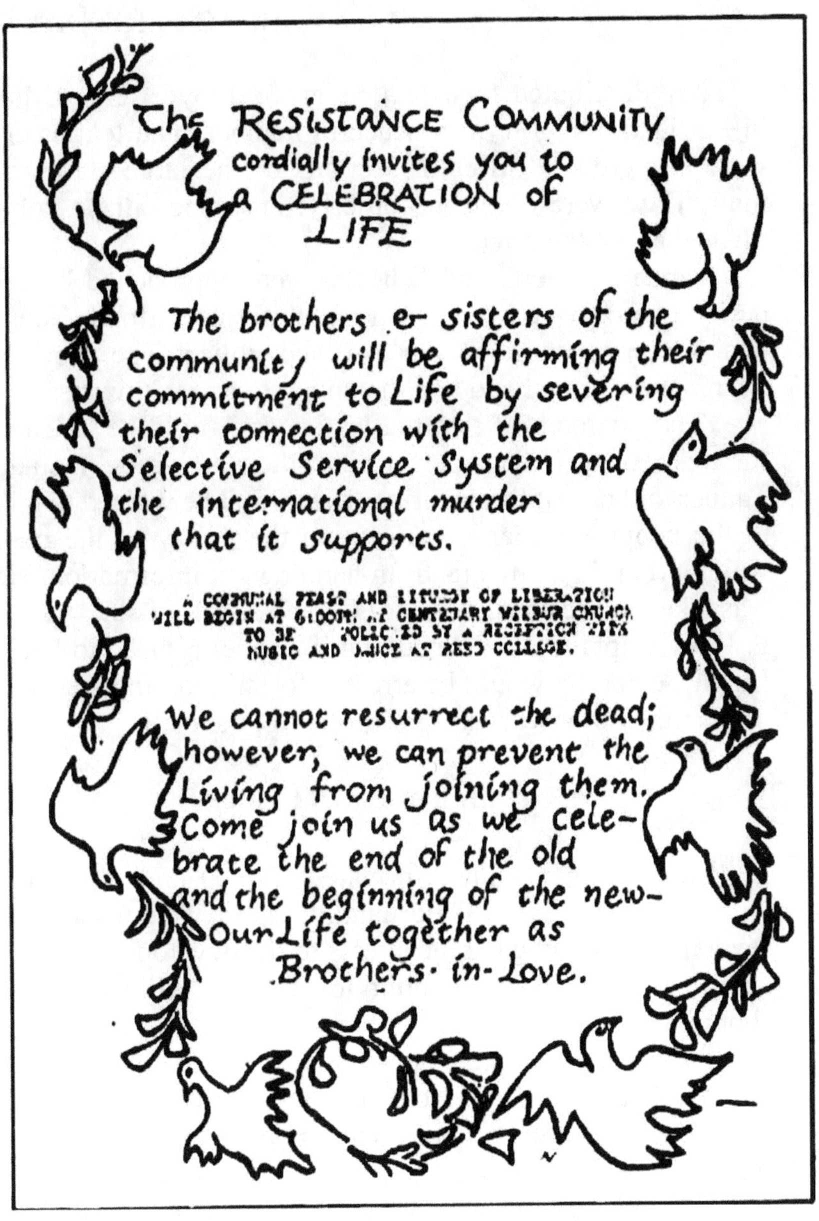

*Invitation to Celebration of Life handed
out at Lloyd Center Mall.*

They distributed their leaflets at the Lloyd Center Mall in Portland, Oregon, in a peaceful manner. The leafleteers were scattered in different sections of the large shopping mall. They were quiet and orderly: only one citizen complained about their activities.

Tanner, Roberts and Wheeler were approached by security guards who were wearing uniforms virtually identical to those worn by the Portland police. The security guards were armed and had the power to arrest citizens.

The guards said that the leafleteers would be arrested for trespassing if they persisted in their activities. Donald Tanner told one of the security officers that he wanted to talk to the people in charge concerning the policy of the mall which prohibited citizens from handing out information. He was taken to see security guard Captain Clifford P. Boss. Captain Boss stated that if Tanner refused to leave Lloyd Center, he would be arrested for trespassing.Because of the threat of arrest, the leafleteers left the mall.

The Mall at Lloyd Center

Lloyd Center Mall is privately owned and is located within the city limits of Portland, Oregon. The city closed several streets and gave the streets to the developers, so that an urban mall could be built to compete with suburban shopping malls.

Lloyd Mall is like many other enclosed malls in the United States with covered climate-controlled pedestrian walkways connecting about sixty retail stores. The mall, which is open to the public twenty-four hours a day, includes twenty-five acres of stores and twenty acres of parking.

The mall is like the city streets that it replaced. On every Veterans' Day, a parade with flags, drummers and color guard units takes place, and a speech is given on the valor of American soldiers. During the 1968 presidential campaign, candidates Eugene McCarthy, Robert Kennedy and Richard Nixon gave speeches at the mall at Lloyd Center. The auditorium at the mall was used to provide television coverage of the 1964 Oregon presidential pri- mary election.

Several politicians and organizations have been denied use of the mall at Lloyd Center. Oregon Governor Tom McCall was denied an opportunity to make a speech there. The March of Dimes and Hadassah, a Jewish organization, were also denied use of the mall.

The Salvation Army has been permitted to use the mall to raise funds during the Christmas season. The American Legion has been permitted to sell "Buddy Poppies," and the Boy Scouts have been allowed to set up displays there. The mall maintains a public information center where pam-phlets on the Portland Zoo, the Sanctuary of Our SorrowfulMother and other topics are available. The Mall has also displayed National Guard weaponry and equipment, and, because of this, some people referred to the mall as "Fort Lloyd."

Malls Across America

In the 1960s enclosed shopping malls were just starting to sprout up around the country. By 1987, enclosed shopping malls dominated the retail market in the United States. There are now 25,000 covered shopping malls in the U.S. They have become our new town squares. Shopping malls now constitute more than fifty percent of the nation's retail sales, excluding sales of automotive products, a total of more than $1.5 trillion dollars every year.

In Federal Court in Oregon

Donald Tanner, Susan Roberts and Betsy Wheeler felt that they had a right to hand out leaflets in the mall. The mall was open to the public and *everyone* went to the Lloyd Center Mall to shop. Leafletting at the mall was the only effective way to reach many people. Handing out flyers has been an American tradition since Thomas Paine handed out his pamphlet *Common Sense* more than 200 years ago.

After being threatened with arrest, the pampleteers left the mall and consulted with Attorney Carl Neil. Mr. Neil advised them that the First Amendment gave them a right to hand out leaflets at shopping malls. He advised them that the *Logan Valley* case had just been decided by the Supreme Court, giving workers the right to picket at a privately owned shopping mall.[1] The Supreme Court's ruling in that case appeared to extend First Amendment protections to private shopping areas.

Neil studied the laws that allowed the Lloyd Corporation to take over city streets and filed a detailed lawsuit against the mall owners in March of 1969. The case was assigned to Chief Judge Gus J. Solomon. After hearing evidence in the case, Judge Solomon ruled that theResistance Community, and other groups, had the right to hand out leaflets at the mall and enjoined the Lloyd Corporation from interfering with people handing out leaflets. He ruled that the mall was the "functional equivalent of a public business district."[2]

The Appeals

The Lloyd Corporation filed an appeal to the Ninth Circuit Court of Appeals. The appeal was heard by a panel of three judges who unanimously upheld the decision of Judge Solomon.[3]

The owners of the mall then sought review in the United States Supreme Court, which the court granted. The nation's highest court heard arguments on April 18, 1972, and issued its opinion on June 22nd of that year.

By the closest of margins, the Supreme Court overturned the rulings of the lower courts and ruled that there is no First Amendment right to hand out leaflets at privately owned shopping malls.[4] The court, which had ruled four years earlier that unions had the right to picket in private shopping malls, decided to limit its earlier ruling. In 1946, the court had ruled that people living in a company-owned town in Alabama had the right to freespeech in the streets of that town.[5]

The court's ruling in *Lloyd v. Tanner* significantly undercuts the court's earlier rulings regarding the exercise of the right to free speech in malls and towns owned by private corporations. Four justices vigorously dissented.

Justice Marshall, joined by Justices Douglas, Brennan and Stewart, wrote:

> In sum, the Lloyd Center is an integral part of the Portland Community. From its inception, the city viewed it as a "business district" of the city and depended on it to supply much needed employment opportunities. To insure the success of the Center, the city carefully integrated it into the pattern of streets already established and planned future development of the streets around the Center. It is plain, therefore, that Lloyd Center is the equivalent of a public "business district". . . .
>
> *   *   *
>
> When there are no effective means of communication, free speech is a mere shibboleth. I believe that the First Amendment requires it to be a reality.

Epilogue

In the fifty plus years that have passed since *Lloyd v. Tanner* was announced by the court, our country has become more suburban and more mall oriented. Enclosed shopping malls have truly becomethe new town centers of the the United States. Political candidates often use malls to leaflet and campaign, but do so solely at the discretion of the mall owners, whose decisions can be based upon their personal biases and prejudices.

The Supreme Court's decision was based on the rights of property owners. However, when enclosed malls invite the public to shop, they are waiving their rights to completely control their own property. The court has recognized that store owners cannot exclude patrons because of their race, sex or religion. Similarly, the mall owners should not be able to restrict peaceful leafletting in the common areas of shopping malls. If a shopping mall security guard overhears a person talking politics, the guard has no right to evict the speaker. Similarly, the guard should have no right to eject someone for handing a written statement to another shopper.

The Framers of the Constitution did not intend so great a role for store owners in regulating free speech. They certainly did not envision corporate-owned, enclosed shopping malls. If we are truly a democracy, then we must return the right of free speech to our shopping districts, either by a new

Supreme Court ruling, by legislative action at the state and local level, or by a constitutional amendment.

So far, the highest court or legislature in six states (California, New Jersey, Colorado, Massachusetts, Washington and Connecticut) have decried that citizens in those states have the right under state law to exercise free speech rights in shopping malls. Our precious right to free speech should not vary from state to state, but if there is no alternative, then our right should be restored one stateat a time.

Endnotes

1. 391 U.S. 308(1968).
2. 308 F. Supp. 128, at 130.
3. 446 F.2d 545.
4. 407 U.S. 551 (June 22, 1972).
5 *Marsh v. Alabama,* 326 U.S. 501.

Chapter Thirteen

The Second Boston
Tea Party

"Where lies the final harbor?"

—Herman Melville in *Moby Dick*

In December of 1979, in an act of unprovoked aggression, the Soviet Union invaded Afghanistan. On January 9, 1980, in protest of the Soviet invasion,Thomas "Teddy" Gleason, president of the International Longshoremen's Association (ILA) ordered its members to stop handling cargoes arriving from or destined for the Soviet Union. The order was effective on grain, food and other cargo. The ILA union controlled allEast Coast and Gulf Coast ports, from New England to Texas. Rank and file union members supported the boycott. Gleason announced that the decision was made necessary by the demands of the workers. He said:

It is their will to refuse to work Russian vessels and Russian cargoes under present conditions of the world. People are upset and they refuse to continue businessas usual so long the Russians insist on being international bully boys.

Thomas W. Gleason

The ILA President

ILA President Gleason wears a diamond-studded ILA tiepin, which he, jokingly, claims stands for "I Love America." Gleason was born in 1900 and began working on the docks at age fifteen. He has seen the union survive wildcat strikes, riots, boycotts and racketeering scandals. In 1915, he dropped out of school and began working on the docks for ten cents an hour. In 1932, he was blacklisted for union activity, which was not then protected by federal law. After the National Labor Relations Act was passed as a part of the New Deal, Gleason returned to the docks and was elected a union organizer. He led wildcat strikes in 1946, 1949 and 1951, each time winning additional benefits for the union.

Gleason rose through the ranks to become president in 1963. He shaped an unruly mob of workers into a labor organization strong enough to influence international politics and brought stability to a strike-prone industry.

Allied International

Allied International is an American company that imported Russian wood products into the United States. Allied contracted with the Waterman Steamship Lines to deliver goods from Leningrad to Boston. As a result of the ILA boycott, Allied's shipments were completely disrupted. Allied was forced to renegotiate its Russian contracts, reducing its purchases significantly.

In Federal Court in Boston

Allied sued the ILA in the federal court in Boston because its members refused to unload Allied's ships. Allied claimed that the boycott was illegal under the labor laws and interfered with Allied's contractual rights. The court dismissed Allied's case holding that the boycott was purely

political, a primary boycott of Russian goods andprotected by
the First Amendment's right to free speech and association.[1]
Judge Walter Skinner stated:

> I   am presented here, however, with
> political activity in the sense of a directpo-
> litical protest against the Soviet Union's
> foreign policy. While commerce   between
> Allied and the Soviet Union and,ultimately,
> the American people is beingrestrained by
> the ILA's refusal to handlecertain cargo, this
> refusal is wholly politically oriented with
> no apparent economic benefit accruing to the
> union or its members.

> Allied is still free to unload its ships by
> non-union personnel. ILA members have not
> boycotted any ships not involved in trade
> with the Soviet Union, including those ships
> owned by carriers who maintain Russian
> trade elsewhere.
> A mere refusal to deal cannot constitute
> an interference as every workermay decline
> to offer his services just as every buyer may
> decide not to purchase.

The court of appeals reversed the dismissal and ruled
that the boycott was not protected by the First Amendment.[2]The dispute was a labor issue, said the court, and the
rights of free speech and association did not apply. The U.S.
Supreme Court agreed to hear the case.

The First Boston Tea Party

The Boston Tea Party took place on December 16,1773. The object of that protest was an overseas power, Britain. The issue was the British tax on tea. A group of forty to fifty Boston patriots, including longshoremen, un- loaded a cargo of tea into the Boston Harbor. As a result of the tea dumping, Britain closed the Port of Boston. The Boston Tea Party was one of the events that led to the American Revolution.

In the Highest Court

The U.S. Supreme Court heard arguments in the longshoremen's case but finally agreed with court of appeals. The case, the court decided, was a "labor law" matter and not a matter of free speech and association.[3] The court said that the U.S. labor laws applied, because an American union was refusing to unload an American ship. The court found that under the labor laws, the boycott was an illegal secondary boycott. A primary boycott, or strike, is when workers are protesting directly against a company because of that company's policies or actions. The labor law outlaws secondary boycotts. The court gave the First Amendment this brief consideration:

> There are many ways in which a union and its individual members may express their opposition to Russian foreign policy without infringing upon the rights of others.

There were also other ways that the citizens of Boston could have protested the British tax on tea without infringing on the rights of others. Consider the harm suffered by the tea drinkers in Boston, as well as the company that imported the tea. If the current labor laws had been in effect in 1773, the Boston Tea Party would have been illegal as a secondary boycott. The patriots who dumped the tea into the Boston harbor were not protesting against the tea company or the tea importer. They were, as here, protesting against the policies of a distant government. If those protesting the British tax on tea had decided to write letters to the editor instead of making an effective protest, we might still be part of the British Empire. Those colonial Americans would have wanted citizens of their new nation to have the right to protest against a government's oppression by means of a secondary boycott.

The First Amendment provides that "Congress shall pass no law abridging the freedom of speech, or of the press, or the right of the people peaceably to assemble." Congress passed the labor laws. The extent to which these labor laws conflict with the right to free speech, to protest, render them unconstitutional.

A political protest is a First-Amendment-protected activity. The Supreme Court has ruled in other cases that symbolic speech, such as the wearing of black armbands in protest of war, is protected speech.

The ILA boycott was the only *effective* way that the union could protest. Does the Constitution only protect *ineffective* means of protest?

The Founding Fathers would have been revolted by this *unanimous* Supreme Court ruling. At least one judge, Boston federal court Judge Walter Skinner, could separate free speech rights from union activities and labor laws.

Epilogue

After the Supreme Court ruling, Judge Skinner held a trial on the damages that Allied suffered because of the boycott. The court ruled that the union must pay about nine million dollars for the damages that the shipping firm suffered.

This damages award is one of the largest ever imposed against a labor union. The courts have punished a labor union for acting in a patriotic protest, one that should have had the full support of the country. Since the judge who first heard the case believed the union's activities werelegal, the union should not have to suffer damages because the judge erred.

ILA president Gleason retired from office in 1987 after twenty-four years of service. Five years later Gleason passed away. The boycott of Russian ships, that he started, lasted just over a year. The boycott began while Jimmy Carter was President of the United States. Gleason lifted the boycott at President Reagan's request, not because of a court order.

Endnotes

1. 492 F. Supp. 334 (1980).
2. 640 F.2d 1368 (1981).
3. 456 US. 212 (1982).

Chapter Fourteen

Citizens Disunited

"Corporations are not people. People have hearts, they have kids, they get jobs, they get sick, they cry, they dance. They live, they love and they die. And that matters. That matters because we don't run this country for corporations, we run it for people."

—Senator Elizabeth Warren

"Both free speech rights and property rights belong legally to individuals."

—Thomas Sowell, Conservative Economist

Corporate contributions to political campaigns and candidates were banned in the United States for more than 100 years. The Tillman Act of 1907 was the first federal legislation that banned corporate political contributions. The Bipartisan Campaign Reform Act of 2002 (known as McCain–Feingold) prohibited corporations and unionsfrom using their general treasury to fund "electioneering communications" (broadcast advertisements mentioning a candidate) within 30 days before a primary or 60 days before a general election.

During the 2004 Bush-Kerry presidential campaign, Michael Moore's film *Fahrenheit 9/11* was promoted. *Fahrenheit 9/11* was a documentary critical of the Bush administration's response to the terrorist attacks on September 11, 2001.

Citizens United, a conservative nonprofit organization, filed a complaint with the Federal Election Commission (FEC) charging that advertisements for *Fahrenheit 9/11* were political ads because they sought to influence thecampaign. The FEC dismissed the complaint because the film, associated trailers and website represented bona fide commercial activity, not "contributions" or "expenditures" as defined by the Federal Election Campaign Act. The FECsaid that Moore's movie was produced and distributed by bona fide commercial film company.

In response to the FEC decision, Citizens United sought to establish itself as a bona fide commercial film maker, producing several documentary films between 2005 and 2007. Citizens United planned to run television commercials to promote its latest political documentary *Hillary: The Movie* and to air the movie on DirecTV.

The movie was highly critical of then-Senator Hillary Clinton, with the District Court describing the movie as an elongated version of a negative 30-second television commercial. Citizens United filed suit against the Federal Election Commission seeking a court order declaring that McCain-Feingold was unconstitutional if it applied to *Hillary: The Movie.*

In the District Court

In January 2008, the United States District Court for the District of Columbia ruled that the television advertisements for *Hillary: The Movie* violated the McCain-Feingold restrictions of "electioneering communications" within 30 days of a primary. Though Citizens United claimed that the film was fact-based and non-partisan, the lower court found that the film had no purpose other than to discredit Clinton's candidacy for president. 530 F. Supp. 2d 274 (D.C. 2008).

Appeal to the Supreme Court

Citizens United appealed directly to the U.S. Supreme Court because the district court had convened a three-judge panel. The Supreme Court docketed the case on August 18, 2008 and heard oral argument on March 24, 2009. *Citizens United v. Federal Election Commission*, 558 U.S. 50 (2010), was a landmark United States Supreme Court case in which the Court held that the First Amendment prohibited the government from restricting independent political expenditures by corporations and unions. In a 5–4 decision, the Court held that portions of McCain-Feingold violated the First Amendment.

The case did not involve the federal ban on direct contributions from corporations or unions to candidate campaigns or political parties, which remains illegal in races for federal office. The Supreme Court could havemerely held that McCain-Feingold did not apply to theairing and promotion of the *Hillary* movie, as the FEC had done with Michael Moore's *Fahrenheit 9/11* movie,without throwing out the nation's system for regulating campaign contributions.

According to a 2012 article in *The New Yorker* by CNN's legal correspondent Jeffrey Toobin, the Court expected to rule after on the narrow issue that had originally been presented. That narrow issue is whether campaign finance laws apply to the airing of a film. At the subsequent conference among the justices, the vote was 5–4 in favor of Citizens United being allowed to show the film.

Chief Justice John Roberts, according to the privilege of that office when in the majority, was in charge of assigning the majority opinion and chose to write it himself. His opinion restricted itself narrowly, holding that the McCain-Feingold allowed the showing of the *Hillary* film. A draft concurrence by Justice Kennedy argued that the court could and should go much further. The other justices in the majority began agreeing with Justice Kennedy, and convinced Roberts to reassign the writingand allow Kennedy's concurrence to instead become the majority opinion.

Airing the Court's Dirty Laundry

On the dissenting side, John Paul Stevens, the most senior justice in the minority, assigned the dissent to Justice David Souter, who had announced his retirement from the Court while he was working on this case. The final draft went beyond critiquing the majority. Jeffrey Toobin described it as "air[ing] some of the Court's dirty laundry," writing that Souter's dissent accused Roberts of having manipulated Court procedures to reach his desired result— an expansive decision that, Souter claimed, changeddecades of election law and ruled on issues neither party to the litigation had presented.

According to Toobin, Roberts was concerned that Souter's dissent, likely to be his last opinion for the Court, could "damage the Court's credibility." Souter agreed with the minority to withdraw the opinion and schedule the case for reargument. However, when he did, the "Questions Presented" to the parties were edited to be more expansive, touching on the issues that Kennedy had identified. According to Toobin, the eventual result was a foregone conclusion from that point on since the same majority had supported it.

On June 29, 2009, the last day of the term, the Court issued an order directing the parties to re-argue the case after briefing whether it might be necessary to overruleearlier Supreme Court cases in order to decide the case. Justice Stevens noted in his dissent that in its prior motion for summary judgment Citizens United had abandoned its challenge of McCain-Feingold §203, with the parties agreeing to the dismissal of the claim. This means that the only issue before the court was how the law applied to the airing of the *Hillary* film, not to the law in general.

Justice Sotomayor sat on the bench for the first time during the second round of oral arguments. This was the first case argued by Solicitor General and future Supreme Court Justice Elena Kagan. Former Bush Solicitor General Ted Olson and First Amendment lawyer Floyd Abramsargued for Citizens United, and former Clinton Solicitor General Seth Waxman defended the statute on behalf of various supporters.

Opinions of the Court

The majority opinion, written by Justice Kennedy, was relatively short, less than 30 pages. Chief Justice Roberts wrote a concurring opinion to address concerns about *stare decisis* (following precedent), and Justice Scalia wrote a concurring opinion about the history and meaning of the First Amendment.

Justice Kennedy's majority opinion found that McCain-Feingold's prohibition of all independent expenditures by corporations and unions violated the First Amendment's protection of free speech. He wrote, "If the First Amendment has any force, it prohibits Congress from fining or jailing citizens, or associations of citizens, for simply engaging in political speech."

Justice Kennedy's opinion for the majority also noted that since the First Amendment (and the Court) do not distinguish between media and other corporations, these restrictions would allow Congress to suppress political speech in newspapers, books, television and blogs. TheCourt overruled *Austin*, a case that had held that a state law that prohibited corporations from using treasury money to support or oppose candidates in elections did not violate the First and Fourteenth Amendments. The Court also over-ruled that portion of *McConnell*, a case that upheld the restriction of corporate spending on "electioneering com-munications." The Court's ruling effectively freed corpor-ations and unions to spend money both on "election-eering communications" and to directly advocate for the election or defeat of candidates (although not to contribute directly to candidates or political parties).

The majority argued that the First Amendment protects *associations* of individuals in addition to individual speakers, and further that the First Amendment does not allow prohibitions of speech based on the identity of the speaker. Corporations, as associations of individuals, therefore, have speech rights under the First Amendment. Because spending money is essential to disseminating speech, as established in *Buckley v. Valeo*, limiting a corporation's ability to spend money unconstitutionally limits the ability of its members to associate effectively and to speak on political issues.

The majority also criticized *Austin's* reasoning that the "distorting effect" of large corporate expenditures con-stituted a risk of corruption or the appearance of corruption. Rather, the majority argued that the governmenthad no place in determining whether large expenditures distorted an audience's perceptions, and that the type of "corruption" that might justify government controls on spending for speech had to relate to some form of "quid pro quo" transaction: "There is no such thing as too much speech."

Concurrences

Chief Justice Roberts, with whom Justice Alito joined, wrote separately "to address the important principles of judicial restraint and *stare decisis* implicated in this case." This concurrence was a list of excuses for allowing the court to overrule earlier decisions, even though Justice Roberts testified in his confirmation hearing that he would be a restrained justice.

The Dissent

A stinging dissenting opinion by Justice Stevens was joined by Justice Ginsburg, Justice Breyer, and Justice Sotomayor. To emphasize his unhappiness with the majority, Stevens read part of his 90-page dissent from the bench. The dissent argued that the Court's ruling "threatens to undermine the integrity of elected institutions across the Nation. The path it has taken to reach its outcome will, I fear, do damage to this institution." He wrote: "A democracy cannot function effectively when its constituent members believe laws are being bought and sold."

Justice Stevens also argued that the Court addressed a question not raised by the litigants when it found McCain-Feingold to be facially unconstitutional, and that the majority "changed the case to give themselves an opportunity to change the law." He argued that the majority had expanded the scope beyond the questions presented by the appellant and that therefore a sufficient record for judging the case did not exist. Stevens argued that at a minimum the Court should have remanded the case for a fact-finding hearing, and that the majority did not consider other compilations of data, such as the Congressional record for justifying the law.

Justice Stevens said,

> In the context of election to public office, the distinction between corporate and human speakers is significant. Although they make enormous contributions to our society, corporations are not actually members of it. ***They cannot vote or run for office.*** Because they may be managed and controlled by nonresidents, their interests may conflict in fundamental respects with the interests of eligible voters. The financial resources, legal structure, and instrumental orientation of corporations raise legitimate concerns about their role in the electoral process. Our lawmakers have a compelling constitutional basis, if not also a democratic duty, to take measures designed to guard against the potentially deleterious effects of corporate spending in local and national races. (emphasis added).

Stevens' lengthy dissent specifically sought to address a number of the majority's central arguments:

First, Stevens argued that the majority failed to recognize the possibility for corruption outside of strict *quid pro quo* exchanges.

Stevens, however, argued that in the past, even when striking down a ban on corporate independent expenditures, the Court "never suggested that such quid pro quo debts must take the form of outright vote buying or bribes."

Furthermore, Stevens argued that corporations could threaten Representatives and Senators with negative advertising to gain unprecedented leverage. Stevens supported his argument by citing *Caperton v. A.T. Massey Coal Co.,*

556 U.S. 868 (2009), where the Court held that $3 million in independent expenditures in a judicial race raised sufficient questions about a judge's impartiality to require the judge to recuse himself in a future case involving the spender. Stevens argued that it was contradictory for the majority to ignore the same risks in legislative and executive elections, and argued that the majority opinion would exacerbate the problem presentedin *Caperton* because of the number of states with judicial elections and increased spending in judicial races.

Second, Stevens argued that the majority did not place enough emphasis on the need to prevent the "appearance of corruption" in elections. Stevens cited recent data indicating that 80% of the public view corporate independent expenditures as a method used to gain unfair legislative access. Stevens predicted that if the public believes that corporations dominate elections, disaffected voters will stop participating.

Third, Stevens argued that the majority's decision failed to recognize the dangers of the corporate form. Stevens argued that the unique qualities of corporations andother artificial legal entities made them dangerous to democratic elections. These legal entities, he argued, have perpetual life, the ability to amass large sums of money, limited liability, no ability to vote, no morality, no purpose outside of profit-making, and no loyalty. Therefore, he argued, the courts should permit legislatures to regulate corporate participation in the political process.

Legal entities, Stevens wrote, are not "We the People" for whom our Constitution was established. Therefore, he argued, they should not be given speech protections under the First Amendment. The First Amendment, he argued, protects individual self-expression, self-realization and the communication of ideas. Corporate spending is the "furthest from the core of political expression" protected by the Constitution, and corporate spending on politics should be viewed as a business transaction designed by the officersor the boards of directors for no purpose other than profit-making.

Justice Stevens attacked the majority's central argument: that the prohibition of spending guards free speech and allows the general public to receive all available information. Stevens argued that corporations "unfairly influence" the electoral process with vast sums of money that few individuals can match, which distorts the public debate. Because a typical voter can only absorb so much information during a relevant election period, Stevens described "unfair corporate influence" as the potential to outspend others, to push others out of prime broadcasting spots and to dominate the "marketplace of ideas." This process, he argued, puts disproportionate focus on this speech and gives the impression of widespread support regardless of actual support. Thus, this process marginalizes the speech of other individuals and groups.

Stevens argued that the majority opinion ignored the rights of shareholders. A series of cases protects individuals from legally compelled payment of union dues to support political speech. *Abood v. Detroit Board of Education*, 431 U.S. 209 (1977). Because shareholders invest money in corporations, Stevens argued that the law should likewise help to protect shareholders from funding speech that they oppose. The majority, however, argued that ownership of corporate stock was voluntary, and that unhappy share-holders could simply sell off their shares if they did not agree with the corporation's speech. Stevens also argued that Political Action Committees (PACs), whichallow individual members of a corporation to invest money in a separate fund, are an adequate substitute for general corporate speech and better protect shareholder rights.

Stevens called the majority's faith in "corporate democracy" an unrealistic method for a shareholder to oppose political funding. Shareholder meetings only happen once a year, not prior to every decision or transaction. Rather, the officers and boards control the day-to-day spending, including political spending. According to Stevens, the shareholders have few options, giving them "virtually nonexistent" recourse for opposing a corporation's political spending.

Stevens concluded his dissent:

> At bottom, the Court's opinion is thus a rejection of the common sense of the American people, who have recognized a need to prevent corporations from undermining self government since the founding, and who have fought against the distinctive corrupting potential of corporate electioneering since the days of Theodore Roosevelt. It is a strange time to repudiate that common sense. While American democracy is imperfect, few outside the majority of this Court would have thought its flaws included a dearth of corporate money in politics.

Criticisms

President Barack Obama, himself a professor of Constitutional law, stated that the decision "gives the special interests and their lobbyists even more power in Washington —while undermining the influence of average Americans who make small contributions to support their preferred candidates." Obama later elaborated in his weekly radio address saying, "this ruling strikes at our democracy itself" and "I can't think of anything more devastating to the public interest." On January 27, 2010, Obama further condemned the decision during the 2010 State of the Union Address, stating that, "Last week, the Supreme Court reversed a century of law to open the floodgates for special interests—including foreign corporations—to spend without limit in our elections. Well I don't think American elections should be bankrolled by America's most powerful interests, or worse, by foreign entities."

Democratic Senator Russ Feingold, a lead sponsor of the 2002 Bipartisan Campaign Reform Act, stated "This decision was a terrible mistake. Presented with a relatively narrow legal issue, the Supreme Court chose to roll back laws that have limited the role of corporate money in federal elections since Teddy Roosevelt was president." Representative Alan Grayson, a Democrat, stated that it was "the worst Supreme Court decision since the *DredScott* case, and that the court had opened the door to political bribery and corruption in elections to come.

Republican Senator John McCain, co-crafter of the McCain-Feingold Act and his party's 2008 presidential nominee, said "there's going to be, over time, a backlash . . . when you see the amounts of union and corporate money that's going to go into political campaigns." McCain said that he was disappointed by the decision of the Supreme Court and the lifting of the limits on corporate and union contributions

Constitutional law scholar Laurence H. Tribe wrote that the decision "marks a major upheaval in First Amendment law and signals the end of whatever legitimate claim could otherwise have been made by the Roberts Court to an incremental and minimalist approach to constitutional adjudication, to a modest view of the judicial role vis-à-vis the political branches, or to a genuine concern with adherence to precedent" and pointed out that "talking about a business corporation as merely another way that individuals might choose to organize their association with one another to pursue their common expressive aims isworse than unrealistic; it obscures the very real injusticeand distortion entailed in the phenomenon of some people using other people's money to support candidates they havemade no decision to support, or to oppose candidates they have made no decision to oppose."

Michael Waldman, director of the Brennan Center for Justice at N.Y.U. School of Law, opined that the decision "matches or exceeds *Bush v. Gore* in ideological or partisan overreaching by the court," explaining how "Exxon or any other firm could spend Bloomberg-level sums in any congressional district in the country against, say, any congressman who supports climate change legislation, or health care."

The *New York Times* stated in an editorial, "The Supreme Court has handed lobbyists a new weapon. A lobbyist can now tell any elected official: if you vote wrong, my company, labor union or interest group will spend unlimited sums explicitly advertising against your re-election."

Former Supreme Court Justice Sandra Day O'Connor, who left the Court in 2006, told the *New York Times,* "I step away for a couple of years and there's no telling what's going to happen." Justice O'Connor continued, *"Citizens United* was an increasing problem for maintaining an independent judiciary." *New York Times*, January 26, 2010.

Justice O'Connor continued, "in invalidating some of the existing checks on campaign spending, the majority in *Citizens United* has signaled that the problem of campaign contributions in judicial elections might get considerably worse and quite soon."

Further Court Rulings

Despite the *Citizens United* ruling, in December, 2011, the Montana Supreme Court, in *Western Tradition Partnership, Inc. v. Attorney General of Montana,* upheld that state's law limiting corporate contributions. Examining the history of corporate interference in Montana government that led to the Corrupt Practices Law, the Montana Supreme Court majority decided that the state stillhad a compelling reason to maintain the restrictions. It ruled that the restrictions on speech were narrowly tailored And withstood strict scrutiny and thus did not contradict *Citizens United v. Federal Election Commission.*

In June, 2012, over the dissent of the same four justices who dissented in *Citizens United,* the Court simultaneously granted certiorari and summarily reversed the decision of the Montana Supreme Court. The U.S. Supreme Court majority rejected the Montana Supreme Court's arguments in a two paragraph, unsigned opinion, stating that these arguments "either were already rejected in *Citizens United,* or fail to meaningfully distinguish that case."

The U.S. Supreme Court's Montana ruling makes clear that states cannot bar corporate and union political expenditures in state elections. Massive corporate contributions to support or oppose California initiatives in 2012 dominated the airwaves and washed out any serious political discourse.

Monsanto, for example, spent millions of dollars on television ads against California's Proposition 37, a proposal to require products containing genetically-modified components to label them. Opinion polls showed broad public support for Proposition 37 until Monsanto and its allies swamped the proponents of the initiative with misleading and deceptive television advertisements. *Citizens United,* until it is overruled, will allow corporations to run roughshod overthe rights of those who have the right to vote. Millions of dollars in television advertising can cause citizens to vote for propositions, and candidates, even when they do not thoroughly understand the issues involved in the campaign.

Chapter Fifteen

Violence Begets Violence

"Violence begets violence."

—Exodus

"We are no longer worried that children are missing school because of video games. We are worried that theyare murdering their classmates because of video games."

—Tom Bissell, Journalist and author
of *Extra Lives: Why Video Games Matter*

"Studies of children exposed to violence have shown that they can become: 'immune' or numb to the horror of violence, imitate the violence they see, and show more aggressive behavior with greater exposure to violence."

—American Academy of
Child and Adolescent Psychiatry

The California legislature, after conducting extensive hearings including testimony from well-known psychologists and psychiatrists found:

(a) Exposing minors to depictions of violence in video games, including sexual and heinous violence, makes those minors more likely to experience feelings of aggression, to experience a reduction of activity in the frontal lobes of the brain, and to exhibit violent antisocial or aggressive behavior.

(b) Even minors who do not commit acts of violence suffer psychological harm from prolonged exposure to violent video games.

The California video game legislation was designed to strengthen the current industry-controlled rating system, and would have placed an outright ban on the sale or rental to those under 18 of video games deemed excessively "violent." As defined by California, such interactive games are those in which the player is given the choice of "killing, maiming, dismembering or sexually assaulting an image of a human being" in offensive ways. It also defined such games as those that would "appeal to a deviant or morbid interest of children and are patently offensive to prevailing community standards."

The Entertainment Merchants Association, a group of video game manufacturers, filed suit challenging the constitutionality of the law. The federal district court in San Francisco ruled that video games, like books and movies, are protected by the First Amendment and ruled that the California video game law was unconstitutional. The Ninth Circuit Court of Appeals affirmed.

In the Supreme Court

The Supreme Court divided in a very peculiar way in this case. Justice Scalia, one the most conservative members of the court, was joined by liberals Ginsburg, Sotomayor and Kagan, as well as centrist Justice Kennedy. Liberal Justice Breyer and conservative Clarence Thomas dissented. The court ruled that the First Amendment protected violent video games concerning sales to minors.

The court ruled that the California law was unconstitutional because video games are protected by the First Amendment and minors have First Amendment rights.

Justice Alito, in a concurring opinion with Chief Justice Roberts, said the majority opinion was too quick to dismiss differences between current video games and other media:

> It also appears that there is no antisocial theme too base for some in the video-game industry to exploit. There are gamesin which a player can take on the identityand reenact the killings carried out by the perpetrators of the murders at Columbine High School and Virginia Tech.The objective of one game is to rape a mother and her daughters; in another, the goal is to rape Native American women. There is a game in which players engagein "ethnic cleansing" and can choose to gun down African-Americans, Latinos, or Jews. In still another game, players attempt to fire a rifle shot into the head of President Kennedy as his motorcade passes by the Texas School Book Depository.

Justice Alito's concurrence was also peculiar because he was warning that video games are not like books or movies. He couldn't quite get himself to say the magic words: ***violent video games are obscene.*** The court has always allowed regulation of obscene material, but obscenity has usually meant sexually explicit material. The definition of obscenity is broader: indecency, lewdness or offensiveness. Under many definitions of obscenity the video games described by Justice Alito are obscene.

Justice Antonin Scalia, writing for five justices in the majority, said:

> Like the protected books, plays and movies that preceded them, video games communicate ideas—and even social messages —through many familiar literary devices (such as characters, dialogue, plot and music) and through features distinctive tothe medium (such as the player's interaction with the virtual world). . . .

Justice Scalia wrote, "That suffices to confer First Amendment protection."

Depictions of violence, Justice Scalia added, have never been subject to government regulation. "Grimm's Fairy Tales, for example, are grim indeed," he wrote, recounting the gory plots of "Snow White," "Cinderella" and "Hansel and Gretel." High school reading lists andSaturday morning cartoons, too, he said, are riddled with violence.

The California law would have imposed $1,000 fines on stores that sold violent video games to anyone under 18. It defined violent games as those "in which the range of options available to a player includes killing, maiming, dismembering or sexually assaulting animage of a human being" in a way that was "patently offensive," appealed to minors' "deviant or morbid interests" and lacked "serious literary, artistic, political orscientific value."

The definitions tracked language from decision upholding laws regulating sexual content. In 1968, in *Gins-*

berg v. New York, the court allowed limits on the distribution to minors of sexual materials like what it called "girlie magazines" (like *Playboy* magazine) that fell well short of obscenity, which is unprotected by the First Amendment. (See Chapter 7.)

Justice Scalia rejected the suggestion that depictions of violence are subject to regulation as obscenity. "Because speech about violence is not obscene," he wrote, "it is of no consequence that California's statute mimics the New York statute regulating obscenity-for-minors that we upheld in the *Ginsberg* decision." Justice Scalia is just plain wrong that violence cannot be obscene.

The Dissent

Justice Breyer pointed out in dissent:

> California's law imposes no more than a modest restriction on expression. The statute prevents no one from playing a video game, it prevents no adult from buying a video game, and it prevents no child or adolescent from obtaining a game provided a parent is willing to help.

There are many scientific studies that support the California legislature's findings. Social scientists, for example, have found causal evidence that playing these games results in harm. Surveys of 8th and 9th grade students have found a correlation between playing violent video games and aggression.

Just like the court has protected minors from exposure to adult films, it should have allowed protection of minors from excessively violent video games. In the obscenity cases the Supreme Court actually wrote the law. In this case, the California legislature wrote the law and the Supreme Court voided it claiming that children have a First Amendment right to buy and use violent video gam.es even if their parents object.

The Media

No newspaper is a stronger advocate for the First Amendment than the *Washington Post*. However, on June 21, 2011, the *Washington Post* blasted the Supreme Court's opinion:

> THE SUPREME COURT has decreed that the government is on solid ground when it bans the sale of "girlie" magazines to a minor but tramples on the Constitution when it tries to block that minor from buying a violent video game in which he can (virtually) mutilate and murder a realistic depiction of a woman.

> The distinction makes no sense — in the real or the virtual world.

> The California law is different because it dealt only with reasonable limitations on minors' access to extremely violent games that even the video game industry ack-nowledges are inappropriate. The rights of minors are often justifiably curtailed in ways that would violate the Constitution if applied to adults. Take, for example, prohibitions against selling alcohol and tobacco products to juveniles. The California law did nothing to infringe on the rights of adults to purchase

violent video games, and manufacturers remained free to create and market these videos. They could even sell them to minors—as long as a parent or legal guardian approved.

Courts have refused to treat violent content as they would sexual material, which the government restricts under longstanding obscenity doctrines.

Justice Breyer's dissent criticized that divergence, saying that it didn't make sense to ban the sale of a magazine showing a nude woman to 13-year-olds while allowing them to buy video games in which they commit virtual violence against women.

Leland Yee, the California state senator who wrote the law, said in a statement that "the Supreme Court once again put the interests of corporate America before the interests of our children." He added: "It is simply wrong that the video game industry can be allowed to put their profitmargins over the rights of parents and the well-being of children."

With increasing violence against children and adults, including the recent outrageous slaughters in Newtown, Connecticut and Aurora, Colorado, the Supreme Court's stubborn insistence that violent video games are entitled to the same First Amendment protections as books is absurd. The primary purpose of the First Amendment was to protect political speech. (Secondarily, the First Amendmentprotects literary works.)

Justice Scalia, remarkably, quotes the *Chaplinski case* (Chapter Eight) for the proposition that the First Amendment is not absolute. *Chaplinski* was solely about political speech. Mr. Chaplinski was arrested for calling an official of Rochhester, New Hampshire "a fascist and a racketeer." Chaplinski's speech was purely political and entitled to First Amendment protection. In strong contrast, a video game urging participants to kill President Kennedy is not protected speech. If someone actually asked a person to shoot the president, he or she would immediately be arrested for criminal activity. Further, the California video game law only prohibited the sale or rental of violent video games to children. Justice Breyer said this prohibition, was a minor inconvenience, not a constitutional violation.

Scientific Studies

The Supreme Court made a scientific determination that violent video games do not cause violence in society. Real scientists disagree. Craig Anderson who has devoted his professional life to proving a link between video game violence and real-life aggression.

In 2010, Iowa State issued a news release claiming that one of Anderson's studies "proves conclusively thatviolent video game play makes more aggressive kids."

Recently, Anderson appeared on CNN to talk about Adam Lanza's (the shooter in Newtown, Connecticut) fondness for violent video games. In the course of the interview, he repeated his claim that the link between video game violence and real-life aggression has been definitively proven. Anderson said:

> Every major scientific society that hasstudied
> the question has come to the same answer, the
> American Medical Association, the Ameri-
> can Psychological Association, most re-
> cently, the International Society for Research
> and Aggression, have all come to the same

conclusion that basically media violence is a
risk factor, is a causal risk factor for increased
aggressive behaviour, including violence.

Social psychologist Brad Bushman at Ohio State University once showed students violent pictures: one of a man shoving a gun down another man's throat; another of a man holding a knife to a woman's throat. "What we found is for people who were exposed to a lot of violent video games, their brains did not respond to the violent images," Bushman said. "They were numb, if you will."

Not all scientists agree. Chris Ferguson, a psychologist at the Texas A&M International University, disagrees. He also found changes in changes in brain activity, but interpreted the results differently. Ferguson could not prove a link between violent video games and violent acts by those who played the games.

However, scientists Bushman and Ferguson agree on one thing: as fathers, they've banned their own kids from playing violent video games. But the problem is that the U.S. Supreme Court takes this authority away from parents because it has decided that violent video games are just fine for children.

PART 4
Equal Protection

Chapter Sixteen

Once a Slave

"There is one thing stronger than all the armies in the world, and that is an idea whose time has come."

—Victor Hugo

Dred Scott was born in 1797 in Southampton County, Virginia, and became the property of Peter Blow. In 1827, he moved to St. Louis with the Blow family. Following the death of his owner in 1832, he became the property of Blow's daughter Elizabeth. The next year, Elizabeth Blow sold Dred Scott to Dr. John Emerson, an assistant surgeon in the Army, for $500. Scott ran away, but was recaptured.

The Missouri Compromise

In 1834, Dr. Emerson was ordered to duty at Fort Armstrong in Rock Island, Illinois, a free state, and Scott accompanied him there. The Army transferred Dr. Emerson to Fort Snelling in 1836, and he, again, took Dred Scott with him.

Fort Snelling was then in the Wisconsin Territory and is now in Minnesota. Under the Missouri Compromise, slavery was outlawed in this northern part of the Louisiana territory. The Missouri Compromise of 1820 provided that slavery was permitted in the Louisiana Territory from Missouri southward and that slavery was prohibited north of Missouri.

On Free Soil

Dred Scott remained on free soil for about five years, from 1834 until 1839. In 1835, he met Harriet, a slave of Major Taliaferro, who was in the U.S. Army. In that year, Major Taliaferro took Harriet to Fort Snelling and kept her as a slave until 1836, when he sold her to Dr. Emerson. In that year, Emerson permitted Dred Scott to marry Harriet.

Dr. Emerson left Fort Snelling in 1838, unaccom-panied by the Scotts. The Scotts raised two daughters, Eliza and Lizzie. Eliza was born in about 1843, aboard the steamboat Gipsey on the Mississippi River. She was born north of the northern border of Missouri, in free territory. Lizzie was born in about 1850. The Scott family departed from the Wisconsin Territory, after Emerson, and, probably, went back to St. Louis.

Dred Scott's New Owner

In 1843, Dr. Emerson died and his widow, Irene Sanford Emerson, inherited his slaves. Mrs. Emerson did what many slaveowners did in those days, she hired out herslaves to various families who needed servants. Then, inthe mid-1840s, she moved to New York and did not take Dred Scott, or any members of his family, with her. She lefthim in St. Louis with Henry and Taylor Blow, two sons of Scott's original owner.

Henry Blow was then in his thirties, a lawyer and a successful businessman. He ran a railroad and was active in lead mining. Henry Blow was also active in the Whig Party, a party which opposed the extension of slavery in the ter-

Photoengraving of Dred Scott, courtesy of the Library of Congress.

Photoengraving of Harriet Scott, courtesy of the Library of Congress.

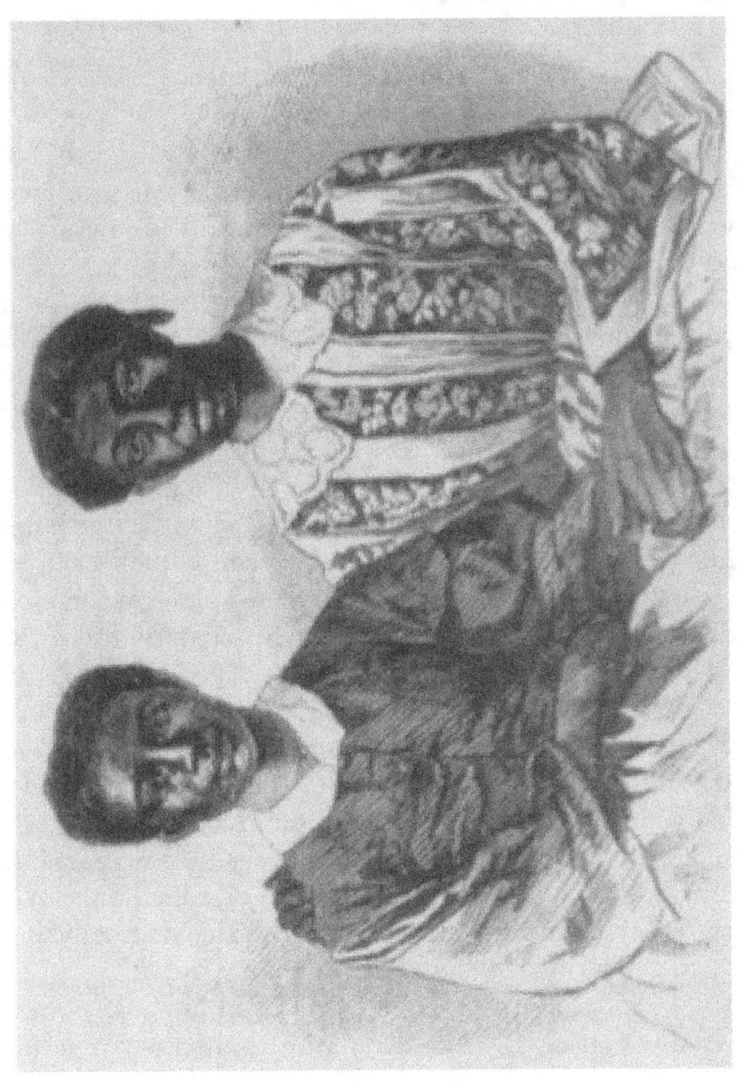

ritories. Blow later organized the Free-Soil movement in Missouri and became a Republican.

The Lawsuit is Commenced

As an opponent of slavery, Henry Blow wanted Scott freed, and, in 1846, he financed a suit in the Missouricourts to have Scott declared to be a free man. The lawsuit was Blow's idea, but Scott signed the necessary papers.

The 1846 lawsuit was filed against Emerson's estate. Scott claimed that he became a free man when he accompanied his master into Illinois and the Wisconsin Territory, and his status could not be reversed by his return to Missouri.

The aim of the lawsuit, although specifically seeking Scott's freedom, was to undercut slavery in the territories. This was important at the time, because the West was opening up for settlement, and many slaveowners were bringing slaves with them into the new territory. From 1846 to 1848, the Mexican-American War raged. At the end of the war, the United States expanded its territory to California. By this time, the question of slavery in the new territories became one of the major issues facing the nation. Mrs. Emerson did not want to retain Scott as a slave. She apparently did not believe in slavery. A few years later, she married Calvin Clifford Chaffee, a radical antislavery Congressman from Massachusetts. She could easily have signed papers emancipating Scott, but she did not.

In 1850, Scott won a jury verdict in his favor, but the case was appealed. After Scott won in the lower court, he came under control of the county sheriff, who hired him out for five dollars a month. During the appeal, Scott was everybody's slave and nobody's slave.

The Missouri Supreme Court in 1852 ruled that Scott became a slave when he reentered Missouri. After losing his case, Scott continued to work on odd jobs and was occasionally farmed out. But, he became an important person because of his lawsuit. Antislavery people were moving into the territories and were looking for a way to revive his lawsuit.

Into the Federal Courts

On November 2, 1853, Scott became the plaintiff in a new lawsuit brought in the federal court in St. Louis. Mrs. Emerson transferred title to Scott over to her brother John Sanford, so the case became known as *Dred Scott v. Sanford*. Harriet Scott and Lizzie and Eliza Scott were also named as plaintiffs. They sued for their liberty and for damages for being wrongfully held as slaves. The Scott's lawsuit sought $16,500 for damages. The case was tried before an all-white jury, who ruled in Mr. Sanford's favor, and who determined that the Scotts were lawfully his property.

In 1854, Senator Douglas of Illinois led the fight to pass the Kansas-Nebraska Act. This law, based on the principle of popular sovereignty, provided that the settlers in these new territories would determine the slavery issue by an election. Meanwhile, slaveowners were free to move into the territories. The importance of Dred Scott's case was growing.

In the Supreme Court

The *Dred Scott* case was argued two times before the Supreme Court. It was first argued in February of 1856, but the court could not reach a decision on the question of whether Scott was a citizen of the United States and entitled to file suit in federal court. Four justices leaned one way, four the other; the swing justice, Justice Nelson, thought it best to set the case for reargument. Reargument was set for December, after the presidential election between James

M. Buchanan, John C. Fremont and ex-President Millard Fillmore. Justice McLean wanted the court to rule early in 1856, so that he could write a stinging dissent to the court's upholding of slavery and run for president himself.

In mid-December, the court heard four days of oral argument The justices did not meet to discuss the case until February 1857. One of the justices, John Catron of Tennessee, took the highly unusual step of writing to his old friend, President-elect Buchanan, for advice. Buchanan tried to steer clear of the decision and, in his inaugural address, said that the nation should support whatever decision at which the Supreme Court arrived.

Two days after Buchanan was sworn in as President, the Supreme Court announced its decision against Dred Scott. All nine justices wrote separate opinions, seven in favor of the decision and two in dissent; all totalled, the justices wrote 250 pages explaining their ruling. Justice Taney wrote that black slaves and their descendants could not become citizens of the United States and ruled that the Missouri Compromise was unconstitutional.[1] The court ruled that slavery could not be prohibited in the territories. This decision widened the breach between the northernand southern states and was one of the causes of the CivilWar.

Justice Curtis, in his dissent, pointed out the Taney was simply wrong:

> At the time of the ratification of the Articles of Confederation (1781), all free native-born inhabitants of the States of New Hampshire, Massachusetts, New York, New Jersey, and North Carolina, though descended from African slaves, were not only citizens of those States, but such of these as had the other necessary qualifications possessed the

franchise of electors, on equal terms with other citizens.

Who were the justices and where were they from? Taney, the Chief Justice, was from Maryland, a slave state. Four other justices were from slave states: Wayne of Georgia, Catron of Tennessee, Daniel of Virginia and Campbell of Alabama. Only three of these southern Justices agreed that Negroes of slave ancestry could not become citizens.

All of the Southern justices along with Nelson of New York decided that Scott's status depended upon the law of Missouri. The five Southerners, along with Grier of Pennsylvania, ruled that the Missouri Compromise was unconstitutional because it deprived citizens of the right to take property (slaves) into the territories. The dissenters, McLean and Curtis, argued that Scott was a citizen, that Missouri law did not control his status and that Congress had a constitutional right to prohibit slavery from a ter- ritory.

Epilogue

John Sanford died before the case was announced. Mrs. Emerson and her husband, Dr. Chaffee, transferred their rights in the Scotts to Taylor Blow, the son of Scott's original owner. Blow emancipated the Scotts in May 1857. Scott was quoted as saying that his lawsuit had brought hima "heap o' trouble" and that had he known that it would last so long he never would have brought it in the first place. Scott became a porter in a St. Louis ho-tel. On September 17, 1858, Scott died of tuberculosis in St. Louis. Henry Blow paid his funeral expenses.

For the nation, the court's decision was an unmitigated disaster. The decision could be changed only by a constitutional amendment (an impossibility given Southern opposition), by the court itself (not likely) or by force

The case, especially Justice Taney's opinion, inflamed the North. The decision also split the Democratic Party. "Popular sovereignty," which had been advocated by Senator Douglas to let the states decide on slavery by themselves, had been ruled unconstitutional. The Northern Democrats could not agree with the South's demands for slavery in the territories. With the collapse of Douglas's compromise, Abraham Lincoln and the Republicans gained the White House.

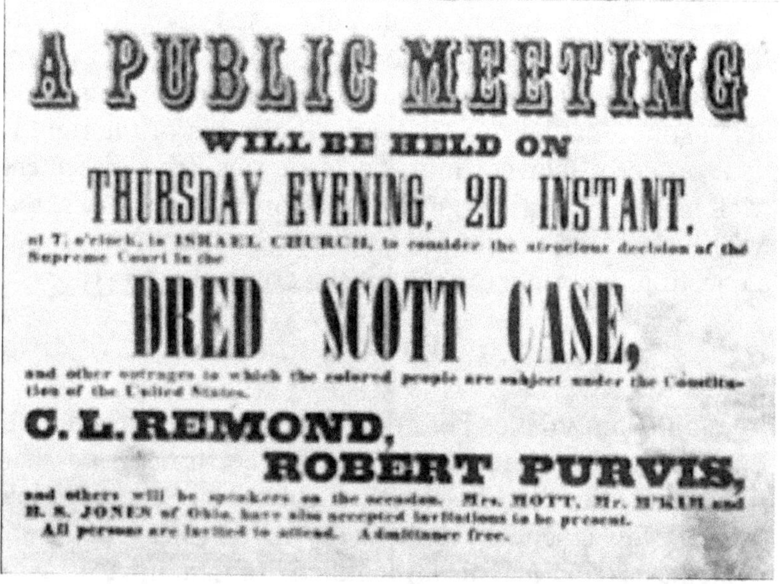

The *Dred Scott* decision, while not the sole cause of the Civil War, certainly contributed to its inevitability. After the Civil War, the Thirteenth and Fourteenth Amendments were passed, which formally overturned the SupremeCourt's ruling in the *Dred Scott* case. Those amendments outlawed slavery and gave Negroes the right to vote.

Endnotes

1. *19 How. 691 (1857).*

Chapter Seventeen

Off Broadway

*"In giving freedom to the slave,
we assure freedom to the free."*

—Abraham Lincoln

"I desired to find an entrance to the palace"

—Victor Hugo in Ruy *Blas*

At 10:00 a.m. Saturday morning November 22, 1879, a light-skinned young woman bought two tickets for that afternoon's matinee at the Grand Opera House in New York City.[1]

The afternoon performance of Victor Hugo's *Ruy Blas* featured Edwin Booth, brother of infamous John Wilkes Booth. A few months earlier, a madman had attempted to shoot Booth during a performance of *Richard II*. Because of the publicity of the shooting attempt and because of the Thanksgiving crowds, the Grand Opera House was jammed.

Ruy Blas is a play in which the main character, Blas, falls in love with a woman of royal blood who lives in the palace. When it is found out that he is a commoner, their relationship ends.

At 1:30 p.m., the young lady and her boyfriend, William R. Davis, Jr, a tall, dark, handsome and well-dressed escort of age twenty-six, arrived at the Grand Opera. Samuel Singleton, the Grand Opera doorkeeper refused admittance to the couple saying "these tickets are no good." The doorkeeper refused them admittance because Mr. Davis was a Negro. Had he known that Davis' girlfriend was one-eighth Negro, he would have refused her admittance as well.

Mr. Davis was offered a refund for his ticket, but he refused it. He saw a small white boy standing near the theater. Davis gave him a dollar plus ten cents for histrouble and had him purchase two more tickets for the matinee. Again, Sam Singleton refused Davis admission but admitted his girlfriend. Davis refused to move out ofthe entrance. Singleton took hold of Davis and forced himout of the theatre and called a policeman for assistance.When Davis protested to the policeman, the officer told Davis that the managers of the theatre, Poole and Donnelly, did not admit colored people and told Davis thathe had better go away. "Perhaps the managers do not,"said Davis, "but the laws of the country do." He announced that he would seek their enforcement at once.

Davis and his girlfriend left the theater and went to a matinee performance at another theater.

The Grand Opera House

The Fourteenth Amendment

After the Civil War, Congress and the States passed the Fourteenth Amendment, giving blacks all rights secured by their fellow citizens, and prohibited the states from depriving Negroes of equal protection under the laws. The amendment also gave Congress the power to enforce the terms of the amendment by appropriate legislation. To enforce the Fourteenth Amendment, Congress passed the Civil Rights Law, which forbade racial discrimination in places of public accommodation, including theaters, restaurants and hotels.

William R. Davis, Jr.

Davis, born a slave in South Carolina, became free with Lincoln's Emancipation Proclamation. He moved to New York City, where he resided at 109 West Twenty-Seventh Street. He was employed as the business agent of the *Progressive American,* a weekly newspaperdevoted to the advancement of black Americans. It was undoubtedly his dedication to the cause of racial equality that led him to file a criminal complaint.

The Criminal Complaint

After consulting with the United States attorney, Mr. Fiero, on Monday, November 24th, Davis filed a criminal complaint. Fiero recommended that Davis file a civil suit against the theater. However, Davis had done this before, in September 1875, after he was denied admission to Booth's Theatre. That case was dismissed because Davis's witnesses failed to appear.

On December 9th, Singleton was indicted. It was the first criminal proceeding in New York State under theCivil Rights Law. The case was heard on January 14,1880. The attorney for Singleton, Louis Post, argued that the Civil Rights Act was unconstitutional, because it interfered with the rights of citizens and their private property. The judge referred the issue to the Circuit Court,which could not reach a decision, and referred the case to the Supreme Court.

The Highest Court's Ruling

On Monday, October 15, 1883, the Supreme Court ruled that the Civil Rights Act was unconstitutional.[2]

Justice Joseph Bradley wrote the opinion for the court. In his opinion he wrote:

> Why may not Congress . . . enact a code of laws for the enforcement and vindication of all rights of life, liberty, and property? . . . . [Because i]t is repugnant to the Tenth Amendment of the Constitution, which declares that powers not delegated to theUnited States by the Constitution, nor prohibited by it to the States, are reserved to the States respectively or to the people.

Justice Bradley, and a majority of the court, held that the Fourteenth Amendment to the Constitution gives the Congress little power to legislate. However, that amendment provides that no State shall deny "any person within its jurisdiction the equal protection of the laws." The amendment further provides that "Congress shall have the power to enforce, by appropriate legislation, the provisions of this article." Under the laws of New York, William Davis should have had an equal right to attend a performance at the Grand Opera House. However, the laws of New York did not protect him. He purchased a ticket, but the New York police were called to evict him, not to help him.Congress passed the Civil Rights Laws for this very reason: in order to protect the citizen's right to equal protection of the laws and for equal access to places of public accomodation, including theaters and hotels.

Once Davis acquired a ticket for admission, it was a breach of contract for the theater to deny his admission. Justice Bradley is saying that the State of New York had nothing to do with the transaction. However, New York police were called to the scene. The State of New York was obligated by the Fourteenth Amendment to see to it that Mr. Davis' rights were protected. Instead, New York's finest police officers ejected Davis from the theater, when they should have escorted him in.

The Tenth Amendment is rarely relied on. The Fourteenth Amendment was passed after the Civil War to remove all vestiges of slavery. The amendment was passed by three-quarters of the States and by Congress, and represented the will of the people.

Further, since the Fourteenth Amendment was enacted after the Tenth Amendment, any conflict between the two should be resolved in favor of the latter amendment. The Supreme Court's finding that the Civil Rights Act was unconstitutional ignores the meaning and intent of the Fourteenth Amendment and was an attempt to overturn the outcome of the Civil War.

Justice John Marshall Harlan of Kentucky, the only Southerner on the Court, wrote the sole dissent:

> Today, it is the colored race which is denied, by corporations and individuals wielding public authority, rights fundamental in their freedom and citizenship. At some future time, it may be that some other race will fall under the ban of race discrimination. If the constitutional amendments be enforced, according to the intent with which, as I conceive, they were adopted, there cannot be in this republic, any class of human beings in practical subjection to another class.

Justice Harlan penned his famous dissent with Justice Taney's inkwell. Taney had authored the majority opinion in the *Dred Scott case.*

The *New York Times* quoted Justice Harlan:[3]

> [U]nder ordinary circumstances and in an ordinary case he [a justice] should hes- itate to set up his individual opinion in opposition to that of his eight colleagues, but in view of what he thought the people of the country wished to accomplish, what they tried to accomplish, and what they believed they had accomplished by means of this legislation, he must express
>
> his dissent from the opinion of the court.

Frederick Douglass, a former slave and civil rights advocate during the era of this decision said:[4]

> The future historian will turn to the year 1883 to find the most flagrant example of national deterioration. Here he will find the Supreme Court of the nation reversing the action of the Government, defeating the manifest purpose of the Constitution, nullifying the Fourteenth Amendment, and placing itself on the side of prejudice, proscription, and persecution.
>
> Whatever this Supreme Court may have been in the past, or may by the Constitution have been intended to be, it has, since the days of the *Dred Scott* decision, been wholly under the influence of slave power, and its decisions have been dictated by that power rather than by what seemed to be sound and established rules of legal interpretation. Although we had, in other days, seen this court bend and twist the law to the will and inter-

rest of slave power, it was supposed that by the late war and the great fact that slavery was abolished, and the further fact that the members of the bench were now appointed by a Republican administration, the spirit as well as the body had been exorcised. Hence the decision in question came to the black man as a painful and bewildering surprise. It was a blow from an unsuspected quarter. The surrender of the national capital to Jefferson Davis in time of the war could hardly have caused a greater shock.

Endnotes

1. Some details were provided by the *New York Times,* November 25, 1879.

2. 109 U.S. 3 (1883).

3. *New York Times,* October 16, 1883.

4. *Life and Times of Frederick Douglass,* MacMillan Publishing Co, New York: 1962.

Chapter Eighteen

American Apartheid

"Each time a man stands up for an idea, or acts to improve the lot others, or strikes out against injustice, he sends forth a tiny ripple of hope . . . those ripples build a current that can sweep down the mightiest walls of oppression and resistance."

—Robert F. Kennedy in Capetown, South Africa

"Jim Crow" was the name of a song sung by Thomas Rice in a Negro minstrel show before the Civil War. Thomas Rice was a white actor who, in black face played the part of Jim Crow. During the minstrel show, he sang, "Wheel about, turn about, do just so. Everytime I wheel about I jump Jim Crow."

Jim Crow came to signify white dominance over blacks, and laws that required segregation of blacks and whites became known as Jim Crow laws. The first Jim Crow law, requiring railroads to carry Negroes in separate cars, was passed by Florida in 1887. The rest of the Southern states joined Florida by passing similar laws.

Louisiana passed its Jim Crow law regarding railroads in 1890, even though negroes in New Orleans had organized against passage of the bill.

The black community in New Orleans had a heritage of several generations of freedom and a high degree of literacy. Louisiana had sixteen black state senators and representatives at the time. A group called the Equal Rights Association of Louisiana Against Class Legislation protested against the law as "unconstitutional, un-American, unjust, dangerous and against sound public policy." Nevertheless, the Assembly passed the bill and the governor signed it into law. The act was titled "An Act to promote the comfort of passengers," and required railroads to provide equal but separate accommodations for colored and white passengers.

A Test Case

In 1891, a group of eighteen black men formed a "Citizens Committee to Test the Constitutionality of the Separate Car Law." Within five weeks, they raised $1,500 for a test case. The committee hired Albion Tourgée as counsel in the case. Tourgee was a well-known, light-skinned black attorney, novelist and former North Carolina judge. Tourgée recommended that a light- skinned Negro be used for the test case.

Railroad officials were cooperative because segregation was inconvenient and expensive for them. The first railroad approached, admitted that it did not enforce the Jim Crow law.

Albion Tourgée, attorney who represented Homer Plessy.

The committee members finally agreed that a white passenger should object to the presence of a negro in a "white" car, that the conductor should send the black passenger to the second-class car, and that the passenger should refuse to go. For the first test case, Daniel Desdunesbought a ticket on the Louisville & Nashville Railroad from

New Orleans to Mobile, Alabama. When the matter was brought to court, the Louisiana judge ruled that the Jim Crow law was unconstitutional, as applied to interstate passengers. However, the law was still valid as to intrastate trains which most blacks used.

Homer Plessy

The committee looked for another plaintiff for a new test case and chose Homer Plessy. He was an octoroon: seven-eighths white and one-eighth black. The East Louisiana Railroad had been informed of the plan and agreed to cooperate. Plessy took a seat in the white coach. The conductor requested that he move to the negro car, which he refused to do. Detective Christopher Cain arrested Plessy and charged him with violating the separatecar law.

Tourgée entered a plea before Judge John H. Ferguson of the Criminal District Court for the Parishof New Orleans, arguing that the law Mr. Plessy allegedly violated was invalid, because it conflicted with the Constitution of the United States. Judge Ferguson ruled against Plessy, and the case of *Plessy v. Ferguson* was born. Plessy was fined twenty-five dollars.

Tourgée argued:

> [T]he statute in question establishes an insidious distinction and discrimination between citizens of the United States, based on race, which is obnoxious to the fundamental principles of national citizenship, perpetuates involuntary servitude, as regards citizens of the colored race, under the merest pretense of promoting the comfort of pas-

sengers on railway trains, and in further respects abridfes the privileges and immunities respects abridges the privileges and
immunities of the citizens of the United
States, and the rights secured by the thirteenth
and fourteenth amendments of the federal
constitution.

An Appeal

The Louisiana Supreme Court granted a hearing. The Chief Justice of this court was Francis Nicholls, who had signed the Jim Crow act into law as governor of Louisiana two years earlier. The case was assigned to Judge Fenner. Judge Fenner ruled that "separate but equal" was a proper law, since the Fourteenth Amendment provided for equal protection under the laws, not undivided protection. Since the statute specifically required equal accommodations, it complied with the Constitution. Judge Fenner relied on *Roberts v. City of Boston,* which upheld segregated public schools in Boston:

> In a case which arose as far back as 1849, the supreme court of Massachusetts, through its great chief justice, Shaw, con- sidered the subject, saying—conceding, therefore, in the fullest manner, that colored persons, the descendants of Africans, are entitled by law to equal rights, con- stitutional and political, civil and social, the question then arises whether the reg- ulations in question which provide for separate schools for colored children, is a violation of any of these rights.

This prejudice, if it exists, is not createdby law, and it cannot be changed by law.

Judge Nicholls granted Plessy's petition for a writ of error. This permitted him to appeal the case to the Supreme Court of the United States.

Plessy v. Ferguson at the Supreme Court

When Tourgée argued the case before the United States Supreme Court, he asked the members of the court toimagine how they would have felt had they been ordered into a Jim Crow car. "What humiliation, what rage would then fill the judicial mind!" he argued. The true intent ofthe Louisiana statute was apparent, Tourgée contended, because it did not apply "to nurses attending children of theother race."

Tourgée argued:

> The exemption of nurses shows that the real evil lies not in the color of the skin butin the relation the colored person sustainsto the whole. If he is a dependent, it may be endured: if he is not, his presence is insufferable. Instead of being intended to promote the *general* comfort and moral well-being, this act is plainly and evidently intended to promote the happiness of one class by asserting its supremacy and the inferiority of another class. Justice is pictured blind and her daughter, the Law, ought at least to be color-blind.

> Why not require all colored people to walk
> on one side of the street and all whites on
> the other? . . . One side of the street may be
> just as good as the other . . . .
> The question is not as to the equality of the
> privileges enjoyed, but *the right of the
> State to label one citizen as white and
> another as colored* in the common
> enjoyment of the public highway.

During the two years that *Plessy v. Ferguson* remained before the Supreme Court, new segregation laws were passed and lynchings had increased. Two states had already disenfranchised negro citizens, and several otherswere planning to take that unconstitutional step.

Separate but Equal

On Monday, May 18, 1896, Justice Henry Billings Brownof Michigan, by way of Massachusetts, delivered the opinion of the court.[1] Only Justice Harlan dissented. Like Justice Fenner of the State Supreme Court, Justice Brown relied on the case of *Roberts v. City of Boston,* a case decided in 1849, before the Civil War and, more importantly, before the Fourteenth Amendment to the Constitution, which guaranteed citizens "equal protectionof the laws." He contended that Congress, which had passed the Fourteenth Amendment, continued to approve of the segregated school system in the District of Co-lumbia and, therefore, must have felt that segregation was consistent with the amendment. Separate but equal be-camethe law of the land.

Epilogue

Separate but equal remained the law of the land until *Brown v. Board of Education*[2] decided that "separate" is "inherently unequal" in 1954. *Plessy v. Ferguson* had remained the law of the land for exactly fifty-eight years, from May 18, 1896 to May 17, 1954. During those fifty-eight years, American Apartheid reined supreme as Homer Plessy's case was cited in scores of cases regarding everyconceivable type of racial discrimination.

Endnotes

1. 163 U.S. 537 (1896).
2. 347 U.S. 483 (1954).

Chapter Nineteen

The Summer of '42

"The great strength of the totalitarian state is that it forces those who fear it to imitate it."

—Adolf Hitler

Fred and Ida

Fred was twenty-three years of age in 1942. He had tried to enlist in the Army the year before but was rejected because he suffered from a stomach ulcer. Fred studied to be a welder and, before Pearl Harbor was attacked, worked in shipyards in California building the Navy's flotilla. He was a patriotic American, a native-born Californian. He lived in the same house in Oakland until he went to Los Angeles to attend college. As soon as he turned twenty-one, he proudly voted for Franklin Roosevelt who was seeking re-election for an unprecedented third term as president.

Fred fell in love with an Italian girl, Ida Boitano. He spent most of his free time with her. Fred had one problem: his parents were born in Japan. Even though Fred Korematsu was a native-born U.S. citizen, he was considered to be "of Japanese ancestry." In December, 1941, Japan nearly destroyed the American naval fleet at Pearl Harbor.Rumors of an imminent invasion of the West Coast made Californians anxious. Now and then, Japanese submarines were sighted off of the coast.

An anti-Japanese hysteria was brewing in California, Oregon and Washington. Many Americans of Japanese ancestry were fired from their jobs. Fred Korematsu was one of them.

The United States declared war on Japan, Italy andGermany soon after Pearl Harbor, but those of Japaneseancestry were treated far worse than Italian-Americans and German-Americans. There were millions Americans of German and Italian ancestry, and they had intermarried with "true" Americans more often than the Japanese. Italians and Germans looked like Americans; they werefair skinned, while Japanese-Americans looked like foreigners. And they were treated like foreigners, enemy aliens.

The War, The Panic

In late November of 1941, shortly before Pearl Harbor was attacked, President Roosevelt, Korematsu's candidate, ordered the names and addresses of all American and foreign born Japanese persons to be compiled. Historianand former Congressman John Toland reports that the secrecy of the census was violated in order to produce the list of addresses of Japanese living in the United States.The list was compiled in one week and was on the president's desk *before* Pearl Harbor was attacked.

After Pearl Harbor, the Pacific Coast was shelled at Santa Barbara, California and at Seaside, Oregon. Near Seattle, a Japanese submarine sank a ship and attacked

Vancouver Island. The Japanese occupied Kiska Island in the Aleutian Islands in Alaska and bombed the U.S. Naval base in nearby Dutch Harbor.

On December 7th, as Pearl Harbor was being attacked, the Japanese simultaneously struck at the Malay Peninsula, Hong Kong, Wake and Midway Islands and the Philippines. The next day, they invaded Thailand. Within a week, Guam fell, and, on Christmas Day, the Japanese captured Wake Island and Hong Kong. General MacArthur was forced to evacuate Manila. MacArthur's troops had become isolated by rapidly advancing Japaneseforces and suffered one of the worst American defeats ofthe war. In February, the Americans were defeated in theBattle of the Java Sea and lost thirteen ships. At that time the U.S. position in the Pacific looked very bleak.

Because of a real fear of invasion based on Japanese military successes, and because of racial differences, there was a growing public clamor for action to be taken against the Japanese who were living in the United States. Earl Warren, then attorney general of California, and planning to run for governor of the state, prepared arguments in favor of imposing restrictions on the Japanese-Americans living on the West Coast.

Warren painted a threatening picture. With use of color-coded, maps he showed the pattern of Japanese land ownership near American Army and Naval bases. The Army and Navy made recommendations, which along with Warren's maps, were submitted to the President.

Similar maps of Italian-American land ownership were never prepared but would have shown an equally threatening picture. Italian restaurants "surround" San Francisco Bay and would appear from a color-coded mapto be part of a grand strategy to capture the bay area.

It was during this period that President Roosevelt signed Executive Order 9066, which gave the secretary of war and the military commanders the power to exclude any person from designated areas in order to secure national defense objectives against sabotage and espionage. Themilitary commander for the western states, Lieutenant General J. L. DeWitt, took full advantage of the powersthat the executive order gave him.

General DeWitt

Lieutenant General DeWitt was designated the military commander for the westernmost parts of the United States. President Roosevelt signed Executive Order 9066 on February 19, 1942. General DeWitt wasted little time, and, on March 2nd, he issued Public Proclamation Number One that established Military Areas Numbers One and Two. Military Area Number One encompassed the western halves of California, Oregon and Washington and the southern half of Arizona. Military Area Number Two was the eastern remainder of California.

DeWitt's plan for the Japanese living in these newly designated "military areas" became apparent On March 24, 1942, from his comfortable headquarters for the Western Defense Command in San Francisco, General DeWitt issued his third public proclamation. This proclamation announced a curfew for enemy aliens (Germans, Italians and Japanese) and for US. citizens of Japanese ancestry. DeWitt imposed a strict curfew between the hours of 8:00 p.m. and 6:30 a.m.

During those hours Japanese-Americans (and enemy aliens) had to remain in their homes. Outsideof those hours, persons of Japanese ancestry were permittedto work, if anyone would hire them, but could not otherwise stray more than five miles from their residences. If they lived in Oakland, they could not go to San Francisco without running afoul of the military proclamation.

In addition, the proclamation prohibited Japanese-Americans from possessing firearms, short-wave radios, radio transmitters, signaling devices and cameras. In the next proclamation, DeWitt required enemy aliens and native-born Japanese-Americans to receive prior approval from the Army, before they could legally change their home addresses.

The Evacuation

Even before the curfew was imposed by General De Witt, the US. Navy forcibly evicted 3,500 Japanese from Terminal Island in Los Angeles harbor. These civilianswere fishermen, their families and local businessmen, but the Navy considered them a serious threat to national security. On February 25th, the Terminal Islanders were given forty-eight hours to leave the island. The residents were forced to sell their belongings for a pittance, or to abandon them. After the evacuation, the island was littered with abandoned household appliances and furniture.

The next Japanese community to be evicted was another fishing village, Bainbridge Island in Puget Sound, near Seattle. During the latter part of March, 1942, the forty-five Japanese-American families who resided on the island were forced to abandon their homes.

Japanese Internment Camps and Relocation Centers

These evacuations sent shockwaves of panic throughthe Japanese communities on the West Coast. Alien fishermen were arrested by the military and sent to the interior of the United States, to Bismark, North Dakota and to otherremote areas. American citizens of Japanese ancestry who were forced to evacuate their homes either moved in with relatives or went to one of the two new "voluntary" relocation centers—Manzanar in the Owens Valley in California or the Northern Colorado Indian Reservation in Arizona.

General DeWitt divided Military Area Number One into ninety-nine zones and ordered the evacuation of Japanese-Americans one zone at a time. The exclusion orders were posted on telephone poles, on storefronts and at bus stops. Fred Korematsu had lived his entire life in Oakland at 10800 Edes Avenue. Civilian Exclusion Number Twenty-Seven made it illegal for him to live in his own home.

The Korematsu Evacuation

In April, 1942, Fred Korematsu left home, telling his family that he was going to start living in Nevada. At the time, Nevada was a legal place of residence for persons of Japanese ancestry. Instead of going to Nevada, however, Fred stayed in Oakland to earn enough money to take his girlfriend, Ida Boitano, with him to the Midwest. Fred and Ida had made plans to marry and dreamed of living a normal life together. But this was not to be.

Fred Korematsu went from place to place, attempting to avoid arrest for violating the curfew and evacuation orders. He routinely violated the curfew by going out with Ida after hours. He changed his name to Clyde Sarah, because he thought that it sounded more American, and even underwent plastic surgery, so that his face did not look Japanese. But, the operation performed on Korematsu in May in San Francisco was not very successful: he still looked Japanese.

Fred Korematsu in 1942, courtesy of Mr. Korematsu.

Fred lived in San Francisco for a few weeks while his face healed from the plastic surgery. He lived in Oakland after noon on Thursday, May 7, 1942, the date by which all Japanese-Americans were required to evacuate. Fred Korematsu knew about the civilian exclusion order but disregarded it, because he wanted to be with his friends, especially Ida. He felt that the exclusion order was illegal. Why did the order apply to him and not to his Italian girlfriend? The United States was at war against both Italy and Japan.

In order to avoid detection, and to prevent ostracism when he moved east with Ida, Fred rented rooms under his assumed name in two rooming houses in Oakland, one at 1428 44th Avenue and the other near the corner of Fruitvale and East 14th Street. "Clyde Sarah" obtained a social security number and worked for one week for the Anderson Trailer Center on MacArthur Boulevard and for amonth for the Trailer Center on MacArthur Boulevard and for a month for the Trailer Company of America in Berkeley at 7th and Gilman Streets.

Korematsu used ink remover to change the name on his draft card to Clyde Sarah and to remove his race and parents' place of birth from his birth certificate. The pressure of being a fugitive, the fear of arrest and the hatred he saw in the faces of white Americans, was getting to him. He missed his family, and he hated to see the white man who took over his father's nursery business.

His family was in Tan-foran, the assembly center in Marin County, north of San Francisco. On May 30, 1942, Fred was with Ida in San Leandro, a few miles south of Oakland. He told her that he had quit his job at the trailer company and was going to turn himself in. He told her th he would challenge the evacuation order and that he would see hersoon. Fred Korematsu, whose only guilt was that his parents were born in Japan, turned himself in at the San Leandro Police Department.

The "Confession"

The San Leandro Police searched Korematsu and had The Oakland Police search his small room of Fruitvale St. The police notified the Federal Bureau of Investigation, which sent in Special Agent Oliver T. Mansfield to interview him. Fred Korematsu voluntarily gave the FBI a full statement. Based on his "confession," a criminal information charge was filed against him on June 12, 1942, and he was held without bail until his trial on September 8, 1942.

Fred Korematsu spent the summer of 1942 interned at the Tanforan Assembly Center, awaiting his chance to prove that he was a patriotic American citizen.

The Trial

The federal government prosecuted Fred Korematsu for violating Civil Exclusion Order Thirty-Four, which applied to military zone thirty-four, San Leandro, Cali-fornia. At the trial, the federal prosecutor introduced the interview with Korematsu, the altered draft card and a certified copy of Korematsu's birth certificate. The birth certificate was introduced to prove Korematsu's Japanese ancestry, the crucial element in the crime that he was charged with committing.

Fred Korematsu testified on his own behalf. He stated that his parents were born in Japan, but that he had never been there. In fact, he said that he had never left the continental

United States. Korematsu testified that he had graduated from Stoner's Grammar School in Oakland and from Castlement High School there. He had attended Los Angeles Junior College in 1938, where he studiedchemistry. He had to work after school hours to pay his college expenses, and he, eventually, had to abandon his studies in order to support himself.

After leaving junior college, Fred Korematsu studied welding. He worked as a welder in a Los Angeles shipyard for two and one-half months. After Pearl Harbor, his employer fired him because he was Japanese.

Korematsu testified that he returned to Oakland to work at his father's nursery and worked there until he left home in April.

Korematsu said that he wanted to fight on behalf of the United States, but that he was rejected because of a stomach ulcer. He registered to vote when he was twenty-one and had never renounced his American citizenship. He testified that he was ready, willing and able to bear arms forthe United States:

> I am willing to enlist. As a citizen of the United States I am ready to render any service that I may be called upon to render to our government in our war against the Axis nations, including the Empire of Japan. I do not owe any allegiance to any country or nation other than the United States of America. I have no dual allegiance. My birth has not, either with my consent or to my knowledge, been registered with any consul of the Empire of Japan. I have never attended and never cared to attend any Japanese school. I am not familiar with the Japanese language . . . . I understand a little Japanese when it is spoken.

WESTERN DEFENSE COMMAND AND FOURTH ARMY
WARTIME CIVIL CONTROL ADMINISTRATION
Presidio of San Francisco, California

INSTRUCTIONS
TO ALL PERSONS OF
JAPANESE
ANCESTRY
LIVING IN THE FOLLOWING AREA:

All of that portion of the County of Alameda, State of California, within that boundary beginning at the point at which the southerly limits of the City of Berkeley meet San Francisco Bay; thence easterly and following the southerly limits of said city to College Avenue; thence southerly on College Avenue to Broadway; thence southerly on Broadway to the southerly limits of the City of Oakland; thence following the limits of said city westerly and northerly, and following the shoreline of San Francisco Bay to the point of beginning.

Pursuant to the provisions of Civilian Exclusion Order No. 27, this Headquarters, dated April 30, 1942, all persons of Japanese ancestry, both alien and non-alien, will be evacuated from the above area by 12 o'clock noon, P.W.T., Thursday May 7, 1942.

No Japanese person living in the above area will be permitted to change residence after 12 o'clock noon, P.W.T., Thursday, April 30, 1942, without obtaining special permission from the representative of the Commanding General, Northern California Sector, at the Civil Control Station located at:

530 Eighteenth Street,
Oakland, California.

Such permits will only be granted for the purpose of uniting members of a family, or in cases of grave emergency.

The Civil Control Station is equipped to assist the Japanese population affected by this evacuation in the following ways:

1. Give advice and instructions on the evacuation.

2. Provide services with respect to the management, leasing, sale, storage or other disposition of most kinds of property, such as real estate, business and professional equipment, household goods, boats, automobiles and livestock.

3. Provide temporary residence elsewhere for all Japanese in family groups.

4. Transport persons and a limited amount of clothing and equipment to their new residence.

Poster giving instructions to persons of Japanese Ancestry.

**Headquarters
Western Defense Command
and Fourth Army**
Presidio of San Francisco, California
April 30, 1942

Civilian Exclusion Order No. 27

1.   Pursuant to the provisions of Public Proclamations Nos. 1 and 2, this Headquarters, dated March 2, 1942, and March 16, 1942, respectively, it is hereby ordered that from and after 12 o'clock noon, P.W.T., of Thursday, May 7, 1942, all persons of Japanese ancestry, both alien and non-alien, be excluded from that portion of Military Area No. 1 described as follows:

All of that portion of the County of Alameda, State of California, within that boundary beginning at the point at which the southerly limits of the City of Berkeley meet San Francisco Bay; thence easterly and following the southerly limits of said city to College Avenue; thence southerly on College Avenue to Broadway; thence southerly on Broadway to the southerly limits of the City of Oakland; thence following the limits of said city westerly and northerly, and following the shoreline of San Francisco Bay to the point of beginning.

2.   A responsible member of each family, and each individual living alone, in the above described area will report between the hours of 8:00 A. M. and 5:00 P. M., Friday, May 1, 1942, or during the same hours on Saturday, May 2, 1942, to the Civil Control Station located at:

530 Eighteenth Street
Oakland, California.

3.   Any person subject to this order who fails to comply with any of its provisions or with the provisions of published instructions pertaining hereto or who is found in the above area after 12 o'clock noon, P.W.T., of Thursday, May 7, 1942, will be liable to the criminal penalties provided by Public Law No. 503, 77th Congress, approved March 21, 1942 entitled "An Act to Provide a Penalty for Violation of Restrictions or Orders with Respect to Persons Entering, Remaining in, Leaving, or Committing any Act in Military Areas or Zones," and alien Japanese will be subject to immediate apprehension and internment.

4.   All persons within the bounds of an established Assembly Center pursuant to instructions from this Headquarters are excepted from the provisions of this order while those persons are in such Assembly Center.

J. L. DeWitt
Lieutenant General, U. S. Army
Commanding

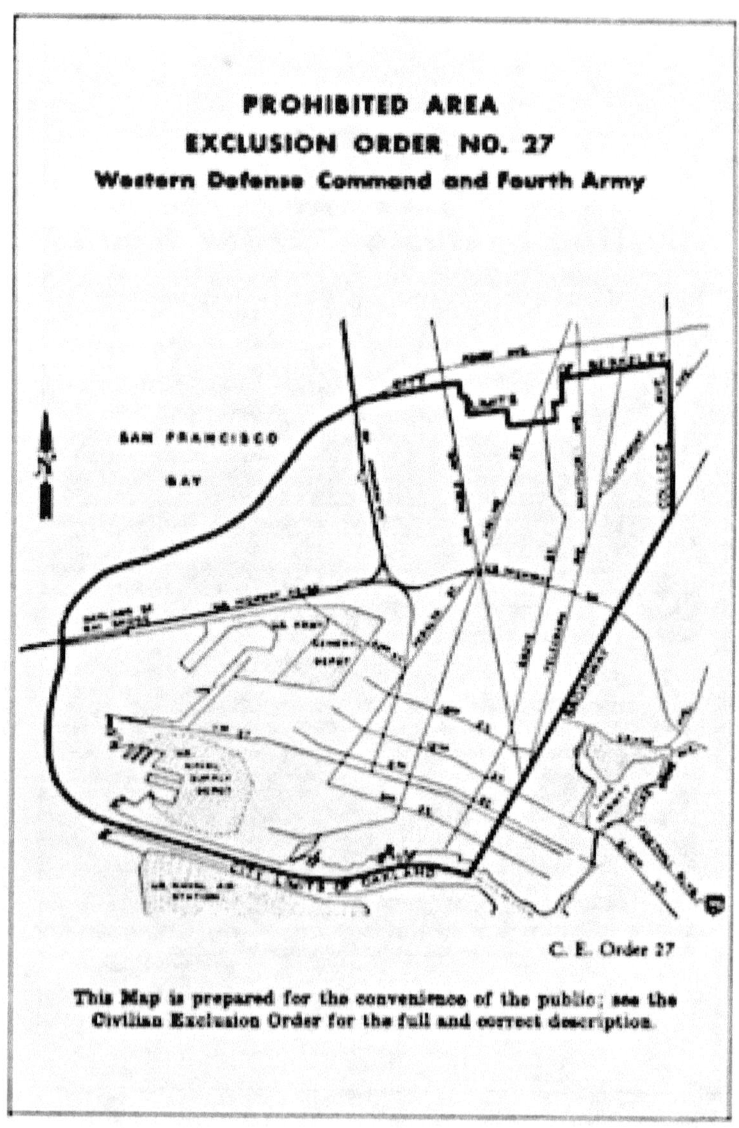

*Map showing an exclusion area in Oakland,
California.*

A typical Japanese internment camp, courtesy of the Library of Congress.

The trial was held before Judge St. Sure without a jury. The judge found Fred Korematsu guilty, but did not fine him, even though the maximum penalty for the offense United States. Korematsu testified that he had charged was a fine of $5,000 and/or imprisonment for one year. The judge sentenced Korematsu to five-years probation and released him to the custody of the U.S. Army. The Army sent him to the Tanforan Assembly Center, where he joined his family. Thereafter, he was moved under military guard to the War Relocation Centerin a desolate desert location near Topaz, Utah.

While his client was confined at Tanforan, Korematsu's attorney, Wayne Collins, appealed the case to the Ninth Circuit Court of Appeals in San Francisco. On December 2, 1942, the court issued a terse decision affirming Korematsu's conviction.

Attorney Collins appealed to the United States Supreme Court. After briefs were filed, the Supreme Court heard extensive oral arguments in October, 1944, at the beginning of the court's term. The arguments were heard over a two-day period, which is most unusual. During the appellate process, Korematsu. was held without bail formore than two years, even though the maximum penalty forthe "crime" alleged was one year's imprisonment. In December, 1944, the court issued its ruling.

The Justification

Justice Hugo Black, one of the court's most liberal jurists, wrote the opinion for the court:

> We uphold the exclusion order as of the time
> it was made and when petitioner [Kore-
> matsu] violated it. In doing so we are not
> unmindful of the hardships imposed by it
> upon a large number of American citizens.

> But hardships are part of war, and war is an aggregation of hardships.

Justice Black was joined in his opinion by Justices William O. Douglas, Stanley Reed, Chief Justice Harlan Stone and Wiley Rutledge. Justice Felix Frankfurter voted with the majority but wrote a separate opinion. However, Justice Owen Roberts, disagreed, pointing out that:

> This is not a case of keeping people off the Streets at night as was in *Hirabayashi v. United States,* nor a case of temporary exclusion of a citizen from an area for his own safety or that of the community. On the contrary, it is the case of convicting a citizen as a punishment for not submitting to imprisonment in a concentration camp, based on his ancestry, and solely because of his ancestry, without evidence or inquiry concerning his loyalty and good disposition towards the United States.[1]

Justices Frank Murphy and Robert Jackson joined Justice Roberts in his courageous dissent. The most disturbing member of the majority was William O. Douglas, later to become of one the court's best and most liberal jurists.

Epilogue

The precedent of the *Korematsu* case is alarming. If the United States and Israel were at war with each other, *Korematsu* would give the U.S. government the authority to intern every Jewish-American, whether he or she was a citizen or not. Similarly, if the United States and Mexico were involved in a border war, every Mexican-American could be held in a concentration camp under this nightmarish ruling.

Over four decades after World War II, various proposals were put forward in Congress to compensate the more than 110,000 Japanese-Americans who were interned during World War II. The first edition, of this book, published in 1987, called upon Congress to provide compensation to the internees. In 1988 Congress apologized for interning Japanese-Americas and awarded compensation of $20,000 to each survivor. Benefits were paid beginning in 1990.

Fred Korematsu and other Americans of Japanese ancestry filed a new lawsuit in 1983, alleging that the Justice Department of the Army fabricated the threat caused by Japanese-Americans. The government joined in Korematsu's petition to have his conviction overturned.The judge stated: "as historical precedent it [the 1944 case] stands as a constant caution that in times of war or declaredmilitary necessity our institutions must be vigilant in protecting constitutional guarantees." The court noted that the decision was overruled by the court of history, but did
not overturn Korematsu's conviction.

Korematsu suffered his entire life because of his conviction. No government agency or large corporation would hire him, because he was convicted of a crime. Korematsu wanted to get a real estate license, but his conviction prevented it. He worked, and continued to work, as a draftsman.

After the war, Fred Korematsu moved to Detroit where he met his wife, Kathryn Parsons. Ida Boitano went to Korematsu's parent's nursery after the war to look for him, but had not seen Fred since 1944. She married someone else. In 1949, Korematsu and his wife moved back to California where they raised their family, a son and a daughter. In 1987, the Korematsus lived in San Leandro, where he was semi-retired at age sixty-eight.

Conclusion

The Supreme Court issued its decision on Monday, December 18, 1944, a day that will live in infamy. While December 7, 1941, as seen in its historical perspective, can be viewed as a day when America slept, and the Japanese took a strategic advantage, the *Korematsu* decision is seen by the entire world as evidence of American discrimination against Asians, and, as evidence of our racism. Fred Korematsu died in Marin County, California in 2005 at age 86.

The State of California, in order to commemorate Korematsu's journey as a civil rights activist, enacted "Fred Korematsu Day of Civil Liberties and the Constitution." Fred Korematsu Day was observed for first time on January 30, 2011 by the state of California, and was the first such commemoration for an Asian-American in the United States.

Endnotes

1. *Korematsu v. United States,* 323 U.S. 214 (1944).

Chapter Twenty

Women's Rights

*"No state shall deny . . . any person within its
jurisdiction equal protection of the laws."*

—Fourteenth Amendment

The much-maligned state of New Jersey was the first state to grant women the right to vote under the Constitution. New Jersey allowed women to vote until 1807. Before the Constitution was enacted, from 1691 until 1780, Massachusetts allowed female property owners to vote.

The woman suffrage movement started to become active after the Civil War. In 1868, an intrepid band of women went to the polls to vote in Vineland, New Jersey. Not much is known about this group except that they inspired Susan B. Anthony into action.

Susan B. Anthony

On November 1, 1872, Susan B. Anthony, following the example of the Vineland group, led fourteen women to register and vote in Rochester, New York. Miss Anthony convinced the inspectors of the registration office that she had a right to vote and they registered her. The two Republican registrars agreed to receive her name while the Democratic official objected. A full report of this scene appeared in the afternoon papers. Because of this publicity, a total of about fifty women registered to vote in Rochester that November.

On November 5th, Susan Anthony and six of the women presented themselves at the polling booth. All of their votes were challenged, but they were all received.

The Rochester newspapers covered these events extensively. The Republican newspaper argued in favor of the women while the Democratic newspaper argued against them. On Thanksgiving Day, the fourteen women were informed that they were going to be prosecuted by the Federal government, and that the Commissioner wishedthat they would voluntarily to come to his office. The ladies refused the invitation.

On the afternoon of Thanksgiving Day, Miss Anthony was summoned to her parlor to receive a visitor. He stated, "The Commissioner wishes to arrest you."

Miss Anthony responded, "Is this your usual method of serving a warrant?"

The Marshal gathered his courage, handed her a summons and meekly escorted her to the Commissioner's office. Anthony was arrested for her part in the Rochester incident. In addition, the male election inspectors who registered Anthony and the other females were arrested for registering the women to vote. Inspectors Hall, Marsh and others were tried and convicted in June, 1873, and fined twenty-five dollars. When they refused to pay the fine, they were jailed. During their short jail terms, the ladies of the Eighth Ward brought home-cooked meals to them. President Grant pardoned the inspectors after they had spent a week in jail.

On June 18, 1873, Susan B. Anthony was tried and pronounced guilty of illegally registering and voting by a hostile judge, Ward Hunt, who took the case away from the jury.[1] He said:

> The Fourteenth Amendment gives no right to a woman to vote, and the voting by Miss Anthony was a violation of the law.
>
> *   *   *
>
> If she believed she had a right to vote, and voted in reliance upon that belief, does that relieve her from the penalty?

> Miss Anthony knew that she was a woman, and that the Constitution of this State prohibits her from voting. She intended to violate that provision, intended to test it, perhaps, but certainly to violate it, and this she is presumed to have intended.

Even though a judge can never constitutionally direct a verdict against a defendant in a criminal case, Judge Hunt did so. He fined Miss Anthony one hundred dollars. Susan B. Anthony stated:

> May it please your honor, I shall never pay a dollar of your unjust penalty. All the stock in trade I possess is a $10,000 debt incurred by publishing my pa*per—The Revolution*—the sole object of which was to educate all women to do precisely as I have

done, rebel against man-made unjust, un-constitutional forms of law that tax, fine, imprison and hang women, while they deny them the right of representation in the government.

Anthony never paid the fine. Her conviction could not be appealed because no steps were taken to enforce her sentence. She was unable, as she had hoped, to appeal her case to the United States Supreme Court. Other women were getting active in the suffrage movement. One of them was Virginia Minor.

Virginia L. Minor

Virginia L. Minor was a Civil War relief worker. She married Francis Minor in Virginia when she was nineteen. Mr. Minor had graduated from Princeton and the University of Virginia Law School.

Despite their Virginia roots, the Minors supported the Union in the Civil War. Mrs. Minor joined the St. Louis Ladies Union Aid Society, which was organized in 1861 to assist wounded soldiers and their families. When the society was disbanded in 1865, Mrs. Minor and several other women turned their attention to their own rights. She said that not only negroes but also women should be given the right to vote. She was the first woman in Missouri to take a stand for suffrage.

In 1867, Mr. and Mrs. Minor circulated a petition to the state legislature that the amendment to the Missouri Constitution permitting male negroes to vote be extended to women. Her proposed amendment was rejected by a vote of eighty-nine to five. After that, she organized the Women's Suffrage Association of Missouri and was elected president.

Virginia L. Minor, courtesy of the Library of Congress.

Francis Minor, a lawyer, believed that the U.S. Constitution granted women the right to vote. The Constitution does not mention the words male or female, only citizens and persons of the United States. The courts had held that women were citizens, were allowed to own property and were required to pay taxes. Mr. Minor felt that state laws prohibiting women from voting were "bills of attainder." Bills of attainder are laws directed at specific individuals or groups and are outlawed by the Constitution. He also believed that the "privileges and immunities" clause of the Constitution applied to men and women alike. That clause provides that "the citizens of each state shall be entitled to all privileges and immunities of citizens in the several states." But his best argument was that the newly enacted Fourteenth Amendment gave women the right to vote. That amendment provides:

> No State shall make or enforce any law which shall abridge the privileges or immunities of citizens of the United States . . .; nor deny to any person within its jurisdiction the equal protection of her laws.

The Challenge

The first step in a legal challenge to Missouri's "male only" voting was to attempt to register to vote. On October 15, 1872, Virginia L. Minor, age forty-six, went to the office of voter registration at 2004 Market Street in St. Louis, Missouri. The registrar, Reese Sappersett, refused to register her to vote. Mr. Sappersett said that she was not entitled to vote because she was not a male citizen, but a woman. He relied on the recently approved Missouri Constitution which declared that only male citizens were permitted to vote.

The law of Missouri did not allow women to file suit unless their husbands agreed to join in and support their case. Mrs. Minor's husband, Francis Minor, agreed withand encouraged his wife's legal tactics. Francis Minor and two other male attorneys (a few years earlier, the Supreme Court had ruled in *Bradwell v. State*,[2] that women had no right to practice law) drafted a lawsuit against Mr. Sappersett. Mrs. Minor sued for $10,000 as damages for deprivation of her right to vote.

The Missouri Supreme Court handed down its decision on August 16, 1873. The court ruled that the Missouri law allowing only men to vote was not a bill of attainder. It further ruled that the provision did not run afoul of the privileges and immunities clause. The court said that the continued denial of a right is the fact that everyone has denied it before. The court considered Minor's Fourteenth Amendment argument to be more substantial. However, the court ruled that the intent of the Fourteenth Amendment was to give former slaves the right to vote and not to give women the right to vote.

A fundamental principle of law is that if a provision is clear on its face, there is no need to seek the intent of the drafters. The Fourteenth Amendment is clear on its face that *all* citizens are to be treated equally.

Woman Suffrage at the Supreme Court

The U.S. Supreme Court agreed to hear Mrs. Minor's appeal. Its decision came on March 29, 1875.[3] The Supreme Court of the United States was *unanimous* in its ruling:

> There is no doubt that women may be citizens. For nearly ninety years the people have acted

upon the idea that the Constitution, when it conferred citizenship, did not necessarily confer the right of suffrage.

The all-male Supreme Court voted that women had no right to vote, as they had ruled that women had no right to practice law. Women's rights were left in the hands of men.

Epilogue

The year after the Supreme Court's ruling in Mrs. Minor's case, the country celebrated its one hundredth anniversary. There was a centennial celebration in Philadelphia where Susan B. Anthony proclaimed a Women's Declaration of Rights. In 1877, Ms. Anthony led a group of women onto the floor of the United States Senate, bearing suffrage petitions. The Senate, after making the standard jokes concerning women's status as property, referred the petition to the Committee on Public Lands.

In the following year Senator Aaron Sargent of California introduced a constitutional amendment:

> The right of citizens of the United States to
> vote shall not be denied or abridged by the
> United States or any State on account of sex.

In 1886, the Senate voted the amendment down by a margin of thirty-four to six, with thirty-two senators not voting. In 1890, the State of Wyoming became the only state to allow women to vote. Colorado followed in 1893, Utah in 1895 and Idaho the following year. Washington State and California followed in 1910 and 1911. Kansas, Oregon and

Arizona approved women's suffrage in 1912, Nevada and Montana in 1914. The only Eastern state to join the trend was New York in 1917.

Forty-one long years after being introduced by Senator Sargent, the Nineteenth Amendment was approved. Thirty-six states ratified the women's rights amendment, and it became a part of the Constitution on August 26, 1920.

During the 1980s, more than one hundred years after the Supreme Court's ruling in Mrs. Minor's case, the Equal Rights Amendment (ERA) failed to become a part of the Constitution. The ERA is still needed because, at any given time, the male-dominated Supreme Court can refuse to give women equal protection of the law, as they did in 1875.

Virginia Minor passed away in 1894 nineteen years after the Supreme Court ruled that she did not have theright to vote.

Endnotes

1. *United States v. Anthony,* Case No. 14,459, 24 Fed. Case 829 (1873).
2. 16 Wall. 130 (1872).
3. *Minor v. Sappersett,* 21 Wallace 162 (1875).

Chapter Twenty-One

Bush v. Gore: A Judicial Coup d'Etat

"All animals are equal, but some are more equal than others."

—George Orwell in Animal Farm

"to be conscious of complete truthfulness while telling carefully constructed lies, to hold simultaneously two opinions . . . knowing them to be contradictory and to believe that democracy was impossible. Even to understand the word 'doublethink' involved the use of doublethink."

—George Orwell in 1984

"Catch-22 says they have a right to do anything we can't stop them from doing."

—Joseph Heller in Catch 22

The worst decision of the United States Supreme Court that was issued after I wrote *Black Mondays* in 1987 was issued in December of 2000. In fact, it was the worst decision in 143 years since the court issued its *Dred Scott* ruling in 1857. It may be the single worst decision ever made by the United States Supreme Court. (However, the Presidential immunity decision, *Trump v. United States*, certainly qualifies as one the worst decisions of all time. See Chapter 40.)

Why is the decision so bad? There are many reasons, but I will limit my list to three. First of all, we have a conservative Supreme Court that claims to believe in States' rights. But when the High Court did not like how the Supreme Court of Florida interpreted the laws of Florida, it jumped into the fray to overturn it.

Secondly, the U.S. Supreme Court granted a stay to stop election boards in Florida from hand recounting un- counted votes. By doing so the Court ignored more than 100 years of precedents and found irreparable injury, one of the requirements for issuing a stay, when there clearly was none.

And finally, the Court entered into the political arena and made a political decision when countless times before it had not taken jurisdiction of a case that it considered political. But the key question used by the Supreme Court for a century has been: has the issue to be decided in a case involving political issues have been committed by the Constitution for a decision by another branch of government? The Twelfth Amendment to the Constitution provides that **Congress** shall count the electoral votes and determine the winner of presidential elections. Nowhere in the Constitution does it provide that the U.S. Supreme Court shall count the votes of the electors and determine the outcome of presidential elections. But that is in fact what the Supreme Court did.

The Election of 2000

In one of the closest elections in American history, Albert Gore won the popular vote by 500,000 votes out of more than 100 million votes cast nationwide. Without including the state of Florida, the electoral vote count was 267 for Vice President Gore to 246 for Governor George W. Bush. There are a total of 538 electoral votes and 270 are required for a majority. Florida's 25 electoral votes controlled the balance of power.

The major television networks first called the election for Florida for Gore at about 9 p.m. Eastern time on election night. Then, about an hour later, the networks declared Florida "too close to call." Later, at about 2:00 a.m. Eastern time, the television networks declared Bush the winner. Once again, the networks reversed themselves and declared the race too close to call. For more than a month after the election, the nation waited patiently for the votes to be counted and recounted in the State of Florida.

After the election, and after the absentee ballots were counted, George W. Bush was leading in the Florida vote count by 1,784 votes. Neither Governor Bush nor Vice President Gore had a majority of the nearly six million votes cast in Florida. Green party candidate Ralph Nader polled more than 90,000 votes in the state, about one and one-half percent. Both major party candidates stood at 49% of the Florida vote.

A manual recount was ordered under Florida law because the difference between Gore and Bush was less than one-half of one percent. Florida has no precise standards for how a manual recount should be conducted. Many voters in the Sunshine State voted with punch-card ballots using a stylus to strike out a rectangle called a "chad." In Miami

Dade County alone more than 9,000 ballots were not counted in the presidential race by the voting machines because the chad was not completely detached from the ballot.

The law in many states, including Texas, provides that an indentation in the ballot (called a pregnant chad) where a presidential candidate's vote was intended to be recorded, was a sufficient indicator of voter's intent to count. The Texas law on pregnant chads was signed into law by Governor Bush.

Judge Robert Rosenberg, a member of the Broward County Canvassing board, closely examines a disputed ballot during that county's recount on Nov. 24, 2000.

After the election totals in the state were certified by the Florida Secretary of State, Vice President Gore filed suit in local Florida courts to require three large Democratic counties to conduct manual recounts. The lower court ruled against Gore. The Vice President appealed to the Florida Supreme Court.

Vice President Gore's legal team argued that every vote must be counted. Governor Bush's lawyers argued that voters should follow the rules and make sure that their chads were punched out cleanly. Bush's legal team also argued that because the recounts were sought in only three out of 67 counties in Florida, that votes in different regions of the state were being counted differently. This differential treatment, the Bush team argued, deprived of voters equal protection of the laws in the 64 other Florida counties.

After hearing the expedited argument, Florida's highest court ruled that the recounts should begin immediately. The court ruled that all uncounted votes should be counted across the state, not just those in the Democratic counties where the Vice President had sought recounts. The decision was not a complete victory for the Gore team because the court found merit in Governor Bush's argument that the recount should be a statewide recount, not just in three heavily Democratic counties.

Governor Bush's legal team also tried to bring this issue directly to federal court. Bush's team had sought a restraining order in a separate federal court case to stop manual recounts. A Florida federal district judge denied the Governor's request for relief. The Eleventh Circuit Court of Appeals, a conservative bench in Atlanta, also denied the Governor's request to stop the counting. The Court of Appeals ruled that there was no irreparable injury and no likelihood that Governor Bush would prevail on appeal.

The decision of Florida's Supreme Court came down on December 8, 2000. The court ordered manual recounting on a statewide basis to address Governor Bush's equal protection argument that allowing recounts only in Democratic areas would be unfair. The electoral college was scheduled to be chosen in Florida on December 12th, so the counters only had four days to complete their work.

The Stay

On December 9th, Governor Bush sought a stay from the United States Supreme Court to order the Florida counters to stop hand-counting ballots. [Bush's team also sought Supreme Court review of the Eleventh Circuit's denial of relief, but review of that decision was denied.] Most legal observers thought that granting a stay by the United States Supreme Court was unlikely because the standards for is- suance of a stay are difficult to meet. A stay is a temporary hold on the effects of a judicial decision. For example, if you win a judgment against someone for $10,000, a stay would prevent you from collecting on the judgment until the appeal was decided.

In a highly unusual action, the nation's highest court reached out and granted a stay, stopping the vote counters in their tracks. By a vote of 5-4, the court stopped the vote counting in Florida, just as many of the uncounted votes were being counted for the first time. The court granted a stay, and by doing so ran afoul of the rule of law that the Court had been following for more than 100 years.

Justice Antonin Scalia, an exceptionally conservative Reagan appointee, said,

The counting of votes that are of questionable

> legality does in my view threaten irreparable
> harm to petitioner, and to the country, by
> casting a cloud upon what he claims to be the
> legitimacy of his election. Count first, and
> rule upon legality afterwards, is not a recipe
> for producing election results that have the
> public acceptance democratic stability re-
> quires.

This is the type of language that George Orwell was referring to in *1984* when he described "doublespeak." What harm is there in counting votes? If a cloud is cast over George W. Bush's presidency, it is because he not only failed to win the national popular vote, he "won" the disputed election in Florida where his brother Jeb Bush was governor. The United States Supreme Court is fully responsible for the cloud over this election. And as Justice Breyer, joined by Justices Stevens, Ginsburg and Souter, remarked in dissent:

> Above all, in this highly politicized matter,
> the appearance of a split decision runs the risk
> of undermining the public's confidence in the
> Court itself. That confidence is a public trea-
> sure. It has been built slowly over many
> years, some of which were marked by a Civil
> War and the tragedy of segregation. It is a
> vitally necessary ingredient of any successful
> effort to protect basic liberty and, indeed, the
> rule of law itself. We run no risk of returning
> to the days when a President (responding to
> this Court's efforts to protect the Cherokee
> Indians) might have said, "John Marshall has
> made his decision; now let him enforce it!"
> Loth, *Chief Justice John Marshall and The*

Growth of the American Republic 365
(1948). But we do risk a self-inflicted
wound—a wound that may harm not just the
Court, but the Nation.

Justice John Paul Stevens, who was appointed to the
High Court by Republican President Gerald Ford, dissented
from the issuance of the stay:

> To stop the counting of legal votes, the
> ma- jority today departs from three venerable
> rules of judicial restraint that have guided the
> Court throughout its history. On questions of
> state law, we have consistently respected the
> opinions of the highest courts of the States.
> On questions whose resolution is committed
> at least in large measure to another branch of
> the Federal Government, we have construed
> our own jurisdiction nar rowly and exercised
> it cautiously. On federal constitutional ques-
> tions that were not fairly presented to the
> court whose judgment is being reviewed, we
> have prudently declined to express an
> opinion. The majority has acted unwisely.
>
> It is clear, however, that a stay should not
> be granted unless an applicant makes a
> substantial showing of a likelihood of ir-
> reparable harm. In this case, applicants have
> failed to carry that heavy burden. ***Counting
> every legally cast vote cannot constitute
> irreparable harm.*** On the other hand, there is
> a danger that a stay may cause irreparable
> harm to the respondents—and, more impor-

> tantly, the public at large—because of the risk that "the entry of the stay would be tantamount to a decision on the merits in favor of the applicants." Preventing the recount from being completed will inevitably cast a cloud on the legitimacy of the election (emphasis added).

A stay of a lower court decision is only granted when four conditions are met. The first condition is that irreparable injury will result if the stay is not granted. Irreparable injury is harm that cannot be undone, such as the death penalty, or a court-ordered blood transfusion or abortion. No one would have been harmed irreparably if the votes had been counted. The only injury that would have resulted is one that stems from the truth. And, as the Supreme Court knows well, there can be no legal injury from telling the truth. In the United States, unlike Great Britain, truth is an absolute defense to a lawsuit for slander or libel. Failing to have irreparable injury means that no stay should have been granted. Period. But I will proceed to review the other three criteria, all of which counsel against granting a stay and stopping the vote counters.

The second condition that must be met for a court to grant a stay is that the party asking for the stay (George W. Bush) is likely to prevail in the case. But for that to happen the United States Supreme Court would have to ignore hundreds of cases which grant to state supreme courts the respect that they are due when construing state law. How could five conservative Justices, Rehnquist, Scalia, Thomas, Kennedy and O'Connor, who profess a respect for states' rights, ignore the right of the states to conduct their own elections? Florida law provides, "No vote shall be declared invalid or void if there is a clear indication of the intent of the voter as determined by the canvassing board."

Florida's Supreme Court properly interpreted that section of Florida law to require a count of the uncounted ballots. That should have been the end of the story.

The third criterion for granting a stay is: "will the stay harm the other party to the case?" Obviously, Al Gore is harmed, possibly irreparably, by the Supreme Court's hasty action. Had the Court allowed the votes to be counted we would all know who really won the election. If Mr. Gore lost, then a Supreme Court ruling, or even a hearing, would have been unnecessary.

The fourth criteria for granting a stay is, "how will the decision affect the public?" Unfortunately, this is where the Court has done lasting harm to the United States in specific, and to democracy in general. The people of the United States have been dealt a cruel injustice by the nation's highest tribunal. Most voters want to know who won. And the only way to know who won the election is to count all the votes. Failing to count all the votes undeniably deprives the uncounted voters of equal protection of the laws.

By ushering in President Bush, the popular vote loser, without a proper vote count, the Supreme Court has committed a judicial coup d'etat. The Republican-controlled court anointed Republican, George W. Bush, President of the United States, the voters be damned.

Political Questions

The Supreme Court has always declined to take cases that present political questions. Of course, many cases have political ramifications, like *Roe v. Wade* (abortions) and *Clinton v. Jones* (right to proceed in a civil case against the President of the United States). Political questions are those which are dedicated by the constitution for a decision by another branch of government. The Twelfth Amendment to the Constitution specifically provides that ***Congress*** shall count the votes of the presidential electors. If two competing slates of presidential electors from one state are presented to Congress, Congress, not the United States Supreme Court, must decide which slate of electors are to be counted. This case presents the ultimate political question that should have been decided by Congress, not the United States Supreme Court.

The Decision

The Supreme Court granted the stay on Friday, December 9 and set argument for Monday, December 11, 2000. Briefs were filed on Sunday. The country waited anxiously for the court to take action.

The scene outside of the court building, a stately Greekcolumned edifice built during the Great Depression, looked like a combination of a protest march and an all-night ticket line for a hot rock concert. Hundreds of demonstrators, partisans for Gore and Bush, held signs and pranced before live television cameras from CNN and the major and not-somajor television networks.

There were three ways to gain entrance to the court to attend the oral argument. There is one line for members of the Supreme Court bar. I was fortunate enough to get in this line so I could hear the case live. To do so I had to leave my home at 4:30 in the morning. Joining me in the line were television commentators, law professors and high- powered Washington attorneys. Every person in line was given a number on a card by a member of the Supreme Court staff. These cards were color coded depending on which line you were in.

The second method for gaining admittance to the court for a brief glimpse of the historic argument was to join the

Public line. To get into the courthouse via the public line required staying in line overnight in twenty-degree weather. Hundreds of students, tourists and government bureaucrats camped out in tents and sleeping bags waiting in the public line.

The best way to gain entrance is to get a special invitation from either the court itself or from one of the parties to the case. Senators and "important" members of the House of Representatives did not have to stand in either of the two lines. Vice President Gore's daughters were granted special admittance. The media was limited to one seat per network or publication. Even CNN's legal correspondents had to wait in the lawyer's line to gain admittance.

Equal Protection of the Laws

Even though the United States Supreme Court certainly does not provide equal protection to the several classes of visitors seeking to gain admittance to the court, it said that it attempted to apply equal protection of the laws to the voters of Florida.

Governor Bush's team argued that by applying different standards for recounts in various Florida counties, the voters were deprived of equal protection the law under the Fifth and Fourteenth Amendments to the Constitution of the United States.

The Fifth Amendment provides that no person shall be "deprived of life, liberty or property without due process of law." This due process clause has been interpreted to create a right to equal protection of the law. The Fourteenth Amendment is more specific. It provides that no state can "deprive any person of life, liberty, or property without due process of law; nor deny to any person within its jurisdiction the equal protection of the laws."

The Supreme Court has previously found constitutional

different methods for voting in different counties within a state. For example, some counties may have punchcard votes and others optically scanned ballots without equal protection principles being violated. The record before the court demonstrated that optically-scanned ballots had one-half the percentage of "undervotes" that the punch-card ballots had. An "undervote" for President means that on a ballot where votes for other offices were recorded, no vote for President registered with the vote-tabulating machines.

Vice President Gore had requested under Florida law that three counties have their votes recounted manually to attempt to find the "intent of the voter," as Florida law specified. Even though Governor Bush had the right to seek similar recounts in Republican counties, he did not do so. Further, Governor Bush's legal team pressed the equal protection argument in federal court, and in the Eleventh Circuit Court of Appeals in Atlanta, and was rejected.
It is interesting to note that Governor Bush's team did not think much of the equal protection argument. The team almost didn't raise the issue. Equal protection claims are usually made by members of minority groups, or by women, who are discriminated against. The class of voters who were discriminated against in *Bush v. Gore* remains difficult to define. Was it Republicans who clearly punched their ballots who were discriminated against in favor of Democrats who were too elderly to completely punch out a chad?

The equal protection argument had been addressed by the Florida Supreme Court. That court had ordered recounts statewide. The new issue to be decided by the Supreme Court had never been addressed by Florida's high court. That issue concerned the recount: what standards for counting the chads should be used?
Ordinarily, the United States Supreme Court will not decide an issue until the lower courts have addressed it. In this case,

obviously because of the compressed time situ- ation, the Supreme Court jumped in where it has been loathe to do so in the past.

The Nation Held Its Breath

Both outside and inside the courthouse, the atmosphere was electric. In the twenty-six years since *United States v. Nixon* was heard by the court no case even came close to the excitement generated by *Bush v. Gore*. The lawyers were nervous, calling justices by the wrong name on several occasions. One lawyer even referred to one justice as Justice Brennan, who had passed away several years earlier.

Vice President Gore's famed attorney, David Boies, was unusually silent in response to several questions. In response to a question on how he would correct the equal protection problem, he said, "That's a difficult question," and never really answered it. That may have been Boies fa- tal mistake. The one-and-one-half-hour oral argument was com- pleted by lunchtime on Monday, and a decision was ex- pected that afternoon. As the country held its breath, the court continued to debate the issues behind the closed doors of its marble sanctuary. The midnight oil was burning at the courthouse where the justices were hard at work. Monday afternoon and evening came and went without a word out of the court. No decision was issued. The country now ex- pected a decision by early Tuesday, December 12th, the day that each state was scheduled to pick its electors for the electoral college.

But no decision was announced Tuesday morning. No word came from the Court Tuesday afternoon or evening. Then finally, at around 10:00 p.m. Eastern time, the Court issued its five-to-four decision:

> Upon due consideration of the difficulties identified to this point, it is obvious that the recount cannot be conducted in compliance

with the requirements of equal protection and due process without substantial ad- ditional work.

*   *   *

That date [the date for determining electors] is upon us, and there is no recount procedure in place under the State Supreme Court's order that comports with minimal con- stitutional standards. Because it is evi- dent that any recount seeking to meet the December 12 date will be unconstitutional for the reasons we have discussed, we reverse the judgment of the Supreme Court of Florida ordering a recount to proceed.

The Court found Florida's vote-recounting methods to be unconstitutional. But it also found that there was nothing it could do about it. Finding an action uncon-stitutional and not taking any corrective action, violates one of the earlier precedents of the Supreme Court, *Marbury v. Madison* (1 Cranch 137, 1803). In *Marbury v. Madison* the court ruled that the courts have a duty to remedy violations of law. A more recent Supreme Court ruling, *Bivens v. Six Unknown Agents*, 403 U.S. 388, 397 (1971), provided "it is well settled that where legal rights have been invaded the federal courts may use any available remedy to make good the wrong done. *Bell v. Hood*, 327 U.S. at 684 (1946)."

The Supreme Court took no action to remedy the equal protection violation that it had found. The Court apparently found there was nothing it could do to count 60,000 Florida votes even though the margin of "victory" was less than 2,000 votes. Because the court stopped the vote counters, and did not allow time for more counting, its ruling in effect appointed George W. Bush the President of the United States by a single vote of a Supreme Court Justice.

By claiming that the right to equal protection of the laws was breached, the court itself was treating voters differently. Instead of applying the law of letting every vote count, the court ruled that only the votes counted to date would be counted. Senior citizens who had trouble piercing the ballot with a dull stylus would be deprived of their equal right to vote. The court ordered no remedy to correct these injustices.

Catch-22

Joseph Heller's book *Catch-22* was about a government policy that could not be met. It concerned the sanity of bomber pilots. The rule was that a pilot was presumed to be sane if he did not want to go on a bombing mission. Because of this rule, there was no way for an insane pilot to be excused from duty for reasons of insanity.

The United States Supreme Court has created a new Catch-22. The court found that equal protection of the law required a uniform standard for recounting across the state of Florida. However, because the court stopped the vote counting for four days, no time was available for such a recount. The court ruled that because there was no time, the pre-existing count would be the final count, even though that earlier count was based on unequal treatment of voters from various counties. Justice Breyer wrote in dissent: "What it does today, the court should have left undone. I would repair damage done as best we can, by permitting the Florida recount to continue under uniform standards."

The Supreme Court had the power to alter the electoral clock to allow all the votes to be properly counted. But the court apparently did not want the votes to be counted. And by a vote of five to four, President Bush was sworn in as President of the United States.

Conclusion

To rule that the votes would never be counted because there was not enough time for votes to be counted, undeniably has cost the country and the Supreme Court its hard-earned credibility. The Supreme Court certainly had the power to adjust timetables to allow time for all of the votes to be counted by a uniform standard. The President of the United States did not have to be sworn in until January 20, 2001. Votes could have been counted until December 31st, or even as late as January 10th, without delaying the inauguration.

The Supreme Court allowed the loser of the popular vote, and the probable loser of the electoral college, to be sworn in as the 43rd President of the United States. This is the first Judicial Coup that has taken place in the United States. Hopefully, it will be the last time that the judiciary interferes in a presidential election. Even Chief Justice Rehnquist, a vestige from the Nixon Administration, stated his desire to avoid judicial intervention in elections again.

By a vote of five to four the Court substituted its votes for the votes of the people of the United States. In the eyes of the world, the United States looks no better than a banana republic. Critics of the decision include both liberals and conservatives. Judge Richard Posner, a well-respected conservative jurist on the 7th Circuit Court of Appeals in Chicago, criticized the Supreme Court's decision in several respects. Writing in the *Supreme Court Review,* Judge Posner criticized the court for judicial activism and for its equal protection findings. Judge Posner writes that the court "cannot avoid the label 'activist' since it expands federal judicial power without clear warrant in con- stitutional text or precedent." In light of the conservatives' dislike for judicial activism, Judge Posner's review should make the Court and President Bush, squirm in their chairs. Posner calls the Court's equal protection ruling "wrong- headed." With criticism from the left and the right, the court's ruling rests on weak pillars. For a conservative court to commit two sins complained of by fellow conservatives, is legal blasphemy. The court committed judicial activism (not necessarily a bad thing) and failed to support the ruling of a state supreme court (also not necessarily a bad thing). But these are two main supporting pillars of the conservative establishment. With this type of inconsistency it is difficult to understand how the court's ruling will be interpreted in years to come.

Only two months after *Gore v. Bush* was decided, the court ruled in another case involving state's rights. This time the issue was whether a citizen could sue his own state under Americans with Disabilities Act. The court ruled in favor of state's rights, holding that states could not be sued. The ruling went beyond the clear language of the Eleventh Amendment. The Eleventh Amendment provides that states cannot be sued in ***federal court*** by citizens of other states. But in that case the state was being sued by one of its own residents. The only clear indication from this Supreme Court is that states rights will be supported, unless they conflict with some other goal of the court. This is not the type of ruling that gives citizens confidence that we live in a nation of laws and that the court is neutral. This Supreme Court clearly has an agenda that rises above principles of law.

The least representative branch of government has taken away the rights of voters and of Congress. The case of *George W. Bush v. Albert Gore* will go down in history as one of the most catastrophic decisions of the United States Supreme Court.

Chapter Twenty-Two
Gerrymandering

"Political gerrymandering makes the incentive for most members of Congress to play to the extremes of their base rather than to the center."

—Barack Obama

"Too much of American politics is decided by efforts to restrict who votes or, as in gerrymandering, to manipulate the weight those votes hold. A more democratic system won't end polarization, but it will create a healthier form ofcompetition."

— Ezra Klein, *Why We're Polarized*
Columnist, *New York Times*

For forty-seven years, the law of the land was "one man, one vote." This was decided by the Supreme Court in *Baker v. Carr,* 369 U.S. 186 (1962). It was a landmark United States Supreme Court case in which the Court districting qualifies as a justiciable question under the Fourteenth Amendment, thus enabling federal courts to hear Fourteenth Amendment-based gerrymandering cases. The court summarized its *Baker* holding in a later decision as follows: "Equal Protection Clause of the Fourteenth Amend-ment limits the authority of a State Legislature in designing the geographical districts from which representatives are chosen either for the State Legislature or for the Federal House of Representatives. *Gray v. Sanders*, 372 U.S. 368 (1963)."

In 2019 in *Rucho v. Common Cause*, the Supreme Court essentially reversed *Baker v. Carr*, holding that Gerrymandering cases were not justiciable.

Gerrymandering

Gerrymandering is the deliberate manipulation of legislative district boundaries to give a disproportional advantage to a political party or racial group. In 1812, the Governor of Massachusetts and future Vice President Elbridge Gerry notoriously approved irregularly-shaped congressional districts that the legislature had drawn to aid the Democratic-Republican Party. The moniker "Gerrymander" was born on March 26, 1812 when an outraged Federalist newspaper, the *Boston Gazette,* observed that one of the misshapen districts resembled a salamander.

Alexander Hamilton founded the Federalist Party, the backbone of which were bankers and businessmen, the same types of people who now make up the Republican Party. It is ironic that the Republican-controlled Supreme Court would allow the same type of gerrymandering that Alexander Hamilton had opposed.

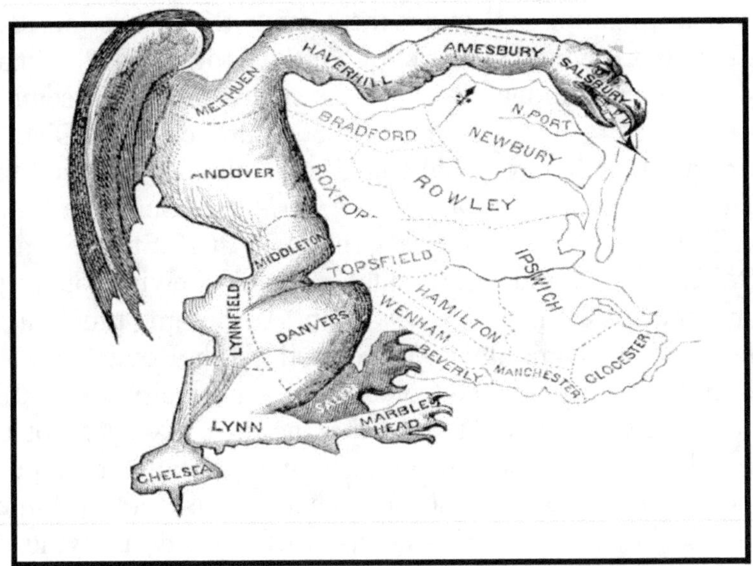

The "Gerrymander" cartoon first appeared in the Boston Gazette, March 26, 1812, and was quickly reprinted in Federalist newspapers in Salem (this copy is from the Salem Gazette from April 2, 1813) and Boston.

North Carolina

Historically, North Carolina has had a nearly-equal split of voters between the Republican and Democratic parties. The political parties, backed by wealthy donors on both sides, have fought over control of the state using Gerrymandering for decades. Prior to 2011, seven of the state's thirteen districts favored Democrats, the rest Republican.

The first redistricting map for North Carolina following the 2010 Census was released in 2011, which resulted in nine districts favoring Republicans. A legal challenge over the new congressional redistricting map shortly followed, claiming that the map utilized racial gerrymandering which was unconstitutional under the Voting Rights Act of 1965. In 2016, the Middle District of North Carolina ruled the map was unconstitutional and gave the state's General Assembly two weeks to revise the map, to be approved by the District Court. The ruling was challenged, and ultimately reached the Supreme Court as *Cooper v. Harris*. The Supreme Court affirmed the District Court's ruling in 2017. State Senator Robert Rucho and Representative David Lewis brought in an expert to help with a new map. At the same time a new redistricting committee was formed by the Republican-led General Assembly and voted on seven principles for this new map. Among them, the new map would not be developed using any data on racial makeup, but that it would use political makeup to strive to keep the same proportion of voters in each district. Lewis was quoted as saying "I propose that we draw the maps to give a partisan advantage to 10 Republicans and three Democrats, because I do not believe it's possible to draw a map with 11 Republicans and two Democrats."

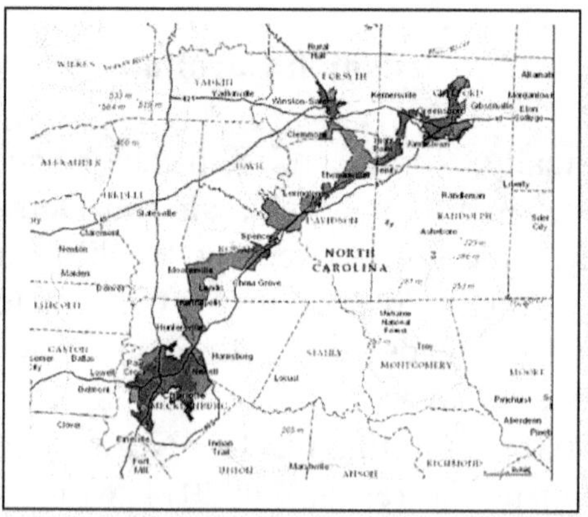

The 12th Congressional district from 2013 to 2017.

The District Court approved the 2016 map, and it was used for both the 2016 and was set to be used in the 2018 general elections.

The new 2016 maps were subject to immediate challenge by Common Cause, the North Carolina Democratic Party, the League of Women Voters, and several individuals in separate lawsuits against Rucho, Lewis, and other state legislators, not only that the redistricting violated the Equal Protection Clause and the First Amendment but also violated two principles of Article I of the United States Constitution. Of particular concern were North Carolina's 1st and 12th congressional district, which had been previously identified as gerrymandered districts in the 2011 maps, and were identified to be disproportionately Democratic with the 2016 maps. The cases were consolidated at the U.S. District Court for the Middle District of North Carolina.

In November 2016, North Carolina conducted congressional elections using the 2016 Plan, and Republican candidates won 10 of the 13 congressional districts. In the 2018 elections, Republican candidates won nine congressional districts, while Democratic candidates won three. The Republican candidate narrowly prevailed in the remaining district, but the State Board of Elections called a new election after allegations of fraud.

After a four-day trial, the three-judge District Court unanimously concluded that the 2016 Plan violated the Equal Protection Clause and Article I of the Constitution. The court further held, with Judge Osteen dissenting, that the Plan violated the First Amendment. *Common Cause v. Rucho*, 279 F. Supp. 3d 587 (MDNC 2018). The defendants appealed directly to this Court under 28 U. S. C. §1253.

While that appeal was pending, the Supreme Court decided *Gill v. Whitford,* 585 U. S. (2018), a partisan gerrymandering case from Wisconsin. In that case, the Supreme Court held that a plaintiff asserting a partisan gerrymandering claim based on a theory of vote dilution must establish standing by showing he lives in an allegedly "cracked" or "packed" district. Id., at (slip op., at 17). A "cracked" district is one in which a party's supporters are divided among multiple districts, so that they fall short of a majority in each; a "packed" district is one in which a party's supporters are highly concentrated, so they win that district by a large margin, "wasting" many votes that would improve their chances in others. (slip op., at 3–4).

After deciding *Gill,* the *Rucho* case was remanded to the lower court for further consideration. 585 U. S. 684 (2018). On remand, the District Court again struck down the 2016 Plan. 318 F. Supp. 3d 777. It found standing and concluded that the case was appropriate for judicial resolution. On the merits, the court found that "the General Assembly's predominant intent was to discriminate against voters who supported or were likely to support non-Republican can-didates," and to "entrench Republican candidates" through widespread cracking and packing of Democratic voters. The court rejected the defendants' arguments that thedistribution of Republican and Democratic voters throughout North Caro-lina and the interest in protecting incumbents neutrally explained the 2016 Plan's discriminatory effects. Id., at 896–899. In the end, the District Court held that 12 of the 13 districts constituted partisan gerrymanders that violated the Equal Protection Clause. Id., at 923.

This litigation began in August 2016, when the North Carolina Democratic Party, Common Cause (a nonprofit organization), and 14 individual North Carolina voters sued the two lawmakers who had led the redistricting effort and other state defendants in Federal District Court. Shortly thereafter, the League of Women Voters of North Carolina and a dozen additional North Carolina voters filed a similar complaint. The two cases were consolidated.

The plaintiffs challenged the 2016 Plan on multiple constitutional grounds. First, they alleged that the Plan violated the Equal Protection Clause of the Fourteenth Amendment by intentionally diluting the electoral strength of Democratic voters. Second, they claimed that the Plan violated their First Amendment rights by retaliating against supporters of Democratic candidates on the basis of their political beliefs. Third, they asserted that the Plan usurped the right of "the People" to elect their preferred candidates for Congress, in violation of the requirement in Article I, §2, of the Constitution that Members of the House of Representatives be chosen "by the People of the several States." Finally, they alleged that the Plan violated the Elections Clause by exceeding the State's delegated authority to prescribe the "Times, interest in protecting incumbents neutrally explained the 2016 Plan's discriminatory effects. Id., at 896–899. In the end, the District Court held that 12 of the 13 districts constituted partisan gerrymanders that violated the Equal Protection Clause. *Id.*,at 923.

The court also agreed with the plaintiffs that the 2016 Plan discriminated against them because of their political speech and association, in violation of the First Amendment. Id., at 935. Judge Osteen dissented with respect to that ruling

Id., at 954–955. Finally, the District Court concludedthat the 2016 Plan violated the Elections Clause and ArticleI, §2. *Id.,* at 935–941. The District Court enjoined the State from using the 2016 Plan in any election after the November 2018 general election. Id., at 942.

The defendants again appealed to the Supreme Court.

At the Supreme Court

The U.S. Supreme Court in *Rucho v. Common Cause* ruled that it would not decide whether gerrymandering was constitutional or not, and left it to the states to decide. This ruling is contrary to more than 200 years of American jurisprudence. In the landmark ruling of *Marbury v. Madison*, 5 U.S. (1 Cranch) 137 (1803), the Supreme Court ruled that the Supreme Court had a duty to say what the law is and a duty to rule on constitutional issues. The Supreme Court has reaffirmed this principle and applied it to elections and the rights of voters to be counted equally. In *Baker v. Carr*, 369 U.S. 186 (1962) the court ruled that the constitution required one man's vote to equal another's. In that case, the court ordered Tennessee to establish equal voting districts so that each constituent's vote weighed the same.

The Supreme Court issued its decision in *Rucho* on June 27, 2019. In the 5–4 majority opinion, the Court ruled that "partisan gerrymandering claims present political questions beyond the reach of the federal courts," vacating and remanding the lower courts' decisions with instructions to dismiss for lack of jurisdiction. Chief Justice John Roberts delivered the majority opinion, joined by Justices Thomas, Alito, Gorsuch, and Kavanaugh. Roberts made clear that partisan gerrymandering can be distasteful and unjust, but that states and Congress have the ability to pass laws to curb excessive partisan gerrymandering.

Justice Elena Kagan wrote the dissenting opinion, joined by Justices Ginsburg, Breyer, and Sotomayor. Kagan's opinion was critical of the majority: "Of all times to abandon the Court's duty to declare the law, this was not the one. The practices challenged in these cases imperil our system of government. Part of the Court's role in that system is to defend its foundations. None is more important than free and fair elections. With respect but deep sadness, I dissent."

In *Rucho v. Common Cause*, the Supreme Court did not say that it was overruling *Baker v. Carr,* but it actually overruled it concerning cases from Maryland and North Carolina. The court ruled that gerrymandering presented a "political question" and that it would not decide the constitutional issues it for that reason.

Political Question Doctrine

The political question doctrine is a judge-made principle that allows courts to duck important issues. In many undemocratic nations, where the courts are not independent, they are controlled by the ruling party, or by a single dictator. In China, for example, courts leave political decisions to the Communist Party. *The People's Court in Transition: The Prospects of the Chinese Judicial Reform*, Qianfan Zhang. In other words, China is the home base for the political questions doctrine—courts there do not decide political questions. By abdicating its authority and ducking the issue of gerrymandering, the United States Supreme Court is undermining democracy and turning the United States into a banana republic.

The Dissent

The dissenting Supreme Court justices in the Gerrymandering case (Kagan, Ginsburg, Breyer and Sotomayor) said,

> For the first time ever, this Court refuses to remedy a constitutional violation because it thinks the task beyond judicialcapabilities.
>
> And not just any constitutional violation. The partisan gerrymanders in these cases deprived citizens of the most fundamental of their constitutional rights: the rights to participate equally in the political process, to join with others to advance political beliefs, and to choose their political representatives. In so doing, the partisan gerrymanders here debased and dishonored our democracy, turning upside-down the core American idea that all governmental power derivesfrom the people.

Light at the End of the Tunnel

Together with the Court's horrendous decision in *Citizens United* (where the court allowed unlimited spendingon elections by wealthy contributors) the Supreme Court has reinforced a wealthy minority's ability to legislate against the majority, turning American's democracy into a wealthocracy.

These two decisions are amongst the worst decisions of the Supreme Court. However, they can be overruled by a constitutional amendment, or by a new Supreme Court, appointed by a new president who is not named Trump, or by state courts. Justices Kavanaugh and Gorsuch, Trump's appointees, joined the other Republicans on the bench and ruled that gerrymandering was a political decision that they would not decide. "One man, one vote," may now be delegated to the garbage dump of history.

One glimmer of hope is that state supreme courts are free to rule that gerrymandering violates their state's constitution. In 2018, the Pennsylvania Supreme Court redrew the map of the state's congressional districts, overturning a Republican gerrymandering scheme that was used in the past three congressional elections. *League of Women Voters v. the Commonwealth of Pennsylvania.*

The Pennsylvania Supreme Court ruled, "It is a core principle of our republican form of government 'that the voters should choose their representatives, not the other way around.' " The Keystone state's highest court ruled that under the Pennsylvania constitution, equal protection of the laws required, "any congressional districting plan shall consist of: congressional districts composed of compact and contiguous territory; as nearly equal in population as practicable; and which do not divide any county, city, incorporated town, borough, township, or ward, except where necessary to ensure equality of population." Hopefully, other states will follow Pennsylvania's well-reasoned example and restore the principle of one man, onevote and end gerrymandering once and for all.

The *Harvard Law Review* found, "Electoral districting creates electoral outcomes. If electoral districting is left to incumbent legislatures, it becomes a tool to stack the political process against disempowered opponents. If courts intervene, they risk wading into the "political thicket" of regulating political representation." 133 *Harvard Law Review 252* (November 8, 2019).

Emmet Bondurant represented Common Cause in the *Rucho* case. In a law review article, he wrote:

> Once upon a time, the right to vote was held by the Supreme Court to be among the most precious of the rights protected by the Constitution, on which all other rights were dependent for their existence. Protection of the right to vote was not a partisan issue. Some of the leading defenders of the right to vote—including Justices Brennan, Powell, Stevens, and Kennedy—had all been appointed by Republican Presidents.
>
> The majority opinion was authored by Chief Justice Roberts, whose entire opinion was based on a misrepresentation of the constitutional basis of the plaintiffs' claims. The Chief Justice also misrepresented the Court's prior precedents and disregarded the factual findings and undisputed evidence of the effectiveness of partisan gerrymandering in favoring candidates and dictating electoral outcomes. The majority opinion is both contradictory and hypocritical. While the Chief Justice self-righteously insisted that the Court

was not condoning partisan Gerrymandering and conceded that partisan Gerrymandering is "incompatible with democratic institutions" and "leads to results that reasonably seem unjust," the Chief Justice, nevertheless, endorsed the constitutionality of partisan gerrymandering—the very issue that the Court had just held it had no jurisdiction to decide." Emmet J. Bondurant, *Rucho v. Common Cause*—A Critique, 70 Emory L. J. 1049 (2021).

Chapter Twenty-Three

Voting Rights and Voting Wrongs

"The vote is the most powerful instrument ever devised by man for breaking down injustice and destroying the terrible walls which imprison men because they are different from other men."

—Lyndon B. Johnson

"Racial discrimination in elections in Texas is no mere historical artifact. To the contrary, Texas has been found in violation of the Voting Rights Act in every redistrictingcycle from and after 1970."

—Ruth Bader Ginsburg

"Americans of our own time—minority and majority Americans alike—need the continued guidance that the Voting Rights Act provides. We have come a long way, but more needs to be done."

—Congressman Elijah Cummings

After successful lobbying by Rev. Martin Luther King and many others in the civil rights movement, on August 6, 1965, President Lyndon B. Johnson signed into law the Voting Rights Act (VRA). This transformative legislation created robust federal oversight to address racial discrimination in elections and voting practices. For decades, voters of color had the full protection of the VRA.

Just eight days after Martin Luther King, Jr. led a peaceful civil rights march in Selma, Alabama, President Lyndon B. Johnson announced his intention to pass a federal Voting Rights Act to ensure that no federal, state, or local government could in any way impede people from voting because of their race or ethnicity.

President Johnson told Congress that voting officials, primarily in Southern states, had been known to force Black voters to "recite the entire Constitution or explain the most complex provisions of state laws," a task most white voters would have been hard-pressed to accomplish. In some cases, even Black people with college degrees were turned away from the polls. Passage of the Voting Rights Act cost the Democrats dearly: the once solidly Democratic south became Republican territory for five decades.

A key provision of the Voting Rights Act was Section 5, which required certain Southern jurisdictions–those determined to have a history of racial discrimination in voting–to preclear any proposed voting change with the Justice Department or a federal court in Washington, D.C. State and localities had to show that a voting change would not have a discriminatory effect on minorities before it could put it into place. The preclearance provision of the law applied to nine states—Alabama, Alaska, Arizona, Georgia, Louisiana, Mississippi, South Carolina, Texas and

Virginia—and to scores of counties and municipalities in other states, including Brooklyn, Man-hattan and the Bronx.

Section 5 was very effective. Black registration rates in the former Confederate states rebounded from 30 percentage points below white registration rates in 1960 to equal or greater than white registration rates by 2010. Black turnout in elections followed a similar pattern. The results are undeniable. In 1965, there were only five African Americans in the U.S. House and Senate combined. Today there are 48. Across all state and local offices, the change is even more remarkable. Since 1965, African-Americans went from holding fewer than a 1,000 offices nationwide to over 10,000.

How the Case Began

Shelby County is a county in the middle of Alabama that includes portions of Birmingham. Alabama is one of the states required by the Voting Rights Act to get pre-clearance for changing to voting laws. Shelby County sued the U.S. Attorney General in the U.S. District Court in Washington, D.C., seeking a declaratory judgment that sections 4(b) and 5 are unconstitutional and sought a permanent injunction against their enforcement. On September 21, 2011, Judge John D. Bates upheld the provisions of the Voting Rights Act, finding that the evidence before Congress in 2006 was sufficient to justify reauthorizing Section 5 and continuing Section 4(b)'s coverage formula. Judge Bates was appointed to the bench by Republican President George W. Bush.

On May 18, 2012, the U.S. Court of Appeals for the D.C. Circuit affirmed the District Court's decision upholding the constitutionality of Section 4(b) and Section 5. After reviewing the evidence in the Congressional record associated with the 2006 reauthorization of Section 5, the appellate court accepted Congress's conclusion that Section 2 litigation by the U.S. Attorney General remained inadequate in the covered jurisdictions to protect the rights of minority voters, that Section 5 was therefore still justified, and that the coverage formula continued to pass constitutional muster.

At the Supreme Court

Shelby County filed a petition with the U.S. Supreme Court to review the court of appeals decision. In a 5–4 decision in *Shelby County v. Holder* (2013), the Supreme Court struck down Section 4(b) as unconstitutional. The court reasoned that the coverage formula violates the constitutional principles of "equal sovereignty of the states" and federalism because its disparate treatment of the states is "based on 40-year-old facts having no logical relationship to the present day," which makes the formula unresponsive to current needs. The court did not strike down Section 5, but without Section 4(b), no jurisdiction may be subject to Section 5 preclearance unless Congress enacts a new coverage formula.

Chief Justice Roberts wrote that Congress remained free to try to impose federal oversight on states where voting rights were at risk but must do so based on contemporary data. But the chances that the current Congress, or a future Congress, could reach agreement on where federal oversight is required are small, most analysts say.

Dissent

Justice Ruth Bader Ginsburg wrote a dissenting opinion that was joined by Justices Stephen Breyer, Sonia Sotomayor, and Elena Kagan. The dissent would have held that Congress had sufficient evidence before it to determine that the coverage formula remained responsive to current needs. The dissent acknowledged that discrimination in voting has decreased in the covered jurisdictions since the Voting Rights Act's enactment, but it attributed much of that decrease to the Act itself, noting that "[t]hrowing out preclearance when it has worked and is continuing to work to stop discriminatory changes is like throwing away your umbrella in a rainstorm because you are not getting wet."

Justice Ginsburg summarized her dissent from the bench, an unusual move and a sign of deep disagreement. She cited the words of the Rev. Dr. Martin Luther King Jr. and said his legacy and the nation's commitment to justice had been "disserved by today's decision."

Justice Ginsburg said the focus of the Voting RightsAct had properly changed from "first-generation barriersto ballot access" to "second-generation barriers" like racial Gerrymandering and laws requiring at-large votingin places with a sizable black minority. She said the law had been effective in thwarting such efforts.

The Blowback

After the decision, several states that were fully or partially covered—including Texas, Mississippi, North Carolina, and South Carolina—implemented laws that were previously denied preclearance. This prompted new legal challenges to these laws under other provisions unaffected by the court's decision, such as Section 2.

President Barack Obama expressed deep disappointment with the decision and called on Congress "to pass legislation to ensure every American has equal access to the polls."

In the 2004 election, the last before the law was reauthorized, the black registration rate in Mississippi was 76 percent, almost four percentage points higher than the white rate. In the 2012 election, Chief Justice Roberts wrote, "African-American voter turnout exceeded white voter turnout in five of the six states originally covered by Section 5."

Data has shown that the coverage formula and the requirement of preclearance substantially increased turnout among racial minorities, even as far as the year before *Shelby County*. Some jurisdictions that had previously been covered by the coverage formula increased therate of voter registration purges after *Shelby County*.

Data also demonstrates that preclearance procedures led to increases in minority congressional representation and minority turnout. Five years after the ruling, nearly 1,000 U.S. polling places had closed, many of them in predominantly African-American counties. Research showsthat changing and reducing voting locations can reduce voter turnout. There were also cuts to early voting, purges of voter rolls and imposition of strict voter ID laws. A 2020 study–need found that jurisdictions that had previously been covered by preclearance substantially increased their voter registration purges after the *Shelby* decision. Virtually all restrictions on voting subsequent to the ruling were enacted by Republicans.

PART 5
Property Rights

Chapter Twenty-Four

A Man's Home
is His Castle

"A man's home is his castle"

—civil rights attorney Clarence Darrow when
defending Ossian Sweet on a charge
of murder in 1925 after an angry
mob approached his home.

*"Nor shall private property be taken for public use
without just compensation."*

—Fifth Amendment to the Constitution

The city of New London, Connecticut sits at the junction of the Thames River and the Long Island Sound, 120
miles northeast of New York City. Decades of economic
decline led a state agency in 1990 to designate the city a
"distressed municipality."

These conditions prompted state and local officials to
target New London, and particularly its Fort Trumbull area,
for economic revitalization. The New London Development Corporation (NLDC), a private nonprofit entity es-

tablished some years earlier to assist the city in planning economic development, was reactivated. Connecticut authorized a \$5.35 million bond issue to support the NLDC's planning activities, and a \$10 million bond issue toward the creation of a Fort Trumbull State Park. Pfizer, the pharmaceutical company known for manufacturing Viagra, announced that it would build a \$300 million research facility on a site immediately adjacent to Fort Trumbull. Local planners hoped that Pfizer would draw new business to the area, thereby serving as a catalyst to the area's rejuvenation.

Susette Kelo and the Other Plaintiffs

Susette Kelo lived in the Fort Trumbull area since 1997. She made extensive improvements to her home, which she prized for its water view. Wilhelmina Dery livedin a house on Walbach Street that has been in her family forover 100 years. She was born in the house in 1918. Her husband, Charles Dery, moved into the house when they married in 1946. Their son lives next door with his familyin the house he received as a wedding gift. None of these properties is blighted or otherwise in poor condition. The city of New London condemned these properties and othersonly because they happen to be located in the development area.

In December 2000, Susette Kelo and other homeowners brought suit in the New London Superior Court. They claimed, among other things, that the taking of their properties would violate the "public use" restriction in the Fifth Amendment. After a weeklong trial before a judge without a jury, the Superior Court granted a permanent restraining order prohibiting the taking of most of the properties.

Suzette Susette Kelo's house in the Fort Trumbull neighborhood of New London.

Both sides appealed to the Supreme Court of Connecticut. That court held four to three that all of the City's proposed takings were valid. The three dissenting justices would have imposed a "heightened" standard of judicial review for takings justified by economic development. Although they agreed that the plan was intended to serve a valid public use, they would have found all the takings unconstitutional because the city had failed to adduce "clear and convincing evidence" that the economic benefitsof the plan would in fact come to pass.[1]

At the United States Supreme Court

The United States Supreme Court, in a five to four ruling, upheld the close ruling of the Connecticut Supreme Court which upholding the taking of plaintiffs' property. Justice O'Connor in a strongly-worded dissent argued:

> Under the banner of economic development, all private property is now vulnerable to being taken and transferred to another private owner, so long as it might be upgraded– *i.e.*, given to an owner who will use it in a way that the legislature deems more beneficial to the public–in the process.

*   *   *

> New London does not claim that Susette Kelo's and Wilhelmina Dery's well-maintained homes are the source of any social harm. Indeed, it could not so claim without adopting the absurd argument that any single-family home that might be razed to make way for an apartment building, or any church that might be replaced with a retail store, or any small business that might be more lucrative if it were instead part of a national franchise, is inherently harmful to society and thus within the government'spower to condemn.

Justice O'Connor warned America: "The specter of condemnation hangs over all property. Nothing is to prevent the State from replacing any Motel 6 with a Ritz Carlton, any home with a shopping mall, or any farm with afactory." She concluded her ringing dissent, claiming,

> Any property may now be taken for the benefit of another private party, but the fallout from this decision will not be random. The beneficiaries are likely to be those citizens with disproportionate influence and power in the political process, including large corporations and development firms. As for the victims, the government now has license to transfer property from those with fewer resources to those with more. The Founders cannot have intended this perverse result.

Justice Stevens warned in the Court's opinion that "[t]here is . . . no principled way of distinguishing economic development from the other public purposes that we have recognized." The Supreme Court handed down the *Kelo* decision on June 23, 2005.

The Nation Reacts

The year after the *Kelo* decision the reaction of the nation was swift and widespread. The case had touched a nerve—how could the Supreme Court not protect the rights of longstanding property owners? Isn't the ownership of private property one of the inviolate rights of being an American? Opinion polls found that the public overwhelmingly disapproved of the ruling. A *Christian Science Monitor* poll found that 93% of Americans disagreed with the ruling. Most other polls, depending on the question posed, reacted negatively in the 65% to 97% range. Opposition to the ruling was announced by groups including the American Association of Retired Persons, theNAACP, the Libertarian Party, and the Institute for Justice. Many owners of family farms also disapproved of the ruling, as they saw it as an avenue by which cities could seize their land for private developments.

New Hampshire libertarians created a plan to seize Justice Souter's "blighted" home in Weare, New Hampshire by eminent domain in order to build a "Lost Liberty Hotel" which would feature a "Just Desserts Café." An amendment to New Hampshire's Constitution limiting eminent domain passed New Hampshire's legislature on March 24, 2006.

The Ohio Supreme Court Responds

In July, 2006 the Ohio Supreme Court unanimously held that the City of Norwood could not use the power of eminent domain to take Carl and Joy Gamble's home of 35 years, as well as the rental home of Joe Horney and tutoringcenter owned by Matthew Burton and Sanae Ichikawa Burton, for private development—specifically, a complex of chain stores, condominiums and office space planned by millionaire developer Jeffrey Anderson and his Rookwood Partners.

In a unanimous decision, Ohio's highest court rejected the U.S. Supreme Court's *Kelo* decision. The Ohio Supreme Court ruled that Ohio courts must apply "heightened scrutiny" to uses of eminent domain, especially when the property is being taken for use by another private party. According to the Court, lower Ohio courts should not simply rubber-stamp decisions by local government to take property. Next, Ohio's highest court held that statutes authorizing the taking of property cannot be vague. The "deteriorating" standard used by Norwood "is a standardless standard," and the Court rejected it. Finally, the Court struck down Ohio's statute that allowed property to be taken even before an appeals court ruled that the taking was legal.

The *Kelo* case has touched off a revolution not only in state supreme courts like Ohio's, but in state legislatures throughout the country. Thus far, 30 state legislatures have passed laws giving greater protections for home and small business owners. In 2006 voters in nine states passed referenda to restrict the power of the states to use their powers of eminent domain.

Endnotes

1. 843 A. 2d, at 587, 588 (Zarella, J., joined by Sullivan, C. J., and Katz, J., concurring in part and dissenting in part).

Chapter Twenty-Five

Outgunned:
How the Second
Amendment
was Turned Upside Down

"I have a very strict gun control policy: if there's a gun around, I want to be in control of it."

—Clint Eastwood

"One man with a gun can control 100 without one."

—Vladimir Lenin

"Force and mind are opposites; morality ends where a gun begins."

—Ayn Rand

"You don't spread democracy through the barrel of a gun."

—Helen Thomas, Associated Press Correspondent

The Second Amendment to the Constitution is ambiguous. It provides simply:

> A well-regulated Militia, being necessary to the security of a free State, the right of the people to keep and bear Arms, shall not be infringed.

For more than 200 years the Supreme Court did not rule that individuals had the right to keep and bear arms. Many constitutional scholars believed that the state militia had the right to keep and bear arms, not individuals.

All of that changed in 2008. Six years earlier a series of meetings at the Cato Institute, a libertarian organization based in Washington, D.C., led to the landmark change.

In 2002, Robert A. Levy, a Senior Fellow at the Cato Institute, began vetting plaintiffs with Clark M. Neilly III for a planned Second Amendment lawsuit that he would personally finance. Although Levy had never owned a gun, as a Constitutional scholar he had an academic interest in the subject and wanted to model his campaign after thelegal strategies of Thurgood Marshall. Marshal had successfully led the challenges that overturned school segregation in *Brown v. Board*.

They aimed for a group that would be diverse in terms of gender, race, economic background, and age, and selected six plaintiffs from their mid-20s to early 60s, three men and three women, four white and two black.

Dick Heller, a licensed special police officer for the District of Columbia became the lead plaintiff. For his job, Heller carried a gun in federal office buildings but was not allowed to have one in his home. Heller had lived in southeast D.C. near the Kentucky Courts public housing complex since 1970 and had seen the neighborhood "transformed from a child-friendly welfare complex to a drug haven." Heller had also approached the National Rifle Association about a lawsuit to overturn the D.C. gun ban, but the NRA declined.

Shelly Parker, a software designer and former nurse had been active in trying to rid her neighborhood of drugs. Parker is a single woman whose life had been threatened on numerous occasions by drug dealers.

Tom G. Palmer, a colleague of Robert A. Levy at the Cato Institute, was the only plaintiff that Levy knew before the case began. Palmer, who is gay, defended himself with a 9 mm handgun in 1982. While walking with a friend in San Jose, California, he was accosted by a gang of about 20 young men who used profane language regarding his sexual orientation and threatened his life. When he produced his gun, the men fled. Palmer believes that the handgun had saved his life.

Gillian St. Lawrence, a mortgage broker who lives in the Georgetown section of Washington, owns several legally registered long guns that she uses for recreation in nearby Virginia. She wanted to be able to use these guns to defend herself in her home and to be able to register a handgun.

Tracey Ambeau (now Tracey Hanson), was an employee of the U.S. Department of Agriculture. She lived in the Adams Morgan neighborhood with her husband. She grew up around guns and wanted one to defend her home.

George Lyon, a communications lawyer, held D.C. licenses for a shotgun and a rifle, but wanted to have a handgun in his home.

For seventy years, the Supreme Court ruling in *United States v. Miller*, 307 U.S. 174 (1939) was interpreted to authorize states and the federal government to restrict regulation of gun ownership by individuals.

In the District Court

In February 2003, the six residents of Washington, D.C. filed a lawsuit in the U.S. District Court for the District of Columbia, challenging the constitutionality of provisions of the Firearms Control Regulations Act of 1975, a local law. This law restricted residents from owning handguns, excluding those grandfathered in by registration prior to 1975 and guns possessed by active and retired law enforcement officers. The law also required thatall firearms including rifles and shotguns be kept "unloaded and dis-assembled or bound by a trigger lock." The plaintiffs filed a motion for an injunction. District Court Judge Ricardo M. Urbina dismissed the lawsuit finding thatgun control was constitutional.

Court of Appeals

On appeal, the U.S. Court of Appeals for the D.C.Circuit reversed the dismissal with a 2–1 decision. The Court of Appeals struck down provisions of the Firearms Control Regulations Act as unconstitutional. Judges Karen L. Henderson, Thomas B. Griffith and Laurence H. Silber-man formed the Court of Appeals panel. Senior Circuit Judge Silberman wrote the court's opinion with Judge Henderson dissenting.

The court's opinion first addressed whether appellants had standing to sue for declaratory and injunctive relief. The court concluded that of the six plaintiffs, only Heller, who applied for a handgun permit but was denied, had standing.

The court then held that the Second Amendment "protects an individual right to keep and bear arms," saying that the right was "premised on the private use of arms for activities such as hunting and self-defense, the latter being understood as resistance to either private lawlessness or the depredations of a tyrannical government (or a threat from abroad)." They also noted that though the right to bear arms also helped preserve the citizen militia, "the activities [the Amendment] protects are not limited to militia service, nor is an individual's enjoyment of the right contingent upon his or her continued or intermittent enrollment in the militia." The court determined that handguns are "arms" and concluded that they may not be banned by the District of Columbia; however, they said that Second Amendment rights are subject to reasonable restrictions.

The court also struck down the portion of the law that requires all firearms including rifles and shotguns be kept "unloaded and disassembled or bound by a trigger lock." The District of Columbia argued that there is an implicit self-defense exception to these provisions, but the D.C. Circuit rejected this view, saying that the requirement amounted to a complete ban on functional firearms and prohibition on use for self-defense, and held it unconstitutional on those grounds.

Henderson's Dissent.

In her dissent, Circuit Judge Henderson stated that Second Amendment rights did not extend to residents of Washington D.C., writing:

> To sum up, there is no dispute that the Constitution, case law and applicable statutes all establish that the District is not a State within the meaning of the Second Amendment. Under *United States v. Miller*, 307 U.S. at 178, the Second Amendment's declaration and guarantee that "the right of the people to keep and bear Arms, shall not be infringed" relates to the Militia of the States only. That

the Second Amendment does not apply to the District, then, is, to me,an unavoidable conclusion.

At the Supreme Court

The defendants petitioned the United States Supreme Court to hear the case. The plaintiffs did not oppose the petition, but, in fact, welcomed it. The Supreme Court agreed to hear the case on November 20, 2007. The court rephrased the question to be decided as follows:

> The petition for a writ of certiorari (review) is granted limited to the following question: Whether the following provisions, D.C.Code §§ 7-2502.02(a)(4), 22–4504(a), and 7-2507.02, violate the Second Amendment rights of individuals who are not affiliated with any state-regulated militia, but who wish to keep handguns and other firearmsfor private use in their homes?

This represented the first time since the 1939 case *United States v. Miller* that the Supreme Court had directly addressed the scope of the Second Amendment.

Oral Arguments

Robert A. Levy and Alan Gura, counsel for Heller, argued for appellants. Walter Dellinger argued for the District of Columbia. The Supreme Court heard oral arguments in the case on March 18, 2008. Each side was initially allotted 30 minutes to argue its case, with U.S. Solicitor General Paul D. Clement allotted 15 minutes to present the federal government's views. During the argument, however, extra time was extended to the parties, and the argument ran 23 minutes over the allotted time, a very unusual occurrence, as the Court generally keeps verystrict time limits.

The Decision

The Supreme Court held that the Second Amendment protects an individual's right to possess a firearm un-connected with service in a militia, and to use that arm for traditionally lawful purposes, such as self-defense within the home.

The court ruled that the Second Amendment's pref-atory clause announced a purpose, but does not limit or expand the scope of the second part, the operative clause. The operative clause's text and history demonstrate that it connotes an individual right to keep and bear arms.

The "militia" comprised all males physically capable of acting in concert for the common defense. The Antifederalists feared that the Federal Government would disarm the people in order to disable this citizens' militia, enabling a politicized standing army or a select militia to rule. The response was to deny Congress power to abridge the ancient right of individuals to keep and bear arms, so that the ideal of a citizens' militia would be preserved.

The court ruled that "Like most rights, the Second Amendment right is not unlimited. It is not a right to keep and carry any weapon whatsoever in any manner what-soever and for whatever purpose: For example, concealed weapons prohibitions have been upheld under the Amend-ment or state analogues."

The Court's opinion should not be taken to cast doubt on longstanding prohibitions on the possession of firearms by felons and the mentally ill, or laws forbidding the carrying of firearms in sensitive places such as schools and government buildings, or laws imposing conditions and qualifications on the commercial sale of arms. *Miller's* holding that the sorts of weapons protected are those "in common use at the time" finds support in the historical tradition of prohibiting the carrying of dangerous and unusual weapons.

The court ruled that the handgun ban and the trigger-lock requirement (as applied to self-defense) violate the Second Amendment. The District's total ban on handgun possession in the home amounts to a prohibition on anentire class of "arms" that Americans overwhelmingly choose for the lawful purpose of self-defense.

Because Heller conceded at oral argument that the D. C. licensing law is permissible if it is not enforced arbitrarily and capriciously, the Court assumes that a license will satisfy his prayer for relief and does not addressthe licensing requirement. Assuming he is not disqualified from exercising Second Amendment rights, the Supreme Court ruled that D.C. must permit Heller to register his handgun and must issue him a license to carry it in the home.

The opinion of the Supreme Court, delivered by Justice Scalia, was joined by Chief Justice John G. Roberts, Jr. and by Justices Anthony M. Kennedy, Clarence Thomas and Samuel A. Alito Jr.

The core holding in *D.C. v. Heller* is that the Second Amendment is an individual right intimately tied to the natural right of self-defense.

The Scalia majority invokes much historical material to support its finding that the right to keep and bear arms belongs to individuals; more precisely, Scalia asserts in the Court's opinion that the "people" to whom the Second Amendment right is accorded are the same "people" who enjoy First and Fourth Amendment protection.

With that finding as its anchor, the Court ruled a total ban on operative handguns in the home is unconstitutional, as the ban runs afoul of both the self-defense purpose of the Second Amendment—a purpose not previously articulated by the Court—and "in common use at the time."

In regard to the scope of the right, the Court wrote, "Although we do not undertake an exhaustive historical analysis today of the full scope of the Second Amendment, nothing in our opinion should be taken to cast doubt on longstanding prohibitions on the possession of firearms by felons and the mentally ill, or laws forbidding the carrying of firearms in sensitive places such as schools and government buildings, or laws imposing conditions and qualifications on the commercial sale of arms."

The Court did not address the level of judicial review that should be used by lower courts in deciding future cases claiming infringement of the right to keep and bear arms: "[S]ince this case represents this Court's first in-depth examination of the Second Amendment, one should not expect it to clarify the entire field." The Court states, "If all that was required to overcome the right to keep and bear arms was a rational basis, the Second Amendment wouldbe redundant with the separate constitutional prohibitionson irrational laws, and would have no effect."

Dissenting Opinions

In a dissenting opinion, Justice John Paul Stevens stated that the court's judgment was "a strained and unpersuasive reading" which overturned longstanding precedent, and that the court had "bestowed a dramatic upheaval in the law." Stevens also stated that the amendment was notable for the "omission of any statement of purpose related to the right to use firearms for hunting or personal self-defense" which was present in the Declarations of Rights of Pennsylvania and Vermont.

The Stevens dissent seems to rest on four main points of disagreement: that the Founders would have made the individual right aspect of the Second Amendment express if that was what was intended; that the "militia" preamble and exact phrase "to keep and bear arms" demands the conclusion that the Second Amendment touches on state militia service only; that many lower courts "collective-right" reading of the *Miller* decision constitutes *stare decisis* (binding precedent), which may only be overturned at great peril; and that the Court has not considered gun-control laws (e.g., the National Firearms Act) unconstitutional. The dissent concludes, "The Court would have us believe that over 200 years ago, the Framers made a choice to limit the tools available to elected officials wishing to regulate civilian uses of weapons. . . . I couldnot possibly conclude that the Framers made such a choice."

Justice Stevens' dissent was joined by Justices David Souter, Ruth Bader Ginsburg and Stephen Breyer.

Justice Breyer filed a separate dissenting opinion, joined by the same dissenting Justices, which sought todemonstrate that, starting from the premise of an individual-rights view, the District of Columbia's handgun ban and trigger lock requirement would nevertheless be permissible limitations on the right.

The Breyer dissent looks to early municipal fire-safety laws that forbade the storage of gunpowder (and in Boston the carrying of loaded arms into certain buildings), and on nuisance laws providing fines or loss of firearm for imprudent usage, as demonstrating the Second Amendment has been understood to have no impact on the regulation of civilian firearms. The dissent argues the public safety necessity of gun-control laws, quoting that "guns were responsible for 69 deaths in this country each day."

With these two supports, the Breyer dissent goes on to conclude, "there simply is no untouchable constitutional right guaranteed by the Second Amendment to keep loaded handguns in the house in crime-ridden urban areas." It proposes that firearms laws be reviewed by balancing the interests of Second Amendment protections against the government's compelling interest of preventing crime.

The Breyer dissent also objected to the "common use" distinction used by the majority to distinguish handguns from machineguns: "But what sense does this approach make? According to the majority's reasoning, if Congress and the States lift restrictions on the possession and use of machineguns, and people buy machineguns to protect their homes, the Court will have to reverse course and find that the Second Amendment does, in fact, protect the individual self-defense-related right to possess a machine-gun . . . There is no basis for believing that the Framers intended such circular reasoning."

Non-Party Involvement

The National Rifle Association (NRA) was initially not supportive of the case because it feared the case might not be successful. The NRA later reconciled and supported the plaintiffs. The Brady Campaign to Prevent Gun Violence lobbied to have the D.C. gun laws changed so the case would not be eligible to be heard by the Supreme Court.

Wayne LaPierre, the NRA's chief executive officer, confirmed the NRA's misgivings. "There was a real dispute on our side among the constitutional scholars about whether there was a majority of justices on the Supreme Court who would support the Constitution as written," Mr. LaPierre said.

Immediately after the Supreme Court's ruling, the NRA filed a lawsuit against the city of Chicago over its handgun ban, followed the next day by a lawsuit against the city of San Francisco over its ban of handguns in public housing.

District of Columbia v. Heller, 554 U.S. 570 (2008), was a landmark case in which the Supreme Court of the United States held that the Second Amendment to the U.S. Constitution protects an individual's right to possess a firearm for traditionally lawful purposes in federal enclaves, such as self-defense within the home. The decision did not address the question of whether the Second Amendment extends beyond federal enclaves to the states, which was addressed later by *McDonald v. Chicago* (2010). It was the first Supreme Court case in United States history to decide whether the Second Amendment protects an individual right to keep and bear arms.

Erwin Chemerinsky, then of Duke Law School and now dean of the University of California, Irvine School of Law, argued that the District of Columbia's handgun laws, even assuming an "individual rights" interpretation of the Second Amendment, could be justified as reasonable regulations and thus upheld as constitutional. Professor Chemerinsky believes that the regulation of guns should be analyzed in the same way "as other regulation of property under modern constitutional law" and "be allowed so long as it is rationally related to achieving a legitimate government purpose."

Even the NRA concedes that you can't have mad men running around with weapons of mass destruction. So, there are some restrictions that are permissible and it will be the task of the legislature and the courts to ferret all of that out and draw the lines.

Richard Posner, judge for the United States Court of Appeals for the Seventh Circuit, compares *Heller* to *Roe v. Wade* inasmuch as it created a federal constitutional right that did not previously exist, and he asserts that the originalist method–to which Justice Antonin Scalia claims to adhere–would have yielded the opposite result of the majority opinion.

The text of the amendment, whether viewed alone or in light of the concerns that actuated its adoption, creates no right to the private possession of guns for hunting or other sport, or for the defense of person or property. Judge

Harvie Wilkinson III, conservative chief judge of United States Court of Appeals for the Fourth Circuit, agrees with Posner's analysis, stating that *Heller* "encourages Americ-ans to do what conservative jurists warned for years they should not do: bypass the ballot and seek to press their political agenda in the courts."

Jeffrey M. Shaman, law professor at DePaul University, delivered a strong criticism of the majority opinion in *Heller*, stating that Scalia's "exposition of the Second Amendment in *Heller* is bad history–simplistic analysis that ignores the complexities of historical research."

McDonald v. Chicago

The NRA filed five related lawsuits since the *Heller* decision. In four Illinois lawsuits, the NRA sought to have the Second Amendment incorporated by the Fourteenth Amendment, causing the Second Amendment to apply to state and local jurisdictions and not just to the federal government. Three Illinois lawsuits have been negotiated and settled out of court involving agreements that repeal gun ban ordinances and did not result in incorporation of the Second Amendment to state and local jurisdictions. The fourth NRA lawsuit against Chicago was rejected. The NRA appealed the case to the 7th Circuit Court of Appeals. On June 2, 2009, the Court of Appeals affirmed the district court's decision, based on the theory that Heller applied only to the Federal Government (including the District of Columbia), and not to states or their subordinate juris-dictions.

On June 28, 2010, the Supreme Court reversed the Court of Appeals for the Seventh Circuit's decision in *McDonald v. Chicago* and remanded it back to Seventh Circuit to resolve conflicts between certain Chicago gun restrictions and the Second Amendment. Chicago's handgun law was likened to the D.C. handgun ban by Justice Breyer.

The decision in *McDonald v. Chicago*, which was brought in response to *Heller* and decided in 2010, invalidated much of Chicago's gun purchase and registration laws, and has called into question many other state and local laws restricting purchase, possession and carry of firearms.

Chicago is now in the midst of an epidemic of firearms deaths. In 2012, Chicago suffered through more than 500 gun-related homicides and more than 2,500 shootings. The U.S. Supreme Court is tying the hands of Chicago and Illinois legislators who are striving to control gun violence there. For a court, whose conservative majority claims to favor state's rights, depriving Illinois and Chicago the right to control firearms contravenes basic state's rights.

PART 6
Criminal Rights

Chapter Twenty-Six
Stripped of our Rights

"The Supreme Court has ruled that anybody can be strip-searched for any kind of arrest. That's something to think about the next time you bring 12 items into a 10-item-or-less lane."

— Jay Leno

On March 3, 2005, the Florence family, Albert, his pregnant wife April and three children, was driving to the home of April's mother in the family's BMW to celebrate their purchase of a new home. A New Jersey state trooper stopped the vehicle in Burlington County. The trooper approached the vehicle and requested the identity of the owner. When Albert Florence identified himself, the trooper removed him from the car, arrested him, hand-cuffed him, and placed him in the patrol car.

When asked, the trooper told Mr. Florence that he was being arrested on an Essex County, New Jersey, bench warrant. Florence had been arrested once before (though never jailed), and pleaded guilty to a minor offense that required him to pay a fine in installments over time. When he fell behind on the payments, a local judge found Albert Florence in civil contempt and granted the county a warrant for petitioner's arrest.

Mr. Florence promptly paid the balance owing on the fine. The judgment underlying the warrant was fully paid and satisfied. Albert Florence kept a copy of the official document certifying that fact in his possession because he felt that he had previously been detained as an African American who drove nice cars and he wanted to avoid being wrongly arrested.

***Albert W. Florence was strip-searched twice
after being wrongly detained over a fine.***

When Mr. Florence was erroneously arrested on the warrant, his wife retrieved the document proving that he had indeed paid the fine and presented it to the New Jersey state trooper. But apparently because the county had failed to remove the warrant from the computer system, the officer continued with the arrest. Even if the warrant had been an outstanding bench order, not paying a court fine in New Jersey is not a crime.

Nonetheless, State troopers transported Mr. Florence to the local detention facility, the Burlington County Jail. Albert Florence was to be held there until retrieved by officers from Essex County, which had issued the warrant and that would resolve his status. Mr. and Mrs. Florence were told that would occur the next day. But Mr. Florence was not retrieved for almost a week.

During his first strip-search, Florence was forced to disrobe in front of an officer and told to lift his genitals. Upon arriving at the second jail, he was made to squat and cough in front of a number of viewers for the purpose of expelling anything that might be hidden in a body cavity.

"Turn around," Mr. Florence, recalled being told by jail officials. "Squat and cough. Spread your cheeks."

"I consider myself a man's man," said Albert Florence, a finance executive for a car dealership. "Six-three. Big guy. It was humiliating. It made me feel less than a man."

Under both New Jersey law and the Burlington County Jail's policy, an individual arrested for a minor offense–a "non-indictable" offense in the terminology of state law–"shall not be subjected to a strip search" absent a search warrant, consent, or reasonable suspicion that the accused may possess contraband.

Mr. Florence filed suit against the two jails alleging that his Fourth and Fourteenth Amendment rights had been violated. The Fourth Amendment provides:

> The right of the people to be secure in their persons, houses, papers, and effects, against unreasonable searches and seizures, shall not be violated, and no Warrants shall issue, but upon probable cause, supported by Oath or affirmation, and particularly describing the place to be searched, and the persons or things to be seized.

Florence argued that "that persons arrested for minor offenses cannot be subjected to invasive (Fourth Amendment-unreasonable) searches unless prison officials have. . . reason to suspect concealment of weapons, drugs, or other contraband." A federal judge agreed. On appeal,the Third Circuit Court of Appeals reversed, two to one, holding that the "jails' interest in safety and security outweighed the privacy interests of detainees – even those accused of minor crimes."

Judge Thomas Bull dissented at the Court of Appeals:

> The majority sweeps away twenty-five years of jurisprudence, giving jailors the unfettered right to conduct mandatory, routine, suspicionless body cavity searches on any citizen who may be arrested for minor offenses, such as violating a leash law or a traffic code, and who pose no credible risk for smuggling contraband into the jail.

The case was subsequently appealed to the United States Supreme Court. The Court granted review on April4, 2011.

At the Supreme Court

Justice Kennedy wrote the opinion for the court. Kennedy ruled that the right of jailers for security overrides the right to be free from unreasonable searches, no matter what the offence is. Kennedy said one person arrested for disorderly conduct in Washington State "managed to hide a lighter, tobacco, tattoo needles and other prohibited items in his rectal cavity." Officials in San Francisco, he added, "have discovered contraband hidden in body cavities of people arrested for trespassing, public nuisance and shoplifting."

The Dissenters

Justice Breyer's dissent was joined by the court's three female members, Justices Ginsburg, Sotomayor and Kagan. Justice Breyer wrote:

> A strip search that involves a stranger peering without consent at a naked individual, and in particular at the most private portions of that person's body, is a serious invasion of privacy.

> * * *

> I cannot find justification for the strip search policy at issue here—a policy that would subject those arrested for minor offenses to serious invasions of their personal privacy. I consequently dissent.

Justice Breyer wrote that there was very little empirical support for the idea that strip searches detect contraband that would not have been found had jail officials used less intrusive means, particularly if strip searches were allowed when officials had a reasonable suspicion that they would find something.

For instance, in a study of 23,000 people admitted to a correctional facility in Orange County, N.Y., using that standard, there was only one instance of contraband detected that would not otherwise have been found, Justice Breyer wrote.

The Court of Public Opinion

In December, 2011, after oral arguments but months before the Court's decision was announced, Fairleigh Dickinson University's PublicMind conducted a nation-wide study to measure the opinion of voters on the constitutional issue of whether strip searches should be conducted on everyone taken to jail. Results showed that a significant majority (65%) of the 855 registered voters polled agreed that if the offense is minor, officials must have reasonable suspicion before conducting a strip search. On the other hand, 31% of voters felt that regardless of the offense, officials should have the authority to strip search anyone taken to jail.

Democrats (67%-30%) and Republicans (65%-31%) shared virtually the same opinion. There were small gender differences. Women (70%-25%) had a tendency to disagree more with strip searches than men (61%-37%). Pollsters observed that the "public did not express uncertainty or pass off the decision to someone else by giving "mixed,""don't know," or refusal responses. They offered a clear ruling on a significant question of civil liberties."

Bruce Peabody, professor of political science at Fairleigh Dickinson University, and editor of *The Politics of Judicial Independence* commented that: "Here we have a perfect storm of public opinion that combines people's misgivings about government power with the great invasiveness of personal searches, and the fact that such searches could occur even after small matters like ticket violations."

The *Harvard Law Review*, Volume 126 at 206 (November, 2012), noted:

> The most remarkable aspect of the (strip-search) ruling was the Court's reliance on the expertise of corrections officials, without any scrutiny of their knowledge, procedure, or diligence in developing the prison's strip search policy. The Court should have critically reviewed the proffered justifications for such an invasive search, examined empirical evidence, and considered clear alternatives, rather than deferring to determinations that affect basic constitutional rights.

The *Trenton Times* criticized the Supreme Court's ruling:

> The 5-4 ruling oversteps the bounds of decency established by international human rights treaties, conventions to which the U.S. subscribes.
>
> It contradicts reason–and it contradicts New Jersey law. As a *Star-Ledger* editorial pointed put last week, New Jersey has a statute on the books that bans automatic strip searches.

Justices Kennedy, Scalia, Alito, Thomas and Roberts, have probably never been arrested. Thirteen million Americans are arrested every year, mostly for petty offenses.

This means that about three percent of the population is arrested annually for some offense, for drunk driving, petty theft, marijuana possession or a more serious matter. Do we as a civilized nation have to subject everyone arrested to the humiliation of a strip search? Is not a pat-down and a scan sufficient, especially for those charged with non-violent offenses? The Fourth Amendment prohibits "unreasonable searches." Isn't a strip search for a non-violent offense unreasonable? Most Americans think so. However, the five justices who have never been arrested and probably never will, have decided that it is reasonable to strip search everyone charged with *any* offense. Had one of the justices' wives, or their teenaged daughter, been strip-searched, I am quite certain that the decision in this case would have been very different.

Chapter Twenty-Seven

The Right to An Attorney

"In all criminal prosecutions, the accused shall . . . have the assistance of counsel for his defence."

—Sixth Amendment

Smith Betts was an unemployed thirty-six-year-old farm worker who was on welfare in 1938, during the Great Depression. He lived in Hagerstown, a small town in rural western Maryland. In the summer, the Maryland hills are covered with acres of corn and other crops, and when Smitty worked, he cut corn or performed other farm duties. But the economy was still in the midst of the Depression, and there isn't much farm work in the winter.

Mr. Betts had lived with Mary Emerson for three years, and she was considered his wife. On the day before Christmas in 1938, Smitty got his welfare check from the Washington County Welfare Fund for ten dollars. Betts paid his landlord, George Uhler, five dollars toward his rent.

Christmas Eve Robbery

Norman Bollinger was a teenager who worked at the Medford Grocery Store, a small rural store in the rolling hills of Carroll County. It was dark when Bollinger closed the store at 5:00 p.m. on that Christmas Eve. A few minutesafter closing, he walked to his car. An old green Chevrolet with red wheels pulled up and slowed down. Bollingerthought it was a last-minute customer. A man, dressed in a dark overcoat, dark amber glasses and a hat, with a handkerchief over his chin, got out of the car.

The man said to the teenaged Bollinger: "Hey, buddy, what do you have there?" He then asked for the bag, which contained twenty-four dollars in bills and twenty-six dollars worth of coins. Bollinger said, "Like fun." The man pulled a gun from his coat pocket, and Bollinger gave him the bag. Bollinger failed to get the license number of the car but phoned ahead to alert others down the highway of the robbery and immediately ran to tell the store owner what had happened

The Senator and the Sheriff

The Medford County Grocery Store was owned byState Senator J. David Baile. When Bollinger told himabout the robbery, Baile called Sheriff Walter Shipley, whobegan an investigation. His investigation led to Smith Betts,whom people in Medford reported seeing in the vicinity of the Medford County Store. Senator Baile placed anadvertisement in the Westminster newspaper as shown on the top of the next page.

> ## $50 REWARD
>
> for information leading to arrest of two men who held up our Clerk, Norman Bollinger, at 5:05 o'clock, Saturday evening at Branch Store.
>
> The man who leveled the gun on Norman and demanded the change bag of $24.00 in silver and $26.00 in paper money was about 35-years-old, 200 pounds and 6 feet tall.
>
> They left in a 1930 Chevrolet Coach with red-disc-orange wheels. If you happened to be passing the branch at 5 minutes after 5 perhaps you can help identify this car.

Several days after the robbery, Bollinger was called to the jail where the State Police had Smith Betts in custody. Norman Bollinger said that he could not identify Betts as the thief. At Bollinger's request, the police put glasses and a handkerchief on Betts' face. After that, Bollinger said that Betts was the robber.

The Trial

Smitty Betts was arraigned at the Carroll County Circuit Court. He was charged with armed robbery, an offense which had a maximum penalty of over ten years.

Betts had had an earlier run-in with the law. He had pleaded guilty to larceny (theft without a weapon) and served a short sentence.

This time Mr. Betts pleaded not guilty. He asked Judge William H. Forsythe to appoint an attorney to represent him because he was poor, on welfare and could not afford to pay an attorney. The judge said that the usual practice was to appoint attorneys to poor defendants who were charged with murder, manslaughter or rape. The judge refused Betts' request and said that he would have to defend himself.

The State called Norman Bollinger as a witness, and he identified Smitty as the gunman. Other witnesses were called to show that Smith Betts was in the vicinity of the crime within a day or two of the robbery.

Betts called six witnesses who stated that he was in his apartment all day when the robbery was took place. His landlord testified that he saw him several times during the day. The landlord's wife confirmed Betts' alibi, as did a neighbor and his common law wife, Mary.

Officer B.C. Mason of the Maryland State Police testified. He said he learned that Smith Betts was in the vicinity of the store Thursday, December 22, two days before the robbery, with another fellow Ells Dunn. Dunn owned a 1928 Chevrolet with a blue body and black fen- ders. Betts did not own a car.

Smith Betts did not testify on his own behalf. The judge found Betts guilty as charged and sentenced him to eight years in the Maryland House of Corrections.

Habeas Corpus

After spending two years in jail, convinced that he was innocent and that he did not get a fair trial, Betts prepared and filed a petition for *habeas corpus.* Smith Betts was not an educated man, but he learned a fair amount about law while he was incarcerated. *Habeas corpus,* means "you must have the body." A *habeas corpus* petition is a document filed by, or on behalf of, a prisoner, who claims that he is wrongfully detained in custody. Betts still was not represented by an attorney.

Judge Joseph Mish, in Hagerstown, granted Betts' writ on June 5, 1941, and ordered a hearing for June 17. After the hearing, Mish returned Betts to the Maryland Penitentiary.

A few months later, Betts filed a new petition for a writ of *habeas corpus* with Judge Carroll Bond, the chief judge of Maryland's highest court. This time, an attorney, Jesse Slingluff of Baltimore, represented Mr. Betts. Slingluff was paid by an organization who wanted a test case to challenge the denial of counsel to poor defendants. Judge Bond denied Betts relief, because he believed that Betts had a fair trial and did a reasonably good job ofdefending himself.

Slingluff then applied to the United States Supreme Court to appeal Judge Bond's decision. The Supreme Court accepted the case.

In the Supreme Court

Attorney Slingluff argued that the Sixth Amendment requires that counsel be appointed to those accused of serious crimes when they cannot afford their own lawyer. By a vote of six to three, the Supreme Court ruled that Betts did not have the right to have an attorney appointed to represent him.[1] Justice Owen Roberts wrote the court's opinion. He ruled that while those accused of federal crimes have the right to have counsel appointed, those accused of state crimes do not.

While some of the amendments to the Constitution specifically apply (at least on their face) to the federal government, the Sixth Amendment does not. The Sixth Amendment begins "in *all* criminal prosecutions theaccused shall . . . have the assistance of counsel. " According to the amendment, accused persons have theright to a speedy and public trial, the right to confrontwitnesses, the right to a jury trial and the right to have the assistance of counsel.

The court could have justified its decision by saying that nothing requires the State of Maryland to pay an attorney to represent every individual charged with a crime.

But the Supreme Court, without foundation in the Constitution, ruled that those accused of state crimes did not
have the right to have attorneys represent them.

Epilogue

Smith Betts served out his sentence. Twenty-one years
later, the same issue again came before the Supreme Court.
In one of the few cases in which the court directly overruled
an earlier decision, the landmark decision of *Gideon v.
Wainwright.*[2] overturned the *Betts* case. The new decision
was approved by all nine members of the court. All of the
six members of the majority in the *Betts* decision had retired
from the court, while two of the three dissenters (Black and
Douglas) joined the new majority. A book and amovie about
Gideon's case, both called *Gideon's Trumpet,* were produced in the 1960s.

The Shipley name is common in the Carroll County. In
1987, the Clerk of the Court was named Shipley, and other
Shipleys are employed in the courthouse. During the same
week as the 1938 Medford robbery, the sheriff's son, Russell
Shipley, was arrested for stealing $3,000 in a break-in.
Russell Shipley was sentenced to three years in jail for
breaking and entering. He got the best legal representation
that money could buy. On the other hand, Smitty Betts was
charged with stealing only fifty dollars, but was sentenced to
eight years in prison. If Betts had had an attorney, he would
have demanded a jury trial and probably would have been
acquitted. Unfortunately, he got all the justice that he could
afford.

Endnotes

1.   316 U.S. 455 (1942).
2.   372 U.S. 335 (1963).

Chapter Twenty-Eight

Cruel and Unusual Punishment

*"My object all sublime I shall achieve in time
To make the punishment fit the crime."*

—Gilbert & Sullivan The Lord High Executioner

The Mikado

William James "Scotty" Rummel hung around with the wrong kind of friends. When he was sixteen, he stole a case of beer. A year later, along with a buddy, he broke into a Western Auto store in Karnes City, Texas.

Rummel was born in 1942 and reared by his grandparents in Karnes City. He dropped out of high school to do construction work and odd jobs in San Antonio. There wasn't a lot of work to go around, so he did what he had to do.

He was six feet tall, blond and weighed two-hundred pounds. His life had not been easy. Rummel was divorced three times. His body is marked by numerous scars and tattoos.

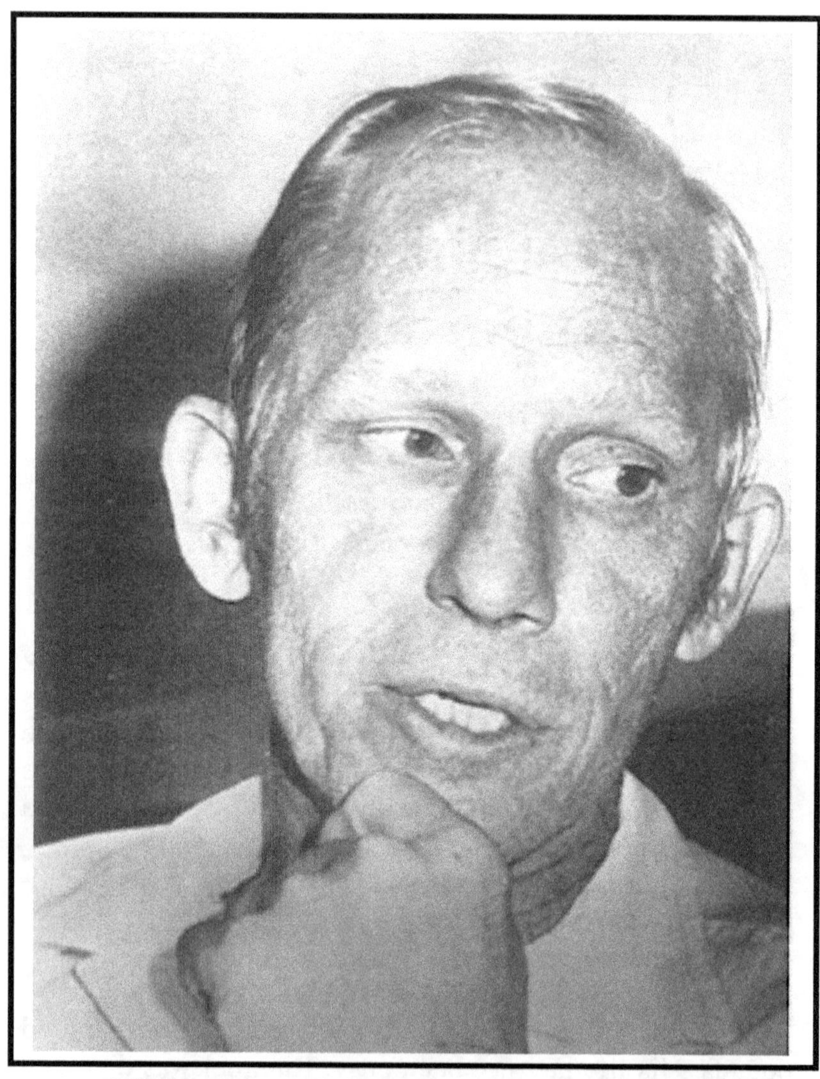

William "Scotty" Rummel, courtesy of the San Antonio Light.

In 1964, at the age of twenty-two, Bill Rummel's well-worn Studebaker badly needed new tires. An acquaintance gave him a credit card, and he charged eighty dollars-worth of tires at Harvey Helton's Enco gasoline station in San Antonio, Texas. The credit card was a stolen card. Rummel claims that he didn't know the card was stolen, but admitted that he had a pretty good idea that it was hot. He pleaded guilty, was sentenced to three years in prison, but was released after twenty-months incarceration. It was his first felony conviction.

Rummel was released in 1966 and spent the next three years working on a series of construction and repair jobs. In 1969, at the age of twenty-seven, Bill Rummel was living in the Angeles Motel in San Antonio. His rent of $28.36 was due weekly. He was having problems paying his bills and had been threatened with eviction. To keep a roof over his head, he forged a check for $28.36. Again, Rummel pleaded guilty. Rummel was sentenced to spend another four years with the Texas Department of Corrections. Rummel was released in 1971 after serving a year and a half. This was his second felony conviction.

In the Heat of San Antonio

On a blazing hot day in August, 1972, Rummel walked into Captain Hook's Lounge in San Antonio. In the bar, he recognized Paul Ellis and headed for the door, but Ellis caught him. "Hey Scotty, come over here." Rummel owed Ellis twenty dollars, and Ellis demanded his money. Bill Rummel had a ten-dollar bill and some change in his pockets and handed Ellis the ten.

Rummel stuck around and watched men playing pool. He overheard Ellis talking to David Shaw, owner of the bar, about getting his air conditioner fixed. Rummel had worked for Mike's Air Conditioning Service and offered his services to repair the air conditioning unit.

The air conditioner needed a new compressor. Rummel called Service Supply, a parts wholesaler, for the price of a replacement compressor. It would cost $120.75. Ellis, not trusting "Scotty," advised Shaw to write a check to Service Supply. Rummel took the check.

Service Supply wouldn't sell the compressor to Rummel because he wasn't an authorized dealer. Rummel went to a drive-in teller at Shaw's bank and cashed the check, signing his name and Service Supply. Rummel claims that he intended to buy a compressor from Montgomery Ward, but it cost more than from Service Supply. Rummel had no extra money of his own, so he tried to reach Shaw at Captain Hook's Lounge.

Bill Rummel was not the most reliable repairman around. On occasion, he would remember his promise to repair the air conditioner, but he never got around to making the repair. It turned out to be the biggest mistake that he made in his life.

In September, Shaw filed a complaint with the police concerning Rummel's theft of the $120.75. Rummel was picked up by the police on a charge of "theft of over $50 by false pretext," concerning the $120.75 that he pocketed for the air conditioner repair. William B. Chenault III was appointed by the court to represent Rummel. Chenault said that "he didn't think that it was the duty of a court-appointed lawyer to go out into a bunch of sleazybars on the bad side of town and look for witnesses I wasn't about to go there for the $250 I was being paid for this case."

The Trial

On the day of trial, April 10, 1973, Rummel's attorney asked to withdraw from the case. The court denied the request. During the trial, Chenault called no witnesses on Rummel's behalf and advised Rummel not to testify.

Two days before trial, Rummel's parents paid Mr. Shaw fifty dollars towards the loss he had incurred when dealing with their son. Shaw signed a nonprosecution agreement in exchange for this payment. But the court refused to admit the document into evidence, because it had no bearing on his innocence or guilt. The jury never got a chance to see it

The trial lasted two days. The government subpoenaed Shaw to testify and called two tellers from the bank to verify that Rummel had cashed the check. Another witness testified that Rummel had never worked for the Service Supply company. Hearsay testimony (testimony given by someone who was not a direct witness) was given to the effect that Rummel had been to Service Supply to discuss purchase of the compressor. The court disallowed the testimony because hearsay testimony is generally not ad- missable in court.

The jury made their decision quickly. Primarily, because Rummel did not testify on his own behalf, the jury convicted him of his third felony, theft by pretext.

The Three-Time Loser Law

The law in Texas provided that once a person is convicted of three felonies, regardless of the severity of the offense, the judge must sentence the "three-time loser" to life imprisonment. Judge John Benavides followed the law, and William James "Scotty" Rummel was sentenced to life with the Texas Department of Corrections.

The Jailhouse Lawyer

Bill Rummel is much smarter than one would assume. Although he never graduated from high school, in prison he became a scholar. Rummel started reading legal books and court decisions, randomly, not certain where to begin. He read through hundreds of legal books in the prison law library at the Texas Department of Corrections facility near Angleton, Texas, and became adept at filing legal briefs.

At first, his legal appeals were rejected. He filed a two-page writ for appeal in 1975 with the state court of criminal appeals. The court rejected this petition, so he filed a forty-five page brief with the U.S. District Court. This court, too, rejected his petitions, appeals and motions. Then the Fifth Circuit Court of Appeals, the federal appeals court for most of the south-central United States, granted him a hearing. This appellate court appointed a young lawyer, Scott Atlas, to represent him. Atlas had recently finished a clerkship with one of the judges on the court and had begun working for the prestigious Houston law firm of Vinson & Elkins.

On Atlas' Shoulders

Scott Atlas knew that he was appointed to a potentially precedent-setting case. He argued that the life sentence given to his client was cruel and unusual punishment, which is prohibited by the Eighth Amendment to the Constitution.

In New Orleans in March, 1978 Atlas won a favorable ruling from a divided three-judge panel of the court of appeals.[1] The court ruled that the life sentence "was so grossly disproportionate to his offenses that it could constitute cruel and unusual punishment."

The State of Texas was not about to take this setback lying down. The attorney general's office in Texas filed an unusual request for the entire Fifth Circuit court to rehear the case, all fourteen judges sitting at once.

The court granted the request, which is normally a hundred-to-one shot. In December of 1978, by a vote of eight to four, the full court of appeals reversed Rummel's victory.

The Court of Last Resort

Atlas filed the necessary papers, and the U.S. Supreme Court agreed to hear the case. The case was set for argument in January of 1980. On March 18, 1980, in a five-to-four decision, the court ruled that Rummel's sentence was not a cruel or unusual punishment.[3] Justice Rehnquist wrote the opinion for the court, explaining that life imprisonment for a traffic offense would be cruel and unusual punishment, but that Rummel's crimes were serious, and that he would not overturn the law of the State of Texas imprisoning him for life.

Justice Powell, joined by Justices Brennan, Marshall and Stevens, dissented, arguing that Rummel's crimes were non-violent:

> It is difficult to imagine felonies that pose less
> danger to the peace and good order of society
> than the three crimes committed by the
> petitioner.

Rummel's third offense, the one that caused him to be sentenced to life in prison was barely a criminal offense at all. Thousands of times every day, repair shops take money for repairs that are not made or are made ineffectively. That is, in essence, what Bill Rummel was convicted of. He was given money (the check for the part) to make an air conditioner repair, and he failed to make the repair. It is the type of offense that is usually handled as a civil claim in small claims court and is not unlike a minor traffic offense. In fact, a minor traffic offense can be more serious because speeding or reckless driving can cause injury or death, and Rummel only caused a small economic loss.

While it is true that Rummel committed an act of poor judgment when he cashed the check, many a driver also uses poor judgment when he or she gets behind the wheel while intoxicated. But, the State of Texas considers DWI a misdemeanor the first time it is committed. Driving while intoxicated is certainly more dangerous to society than failing to fix an air conditioner.

Epilogue

In 1983, the State of Texas amended its "three-time loser" law, deleting its mandatory life sentence provision. Also in 1983, the U.S. Supreme Court overturned the *Rummel* precedent and ruled that a life sentence for a series of minor crimes constitutes cruel and unusual punishment.[4] Justice Harry Blackmun apparently changed his mind and made up part of the new five-to-four majority. Justice Powell wrote the new opinion, "We conclude that his sentence is significantly disproportionate to his crime, and is therefore prohibited by the Eighth Amendment." In one of the quickest reversals in U.S. history, the Supreme Court changed its mind in three years.

William James Rummel won his release from the Texas prison system on other grounds. After the defeat in the Supreme Court, his attorney went back to court and successfully argued that Rummel's first attorney provided him with an ineffective defense. After serving seven years, nine months and fifteen days of his life sentence, William Rummel left prison as a free man.

Endnotes

1.   568 F.2d 1193 (1978).
2.   587 F.2d 651 (1979).
3.   445 U.S. 263 (1980).
4.   *Solem v. Helm*, 463 U.S. 277 (1983).

Chapter Twenty-Nine

The Presumption of Innocence

"You don't have many suspects innocent of a crime."

—Former Attorney General Edwin Meese

Our criminal justice system, based on the Constitution, has always presumed those charged with crimes to be innocent until proven guilty. The Eighth Amendment provides that "Excessive bail shall not be required." For more than 200 years, our courts have allowed persons charged with crimes to be set free on bail or on their personal recognizance.

There is an expression used by lawyers that is fitting here: "bad facts make for bad law." The individuals involved in the case described in this chapter are not very appealing.

Fat Tony and Friends

Anthony "Fat Tony" Salerno was the "boss" of the Genovese Family of La Cosa Nostra, the Mafia. Vincent "Fish" Cafaro was a captain in the organization. In 1986, Salerno and Cafaro were arrested after being charged in a twenty-nine-count indictment alleging extortion, mail fraud, gambling violations and conspiracy to commit murder. The government sought to have Salerno and Cafaro detained in jail on the grounds that no condition of release could assure the safety of the community. The government claimed that Salerno had participated in two murder conspiracies.

Salerno was then seventy-four years old and suffered from high blood pressure, complicated by congestive heart failure. In 1981, Salerno suffered from a stroke from which he had recovered with limited residual disability.

In the Lower Courts

Salerno and Cafaro were arrested on March 21, 1986. They were incarcerated without bail. At their arraignment a week later, the government moved for their "pre-trial detention." The federal government contended that because the defendants represented a danger to society, they should be held in jail, without bail, until after trial. Judge John Walker, Jr. agreed with the prosecutor that Salerno could order a murder merely by voicing his assent andordered both defendants held in preventive detention until trial.[1]

The district court granted the government's motion for preventive detention and ordered Salerno and Cafaro to jail pending trial. Judge Walker stated:

> The activities of a criminal organization such as the Genovese Family do not cease with the arrest of its principals and their release even on the most stringent of bail conditions. The illegal businesses, in place for many years, require constant attention and protection, or they will fail. Under these circumstances, this court recognizes a strong incentive on the part of its leadership to continue business as usual. When business as usual involves threats, beatings, and murder, the present danger such people pose in the community is self-evident.

It was never mentioned that even while in jail, Salerno could order someone to be murdered. Salerno and Cafaro appealed. The United States Court of Appeals sitting in New York took the case up promptly and issued its opinion in July.[2]

By a vote of two to one, the court of appeals reversed the order of preventive detention. The court ruled that the Bail Reform Act, passed in 1984, which authorized preventive detention, was unconstitutional, because the detention order was based on the likelihood of Salerno and Cafaro committing crimes in the future. Judge Kearse, of the court of appeals, stated that preventive detention to prevent future crimes is:

> repugnant to the concept of substantive due process, which we believe prohibits the total deprivation of liberty.

The court of appeals ruling freed Anthony Salerno, as well as Cafaro, from prison. The government appealed to the United States Supreme Court.

"Fish" Gets Off the Hook

In early October 1986, Cafaro became a cooperating witness for the government, and the government agreed to let him post a personal recognizance bond of one million dollars for his continued freedom. Apparently, the government felt that once Cafaro agreed to cooperate, his threat to society vanished. This was what happened, but this was not what Salerno, nor the Supreme Court justices, then determining whether they would hear the case, were told. The Solicitor General told the court that Cafaro was "temporarily released for medical treatment." As Justice Marshall later wrote, "I do not understand how the Solicitor General's representation that Cafaro was "still subject to the pretrial detention order" can be reconciled with the fact of his release on a $1,000,000 personal recognizance bond.

Fat Tony Avoids the Slammer

Not long afterward, on November 19, 1986, Salerno was convicted of other federal charges, and, on January 13, 1987, he was sentenced to prison for one hundred years. With the agreement of the federal government, Salerno was not jailed pending appeal, apparently in order to keep Salerno's other case alive before the Supreme Court. The Justice Department wanted to take the issue of pretrial detention before the Supreme Court, and they wanted to do so in a case involving a very undesirable, even despicable defendant, and Salerno fit the part perfectly.

Anthony "Fat Tony" Salerno, courtesy of the New York Daily News.

At the Supreme Court

The Supreme Court agreed to hear the appeal. On May 26, 1987, the court, by a vote of six to three, handed down its decision. The nation's highest court reversed the case once again and upheld the preventive detention law.[3]

Justice William Rehnquist, a former Justice Department official, wrote the opinion for the court. He contended that pretrial detention is not punishment; it is a "regulatory" procedure. Rehnquist stated: "the mere fact that a person is detained does not inexorably lead to the conclusion that the government has imposed punishment." Rehnquist was playing a semantic game with the Constitution which can lead to no long-term good. UnderRehnquist's view of the Constitution, the judge is not finding the defendant guilty of anything but is acting as a regulatory agency. Much like the Federal Aviation Administration regulates air travel to protect air travelers, the judge regulates the defendant's conduct by ordering him or her detained to protect the public. Rehnquist quotes the constitutional ban on deprivation of liberty without due process, but explains how a man can be deprived of liberty without a jury finding him guilty. However, whether he is held because of a regulatory finding, or a jury verdict does not matter to the defendant who remains, nevertheless, locked in a jail cell.

Justice Thurgood Marshall, joined by Justice William Brennan in dissent, stated:

> Honoring the presumption of innocence is often difficult; sometimes we must pay sub-stantial social costs as a result of our com-mitment to the values we espouse. But at the end of the day the presumption of innocence

protects the innocent; the short-cuts we take with those whom we believe to be guilty injure only those wrongfully accused and, ultimately, ourselves.

Throughout the world today there are men, women, and children interned indefinitely, awaiting trials which may never come or which may be a mockery of the world, because their governments believe them to be "dangerous." Our Constitution, whose construction began two centuries ago, can shelter us forever from the evils of such unchecked power. Over two hundred years it has slowly, through our efforts, grown more durable, more expansive, and more just. But it cannot protect us if we lack the courage, and the self-restraint, to protect ourselves. Today a majority of the Court applies itself to an ominous exercise in demolition. Theirs is truly a decision which will go forth without authority, and come back without respect.

Justice John Paul Stevens wrote a separate dissenting opinion. He felt that in some case in the future it might be appropriate to detain someone who had not committed a crime. Justice Stevens gave the example of a demented hijacker who was found innocent because of his insanity. However, we could hold such a man under a commitment proceeding, an emergency one if necessary, and not under the preventive detention provision of the Bail Reform Act.

Epilogue

Today, thousands of Americans charged with federal crimes are held in preventive detention. Some of them may be found guilty. Many will not. All defendants should be presumed innocent until proven guilty, as those charged with crimes in America have been for more than 240 years.

Mr. Salerno was held in federal detention in New York before trial. He was convicted of racketeering. Salerno died in prison of natural causes, just five years into his 100-year sentence in Springfield, Missouri on July 27, 1992, at age 80. Added to his crimes is the destruction of the presumption of innocence in the United States.

Endnotes

1. 631 F.Supp. 1364 (1986).
2. 794 F.2d 64 (1996).
3. 481 U.S. 739 (1987).

Chapter Thirty

The World is Watching: When the Government Breaks International Law

"All treaties made, or which shall be made, under the authority of the United States, shall be the supreme the law of the land."

—Article Six of the Constitution of the United States.

"We are under the Constitution, but the Constitution is what the judges say it is."

—Charles Evans Hughes
(Chief Justice of the United States, 1930–1941)

"Injustice anywhere is a threat to justice everywhere."

—Martin Luther King Jr. (1929-1968)
Letter from Birmingham Jail, April 16, 1963

"When government violates the law, it will be impossible to declare that behaviour proper."

—Marten Oosting National
Ombudsman of the Netherlands

The United States entered into two treaties that are the subject of the two cases in this chapter. The first case involved a treaty between the United States and Mexico that provided that we would respect each other's sovereignty. The second concerned a treaty that provides that when a national of a foreign country is arrested in any of the countries signing the treaty, that the arresting government will notify the foreigner's consulate.

What makes these stories disturbing is that the United States violated both treaties. Further, the United States Supreme Court did not require the United States government or the states to comply with these treaties. These cases were decided in 1992 and 2006.

The Vienna Convention on Consular Relations provides that when the police of a signatory nation arrest a foreign national, the detaining "authorities shall inform" the foreign national "without delay" of his "righ[t]" to communicate with his nation's consular officers.[1]

Special Agent Enrique Camarena was a member of the U.S. Drug Enforcement Agency (DEA) operating in Guadalajara, Mexico. Camarena was working in a cooperative project with the Mexican government to capture top drug traffickers. On February 7, 1985, members of the Guadalajara drug cartel kidnapped him. Taking him to a house in the city, they brutally tortured him to death while questioning him about DEA activities.

Back in the United States, DEA and other U.S. government officials demanded to participate in the murder investigation. U.S. officials had little faith in the Mexican police, believing that they had been bribed by the drug cartel.

American DEA leaders began investigating the involvement of Dr. Humberto Alvarez-Machain. Dr. Alvarez reportedly had been hired by the Guadalajara drug traffickers to provide medical services as needed. The DEA claimed it had evidence that Alvarez injected Camarena with a stimulant to keep him conscious during the torture. On January 31, 1990, a Los Angeles federal grand jury indicted Alvarez for his alleged part in the Camarena killing. But Dr. Alvarez was in Mexico.

Government Kidnapping

DEA agents in charge of the Camarena investigation offered their Mexican contacts a $50,000 reward for delivering Alvarez to the United States. A group of about a half-dozen former and current Mexican police officers agreed to arrange the abduction. This team of Mexican kidnappers, as determined later by a U.S. federal court, had actually become paid agents of the U.S. government.

On April 2, 1990, members of the team kidnapped Alvarez at gunpoint from his Guadalajara medical office. They took him to a house where he claimed he was tortured and injected with some substance. The next day, they flew him in a private plane to the El Paso, Texas, airport where DEA agents arrested the six foot one, 310-pound Mexican gynecologist.

Mexico protested the kidnapping as a violation of its territory and laws. Mexican newspapers and politicians let loose a torrent of anti-American protests against high-handed "Yanqui" tactics. "The intervention in Mexican territory, once again, is extremely dangerous for the sovereignty of the nation," complained the national daily *Excelsior*.

Mexican police, however, continued investigating Camarena's murder and eventually made a number of other arrests.

In the meantime, Alvarez was brought before a federal district court in Los Angeles. The judge, however, ruled that the kidnapping of Alvarez violated the U.S. extradition treaty with Mexico and, therefore, he should be returned home. An extradition treaty is an agreement between nations to follow certain procedures when one country is seeking a criminal suspect in the other's territory. The U.S. government appealed this ruling all the way to the Supreme Court. Strongly opposed to the DEA actions, the Mexican government filed an *amicus curiae* ("friend of the court") brief that argued the kidnapping was a violation of international law.

Before the Supreme Court

On June 15, 1992, the U.S. Supreme Court decided by a 6–3 majority that the kidnapping of Dr. Alvarez from Mexico did not prohibit his trial in a U.S. court. Writing for the majority, Chief Justice William H. Rehnquist cited an 1886 Supreme Court decision that the authority of a court is not weakened if a defendant is brought before it as a result of "forcible abduction."[2] Rehnquist went on to hold that the U.S. extradition treaty with Mexico was not a factor in the case because it "says nothing about the obligations of the United States and Mexico to refrain from forcible abductions "[3]

Writing in dissent, Justice John Paul Stevens pointed out that the 1886 case used by Chief Justice Rehnquist to justify his opinion actually involved a private bounty hunter, not U.S. government agents. Justice Stevens found this difference to be important. In the Alvarez kidnapping,it was agents of the U.S. government, not a private citizen without government support who illegally violated Mexican territory. By being involved in the kidnapping Stevens concluded, the United States violated the extradition treaty with Mexico. The treaty, he said, "would serve little purpose if the requesting country could simply kidnap the person."

Justice Stevens called the majority opinion a "monstrous decision" that disregards the rule of law and sets a poor example for other countries to follow.

Negative Reactions

Many countries, especially in Latin America, condemned the Supreme Court's ruling. Mexico announcedthat it was suspending a major part of its role in cooperating with the United States to stop drug traffickers.

Argentine President Carlos Menem called the decision "a horror." Canada declared that it would not tolerate similar abductions from its soil. In August 1992, a special committee of the Organization of American States (of which the United States is a member) criticized the *Alvarez-Machain* decision as ignoring "the fundamental principle of international law, namely, respect for the territorial sovereignty of states."

A spokesman for the U.S. Department of State replied that the *Alvarez-Machain* decision did not "represent a 'green light' for the United States to conduct operations on foreign territory." But the spokesman went on to say, "At the same time we are not prepared categorically to rule out unilateral action." He explained that in "extreme cases," like when another country protects a terrorist who has attacked Americans, a kidnapping may be justified as a matter of "self-defense."

In December 1992, Alvarez was finally put on trial in Los Angeles. But, in a final twist, the judge threw out the case after ruling that the prosecution's evidence was based on "the wildest speculation." Dr. Alvarez was then returned home to Mexico.

The Right to Have Your Embassy
Notified of Your Arrest

Article 36 of the Vienna Convention on Consular Relations[4], addresses communication between an individual and his consular officers when the individual is detained by authorities in a foreign country.

Article 36 of the Convention concerns consular officers' access to their nationals detained by authorities in a foreign country. The article provides that "if he so requests, the competent authorities of the receiving State shall, **without delay,** inform the consular post of the sending State if, within its consular district, a national of that State is arrested or committed to prison or to custody pending trial or is detained in any other manner."[5] (emphasis added.) In other words, when a national of one country is detained by authorities in another, the authorities must notify the consular officers of the detainee's home country if the detainee so requests. The treaty also provides that "[t]he said authorities shall inform the person concerned [*i.e.*, the detainee] without delay of his rights under this subparagraph."

Mario Bustillo

Mario Bustillo, a Honduran national, was with several other men at a restaurant in Springfield, Virginia on the night of December 10, 1997. That evening, outside therestaurant, James Merry was struck in the head with a baseball bat as he stood smoking a cigarette. He died several days later. Several witnesses at the scene identified Bustillo as the assailant. Police arrested Bustillo the morning after the attack and eventually charged him with murder. Authorities never informed him that he could request to have the Honduran Consulate notified of hisdetention.

The evidence in Mario Bustillo's trial was inconclusive. Several witnesses testified that it was not Bustillo, but another Honduran man who went by the nickname "Sirena," who murdered James Merry with a baseball bat outside a Springfield, Virginia, Popeye's restaurant in December 1997.

Bustillo was convicted of the murder four months later and sentenced to 30 years in prison. While he was appealing, he was contacted by the Honduran consulate. The consulate said that had it been informed of Bustillo's arrest, it had it would have provided him with assistance.

The *Washington Post* found that "Mr. Bustillo may well be innocent. Virginia Gov. Timothy M. Kaine ought to review his case."[6]

On the strength of testimony by three eyewitnesses, a jury convicted Mr. Bustillo of bashing James Merry on the head with a baseball bat in 1997. At trial, Mr. Bustillo's defense claimed that a different man, identified only by his street name, "Sirena," was the guilty party. One witness claimed to have been with Sirena on a flight to Honduras just after Mr. Merry's death. But he could not be located, and prosecutors successfully ridiculed the defense, "This whole Sirena thing. I don't want to dwell on it too much. It's very convenient that Mr. Sirena apparently isn't available," a prosecutor argued to the jury.

In the years after the killing, however, it has emerged that police saw this man, since identified as Julio Osorto, in the vicinity of the crime and that he had—as a police report recorded—ketchup-like stains on his clothes. Honduran immigration records verify that Osorto did arrive back in Honduras the very day the defense claimed. What's more in a surreptitiously-recorded videotape, he confessed to the killing. The Virginia courts ruled that the police report concerning Mr. Osorto was exculpatory and that the commonwealth had improperly withheld it from thedefense. Yet, amazingly, they went on to determine that it would not have made a difference at trial. So Mr. Bustillo'sconviction stands and he remains incarcerated.

After his conviction became final, Bustillo filed a petition for a writ of habeas corpus in state court. There, for the first time, he argued that authorities had violated his right to consular notification under Article 36 of the Vienna Convention. He claimed that if he had been advised of his right to confer with the Honduran Consulate, he "would have done so without delay." Moreover, the Honduran Consulate executed an affidavit stating that "it would have endeavoured to help Mr. Bustillo in his defense" had it learned of his detention prior to trial. Bustillo insisted that the consulate could have helped him locate Sirena prior to trial. His habeas petition also argued, as part of a claim of ineffective assistance of counsel, that his attorney should have advised him of his right to notify the Honduran Consulate of his arrest and detention.

The Virginia court dismissed Bustillo's Vienna Convention claim as "procedurally barred" because he had failed to raise the issue at trial or on appeal. The court also denied Bustillo's claim of ineffective assistance of counsel,ruling that his belated claim that counsel should have informed him of his Vienna Convention rights was barred by the applicable statute of limitations. In an order refusing Bustillo's petition for appeal, the Supreme Court of Virginia found "no reversible error" in the habeas court's dismissal of the Vienna Convention claim.

The United States Supreme Court ruled that the state court proceedings convicting Bustillo would not be overturned because of violations of the treaty. Justice Breyer, joined by Justices Ginsburg and Souter, quoted from the language of the treaty: "when the police of a signatory nation arrest a foreign national, the **detaining 'authorities shall inform' the foreign national "without delay"** of his 'righ[t]' to communicate with his nation's consular officers."

Breyer continued, "The Convention is a treaty. And 'all Treaties made ... under the Authority of the United States, shall be the supreme Law of the Land; and the Judges in every State shall be bound thereby." U. S. Const.,Art. VI, cl. 2.

The dissenters noted:

> Today's decision interprets an international treaty in a manner that conflicts not onlywith the treaty's language and history, but also with the ICJ's (International Court of Justice's) interpretation of the same treaty provision. In creating this last-mentioned conflict, as far as I can tell, the Court's decision is unprecedented.

The dissenters did not have the fire in their bellies that many dissenters in other historic decisions have had. They also failed to explain the harm that the decision would cause the United States. The effect of the *Bustillo* decision is that U.S. citizens can be arrested anywhere in the world and that maybe the U.S. consulate will be notified and maybe it will not. If Russia or China wants to arrest U.S. citizens, the treaty will likely be ignored.

Conclusion

The *Alvarez* and *Bustillo* cases are announcing to the world that the United States does not give a damn about international obligations. The United States is above the law. If a treaty prohibits the United States from kidnapping alleged criminals in a foreign country, the United States will ignore the treaty. If a treaty requires that foreigners arrested in the United States have international rights, U.S. courts do not have to comply with international law.

Both of these decisions harm the reputation of the United States in the court of world opinion. They also harm U.S. citizens who run afoul of the law in a foreign country, because if the United States can ignor a treaty and international law, so can other countries.

Endnotes

1. Vienna Convention on Consular Relations (Vienna Convention or Convention), Arts. 36(1)(a), (b), Apr. 24, 1963, [1970] 21 U. S. T. 77, 100–101, T. I. A. S. No. 6820.
2. *Ker v. Illinois*, 119 U.S. 436 (1886).
3. United States v. Humberto Alvarez-Machain, 112 S.Ct. 2188 (1992).
4. Vienna Convention or Convention), Apr. 24, 1963, [1970] 21 U. S. T. 77, 100–101, T. I. A. S. No. 6820.
5. Art. 36(1)(b), *id.,* at 101.
6. *Washington Post*, July 10, 2006; Page A16.

Chapter Thirty-One

Double Jeopardy

"The 5th Amendment guarantees that defendants can't face "double jeopardy," which means the government can't prosecute a person a second time for the same crime if the jury returns a verdict. Only if the jury doesn't reach a decision can prosecutors elect to retry the case."

—Robert Shapiro, criminal defense attorney
who represented O.J. Simpson in his murder trial.

"When people make mistakes, the . . . job at this point is to restore self-confidence. I think "piling on" when someone is down is one of the worst things any of us can do."

—Jack Welch, former CEO, General Electric Co.

The Double Jeopardy Clause of the Fifth Amendment protects a person from being prosecuted twice "for the same offence." The Fifth Amendment provides: "No person shall . . . be subject for the same offence to be twice put in jeopardy of life or limb." In these two cases, *Gamble* and *Denzpi*, the Supreme Court continues to apply the so-called dual sovereignty doctrine which undermines the ban on double jeopardy by allowing two charges for the same offense. In *Gamble*, one charge was in state court and the other was in federal court. In *Denzpi*, one charge was in an Indian court (a federal one) and the other in regular federal court. In reality, in *Denzpi*, there were not two sovereigns, since he was prosecuted in two different federal courts.

In November, 2015, a local police officer in Mobile, Alabama, pulled Terance Gamble over for a damaged headlight. Smelling marijuana, the officer searched Gamble's car, where he found a loaded 9-mm handgun. Since Gamblehad been convicted of second-degree robbery, his possessionof the handgun violated an Alabama law providing that no one convicted of "a crime of violence" "shall own a firearmor have one in his or her possession."

After Gamble pleaded guilty to this state offense, federal prosecutors indicted him for the same instance of possession under a federal law—one forbidding those convicted of "a crime punishable by imprisonment for a term exceeding one year . . . to ship or transport in interstate or foreign commerce, or possess in or affecting commerce, any firearm or ammunition."

Gamble pleaded guilty to the federal offense but on double jeopardy grounds. The Eleventh Circuit affirmed. The United States Supreme Court reaffirmed the separate sovereigns doctrine. The alleged offender, in that case, pleaded guilty in state court to the crime of possessing a firearm as a appealed felon and the federal government also charged the man for the same incident, but under an equivalent federal law.

The Supreme Court noted that sovereigns have their own offenses, meaning that in this kind of case the defendant really isn't being prosecuted twice for the same crime. Samuel Alito delivered the opinion of the Court, in which Chief Justice John Roberts, Justice Clarence Thomas, Justice Stephen Breyer, Justice Sonia Sotomayor, Justice Elena Kagan, and Justice Brett Kavanaugh joined. Justice Ruth Bader Ginsburg and Justice Neil Gorsuch filed dissenting opinions.

Alito wrote, "Although the dual-sovereignty rule is often dubbed an "exception" to the double jeopardy right, it is not an exception at all. On the contrary, it follows from the text that defines that right in the first place." In his concurrence, Thomas wrote, "Our judicial duty to interpret the law requires adherence to the original meaning of the text. For that reason, we should not invoke stare decisis to uphold precedents that are demonstrably erroneous."

Justice Ginsburg, in dissent, wrote, "Had either the Federal Government or Alabama brought the successive prosecutions, the second would have violated Gamble's right not to be 'twiceput in jeopardy… for the same offense.' U.S. Const., Amdt. 5,cl. 2. Yet the Federal Government was able to multiply Gamble's time in prison because of the doctrine that, for doublejeopardy purposes, identical criminal laws enacted by 'separatesovereigns' are different 'offense [s].' "

"I dissent from the Court's adherence to that misguided doctrine," Ginsburg wrote. "Instead of 'fritter[ing] away [Gamble's] libert[y] upon a metaphysical subtlety, two sover- eignties,' Grant, The Lanza Rule of Successive Prosecutions, 32 Colum. L. Rev. 1309, 1331 (1932), I would hold that the Double Jeopardy Clause bars 'successive prosecutions [for thesame offense] by parts of the whole USA.' "

She continued,

> Justification for the separate-sovereigns doctrine centers on the word "offence": An "offence," the argument runs, is the violation of a sovereign's law, the United States and each State are separate sovereigns, ergo successive state and federal prosecutions do not place a defendant in "jeopardy. . . for the same offence." Ante, at 1963, 1964-1965 (internal quotation marks omitted).
>
> This "compact syllogism" is fatally flawed. See Braun, *Praying to False Sovereigns: The Rule Permitting Successive Prosecutions in the Age of Cooperative Federalism*, 20 Am. J. Crim. L. 1, 25 (1992). The United States and its constituent States, unlike foreign nations, are "kindred systems," "parts of ONE WHOLE." *The Federalist* No. 82, p. 493 (C. Rossiter ed. 1961) (A. Hamilton). They compose one people, bound by an overriding Federal Constitution. Within that "WHOLE," the Federal and State Governments should be disabled from accomplishing together "whatneither government [could] do alone—prosecute an ordinary citizen twice for the same offence." Amar & Marcus, *Double Jeopardy Law After Rodney King*, 95 Colum.L. Rev. 1, 2 (1995).

Justice Gorsuch, also in dissent, wrote, "A free society does not allow its government to try the same individual for the same crime until it's happy with the result."

He continued,

> Unfortunately, the Court today endorses a colossal exception to this ancient rule against double jeopardy. My colleagues say that the federal government and each State are"separate sovereigns" entitled to try the same person for the same crime. So if all the might of one 'sovereign' cannot succeed against the presumptively free individual, another may insist on the chance to try again. And if both manage to succeed, so much the better; they can add one punishment on top of the other. But this "separate sovereigns exception" to the bar against double jeopardy finds no meaningful support in the text of the Constitution, its original public meaning, structure, or history. Instead, the Constitution promises all Americans that they will never suffer double jeopardy. I would enforce that guarantee.

United States v. Denezpi

Merle Denezpi and V. Y., both members of the Navajo Nation, traveled to Towaoc, Colorado, a town within the Ute Mountain Ute Reservation. While the two were alone at a house belonging to Denezpi's friend, Denezpi barricaded the door, threatened V. Y., and forced her to have sex with him. After Denezpi fell asleep, V. Y. escaped from the house and reported Denezpi to tribal authorities.

An officer with the federal Bureau of Indian Affairs filed a criminal complaint in CFR court. The CFR Court is a trial court for offenses against Indian law where parties present their cases before a Magistrate Judge.

The complaint charged Denezpi with three crimes: assault and battery, terroristic threats, and false imprisonment. Denezpi pleaded guilty to the assault and battery charge, and the prosecutor dismissed the other charges. The Magistrate sentenced Denezpi to time served—140 days' imprisonment. Merle Denezpi entered an Alford guilty plea, which waived a trial but did not admit guilt, to an assault charge in 2017, in violation of tribal law in the Court of Indian Offenses of the Ute Mountain Ute Agency. An Alford Plea is a guilty plea in criminal court, whereby a defendant does not admit to the criminal act and asserts innocence, but admits that the evidence presented by the prosecution would be likely to persuade a judge or jury to find the defendant guilty beyond a reasonable doubt.

Six months later, Denezpi was indicted in the United States District Court for the District of Colorado for aggravated sexual assault based on the same underlying crime as the earlier conviction in the CFR Court. Denezpi moved to dismiss the indictment, arguing that the Double Jeopardy Clause barred the consecutive prosecution, but the District Court denied the motion. After a jury convicted Denezpi, the District Court sentenced him to 360 months' imprisonment.

The Tenth Circuit affirmed. It concluded that the second prosecution in federal court did not constitute double jeopardy because the Ute Mountain Ute Tribe's inherent sovereignty was the ultimate source of power undergirding the earlier prosecution in CFR court. 979 F.3d 777, 781–783 (2020).

The U. S. Supreme Court issued its opinion in *Denezpi v. United States*, ruling in favor of the dual sovereignty doctrine. The dual sovereignty doctrine undermines the double jeopardy clause of the Fifth Amendment, allowing for two sovereign entities to charge one defendant under the same set of facts under two different laws and legal authorities.

The majority opinion, written by Justice Amy Coney Barrett, reasons that the clause protects defendants from "successive prosecutions" for the same offense but "does not prohibit twice placing a person in jeopardy" for the same conduct. Barrett goes on to conclude that, "Denezpi's single act led to separate prosecutions for violations of a tribal ordinance and a federal statute. Because the Tribe and the Federal Government are distinct sovereigns, those 'offence[s]' are not 'the same.' "

Conservative Justice Neil Gorsuch dissented, joined in part by Justices Sonia Sotomayor and Elena Kagan. Gorsuch raised concerns about the majority ruling, saying:

> Once more, the Court's reply is unpersuasive. It admits that, in case after case, this Court has emphasized that the dual-sovereignty doctrine does not permit successive prosecutions by the same sovereign....Yet the Court today tries to brush all these precedents aside, offhandedly suggesting that each was mistaken… .If taken to its extreme, the Court's reasoning could seemingly allow a State to punish an individual twice for identical offenses, so long as one is proscribed by state law and the other by federal law.

Both the *Gamble* and *Denezpi* cases violate the spirit of the Fifth Amendment's Double Jeopardy clause. The *Denezpi* decision is even more egregious because the two courts were both federal, and thus there was only one sovereign.

Chapter Thirty-Two

The President is Above the Law

"No man is above the law."

--President Theodore Roosevelt. State of the Union, 1903.

On August 1, 2023, a federal grand jury in the District of Columbia indicted former President Donald J. Trump on four felony counts for conduct that occurred during his Presidency following the November 2020 election. The indictment alleged that after losing that election, Trump conspired to overturn it by spreading knowingly false claims of election fraud to obstruct the collecting, counting and certifying of the election results. Trump moved to dismiss the indictment based on Presidential immunity, arguing that a President has absolute immunity from criminal pro-secution for actions performed within the outer perimeter of his official responsibilities, and that the indictment's allegations fell within the core of his official duties. The District Court denied Trump's motion to dismiss, holding that former Presidents do not possess federal criminal immunity for any acts. The D. C. Circuit affirmed.

In the District Court

Defendant Trump contended that the Constitution granted him "absolute immunity from criminal prosecution for actions performed within the 'outer perimeter' of his official responsibility" while he served as President of the United States, so long as he was not both impeached and convicted for those actions. On December 1, 2023, U.S. federal district court Judge Tanya Chutkan ruled, "The Constitution's text, structure, and history do not support that contention. No court—or any other branch of government—has ever accepted it. And this court will not so hold. Whatever immunities a sitting President may enjoy, the United States has only one Chief Executive at a time, and that position does not confer a lifelong 'get-out-of-jail-free' pass."

Judge Chutkan continued,

> Former Presidents enjoy no special conditions on their federal criminal liability. Defendant may be subject to federal investigation, indictment, prosecution, conviction, and punishment for any criminal acts undertaken while in office. A. Text In interpreting the Constitution, courts ordinarily 'begin with its text,' *City of Boerne v. Flores*, 521 U.S. 507, 519 (1997), but there is no provision in the Constitution conferring the immunity that Defendant claims. The Supreme Court has already noted 'the absence of explicit constitutional . . . guidance' on whether a President possesses any immunity. *Nixon v. Fitzgerald*, 457 U.S. 731, 747 (1982); *see also United States v. Nixon*, 418 U.S. 683, 705–06 n.16 (1974) (observing "the silence of the Constitution"

regarding a President's immunity from criminal subpoenas)." Judge Chutkan completely and flatly denied Trump's claim of presidential immunity.

Former President Trump appealed. In most criminal cases an appeal waits until after the case is tried. In this case an "interlocutory" appeal was allowed. Former President Trump has used the system to delay the trial in this case.

In the Court of Appeals

Judge Karen Henderson was appointed by Republican President George H. W. Bush. Judge J. Michelle Childs was appointed by President Joseph Biden. Judge Florence Pan was appointed by President Barack Obama. Three women decided the fate of former President Donald Trump, two appointed by Democratic Presidents and one apponted by a Republican President. The case was put on a fast track, argued on January 9, 2024 and decided on February 6, 2024.

During oral argument Judge Pan asked, "A president could sell pardons, could sell military secrets, could order SEAL Team 6 to assassinate a political rival? Would such a president be subject to criminal prosecution if he's not impeached?"

D. John Sauer, representing former President Trump, insisted that for any crime connected to a president's "official duties," the "political process" of impeachment and conviction by the Senate "would have to occur" before criminal prosecution. He predicted that if a president was involved in murder, he would be "speedily" impeached

The appellate court early in its opinion noted that judges are not immune from criminal liability. The court also ruled, "We note at the outset that our analysis is specific to the case before us, in which a former President has been indicted on federal criminal charges arising from his alleged conspiracy to overturn federal election results and unlawfully overstay his Presidential term." Opinion at 31. The court of appeals also noted, "The President has a constitutionally mandated duty to "take Care that the Laws be faithfully executed." U.S. Constitution, Article II, § 3." The court continued, "It would be a striking paradox if the President, who alone is vested with the constitutional duty to 'take Care that the Laws be faithfully executed,' were the sole officer capable of defying those laws with impunity." Opinon at 39. "We conclude that "[c]oncerns of public policy, especially as illuminated by our history and the structure of our government" compel the rejection of his claim of immunity in this case." Opinion at 57. Trump appealed to the U.S. Supreme Court.

At the U.S. Supreme Court

The Supreme Court, with no basis in the Constitution, gave former President Trump immunity from prosecution for "official acts." It ruled that under our constitutional structure of separated powers, the nature of Presidential power entitles a former President to absolute immunity from criminal prosecution for actions within his conclusive and preclusive constitutional authority. And he is entitled to at least presumptive immunity from prosecution for all his official acts.

This new official-acts immunity now acts like a loaded gun for any President that wishes to place his own interests, his own political survival, or his own financial gain, above the interests of the Nation. The President of the United States is the most powerful person in the country, and possibly the world.

When he uses his official powers in any way, under the majority's reasoning, he now will be insulated from criminal prosecution. Orders the Navy's Seal Team 6 to assassinate a political rival? Immune. Organizes a military coup to hold onto power? Immune. Takes a bribe in exchange for a pardon? Immune. Immune, immune, immune.

The court seems to have recognized that it was overturning historic precedents. It noted, "By contrast, when prosecutors have sought evidence from the President, we have consistently rejected Presidential claims of absolute immunity. For instance, during the treason trial of former Vice President Aaron Burr, Chief Justice Marshall rejected President Thomas Jefferson's claim that the President could not be subjected to a subpoena. Marshall reasoned that "the law does not discriminate between the president and a private citizen." But the court does discriminated between the former President and every other human being.

The Dissent

Justice Sotomayor wrote the dissent with Justices Kagan and Jackson joining her. Justice Sotomayor wrote,

> Today's decision to grant former Presidents criminal immunity reshapes the institution of the Presidency. It makes a mockery of the principle, foundational to our Constitution and system of Government, that no man is above the law. Relying on little more than its own misguided wisdom about the need for 'bold and unhesitating action' by the President, ante, at 3, 13, the Court gives former President Trump all the immunity he asked for and more. Because our Constitution does not shield a former President from answering for criminal and treasonous acts, I dissent.

The dissent continued, "In the weeks leading up to January 6, 2021, then President Trump allegedly "spread lies that there had been outcome-determinative fraud in the election and that he had actually won," App. 181, Indictment ¶2, despite being "notified repeatedly" by his closest advisers "that his claims were untrue," id., at 188, ¶11. The dissent continued,

> When dozens of courts swiftly rejected these claims, Trump allegedly 'pushed officials in certain states to ignore the popular vote; disenfranchise millions of voters; dismiss legitimate electors; and ultimately, cause the ascertainment of and voting by illegitimate electors' in his favor. Id., at 185–186, ¶10(a). It is alleged that he went so far as to threaten one state election official with criminal prosecution if the official did not "find 11,780 votes" Trump needed to change the election result in that state. Id., at 202, ¶31(f). When state officials repeatedly declined to act outside their legal authority and alter their state election processes, Trump and his co-conspirators purportedly developed a plan to disrupt and displace the legitimate election certification process by organizing fraudulent slates of electors. See id., at 208–209, ¶¶53–54.

In conclusion the dissent warned, "Never in the history of our Republic has a President had reason to believe that he would be immune from criminal prosecution if he used the trappings of his office to violate the criminal law. Moving forward, however, all former Presidents will be cloaked in such immunity. If the occupant of that office misuses official power for personal gain, the criminal law that the rest of us must abide will not provide a backstop.

With fear for our democracy, I dissent."

Critics

Professor Laurence Tribe, Harvard University professsor of Constitutional law: "the Supreme Court dispensed with the rule of law by effectively depriving the American people of crucial information we should have had before the November election."

The question before the justices in *Trump v. United States*: Was Donald Trump immune from prosecution for the crimes the special counsel Jack Smith accused him of committing while president? Prof. Tribe continued, "The answer should have been obvious: No, presidents cannot commit crimes aimed at obstructing the peaceful transfer of power without facing consequences. Indeed, to my knowledge, no court has ever held that a president could be criminally immune under any circumstances."

Tribe continued:

Instead of delivering that judgment many months ago and allowing the trial to proceed, the justices have given Mr. Trump the gift of delay piled upon delay. By taking nearly 10 weeks to deliberate before returning the case to the district court — and by sending it back not even for immediate trial but for preliminary determinations that could trigger yet another round of appeals — they have extinguished any realistic hope of getting a verdict in the Jan. 6 case before November. American voters will enter ballot booths to choose between Donald Trump and President Biden without knowing whether Mr. Trump is guilty of the crimes with which a grand jury of his fellow citizens charged him.

This decision may seem like a reflection of a rogue conservative majority that can, in time, be changed. But it is a sign of a much deeper problem—one that, when the time is ripe, will require constitutional reforms to solve and perhaps even a new branch of government.

Although the opinion features a high-minded disclaimer that the court is not granting Mr. Trump or any future president complete immunity, the practical effect of this decision is presumptive immunity for all future presidents and complete immunity by delay for Mr. Trump.

This prospect was not lost on Mr. Trump. He repeatedly obtained delays to avoid trial, turning the legal machinery of the court system against itself to buy what he needed most: time — time to distract, delay and spin his own version of the story as he sought to find a way to make these devastating charges disappear. If he becomes president again, he could have his new attorney general fire Mr. Smith and deep-six the entire prosecution.

Regardless of whether you think Mr. Trump would have been acquitted or convicted in a trial, immunity by running out the clock is justice delayed and thus justice denied.

So how did our legal system get tripped up by his persistent delay strategy? And why does it have such perilous ramifications for the rule of law?

The Constitution's framers erected a structure they hoped would ensure, as far as humanly possible, that no person, including a president, would be above the law. But they also designed the prosecutorial arm of government—which now includes the attorney general and the special counsels—to be dependent on the president. As centuries passed, this has created serious problems.

The attorney general, for his part, serves at the president's pleasure. That probably explains why Merrick Garland waited about 20 months to appoint a special counsel in this case. The *New York Times* reported that in the early days of his presidency, Mr. Biden adamantly opposed bringing charges against his predecessor, most likely worried that they would backfire politically. An attorney general unconstrained by the political pressures of presidential politics might well have brought charges earlier, ensuring that we had answers before Election Day.

All this is generally accepted. But this case has exposed an even more insidious problem caused by the structural relationship between any president and the Justice Department. During the oral arguments, Michael Dreeben, the able Justice Department advocate, had to acknowledge that,

> because the attorney general serves at the president's pleasure, any president can effectively secure the equivalent of immunity for whatever crimes he might choose to commit. All a chief executive must do is pick an attorney general who would give him a formal opinion stating that whatever he planned to do would be legal — up to and including a coup reversing his own election loss. That advice of counsel would, under settled principles of due process, give the president an ironclad defense every bit as good as judicially conferred immunity.

Should Mr. Trump return to the Oval Office, he could act with even greater impunity than he did in his first term, either by immunizing himself with an attorney general's opinion (which would give him license to commit whatever crimes he chose to commit) or by using the Justice Department to engage in politically motivated prosecutions.

Congressman Jamie Raskin (D-Md.), a former constitutional law professor and member of the January 6th Committee, railed against the U.S. Supreme Court's decision to take up Donald Trump's argument that he is immune from prosecution for actions he took while president. "This was an obvious case not to take up, and just let the D.C. Circuit Court ruling stand," Raskin said during an interview on MSNBC's "Inside with Jen Psaki."

The D.C. Circuit Court's decision, Raskin said, was "completely exhaustive and totally compelling," and Trump's claims that a president could commit crimes with impunity while in office is "utterly antithetical to everything that we know about our Constitution."

"We don't have a king here, we had a revolution against a king and the Constitution is written so that [the] president's main job is to take care [that] the laws are faithfully executed, not faithfully violated in his own interest," Raskin said.

Raskin also claimed that political motivations may be guiding the justices on the Supreme Court, three of whom were appointed by Trump.

"Do you look at this court and say some of these justices want to delay these trials?," Psaki asked. Raskin replied, "Well, yeah. If you don't believe that you're too innocent to be let out of the house by yourself at this point."

The Supreme Court's decision in the *United States v. Donald Trump* will go down in history as one of the Court's worst decisions. Together with *Bush v. Gore*, the Supreme Court has shown its political bias.

PART 7

Access to Justice

Chapter Thirty-Three

Storming the Castle

"The house of everyone is to him as his castle and fortress,
as well for his defence against injury
and violence as for his repose."

—Sir Edward Coke, *Semayne's Case*

"The right of the people to be secure in persons,
houses, papers . . . against unreasonable
searches . . . shall not be violated."

—Fourth Amendment

It was a quiet Friday evening in St. Paul, Minnesota in November of 1983. November 11th—Veteran's Day. The Creighton family, Robert and Sarisse, and their two young daughters, Shaunda and Tiffany, were watching television. Their home was on West Minnehaha Street, within a mile and a half of the Capitol dome. It was calm and peaceful. Mrs. Creighton fell asleep.

Robert Creighton worked in the stockroom for the local telephone company. Mrs. Creighton worked in the

Chancellor's office of the state university system. The Creighton family was a hardworking, middle-class, African-American family.

A Light in the Window

Near the end of the television show *Webster,* a bright spotlight suddenly flashed through the Creightons' front window. Mr. Creighton opened the door and was confronted with seven police officers and an FBI agent, many of them brandishing shotguns. All of them were white.

One of the officers told Creighton "to keep his hands in sight" while the others rushed through the front door. Creighton asked if they had a search warrant and one of them told him, "We don't have a search warrant and don't need one; you watch too much TV."

Robert Creighton told the men to put their guns away because they were frightening the children, but they refused. Sarisse Creighton awoke to the shrieking of her children and was confronted by an officer who pointed a shotgun at her. She overheard an officer yelling at herdaughters to "sit their damn asses down and stop screaming." Mrs. Creighton asked the officer, "What the hell is going on?"

The officer did not explain the situation and simply said to her, "Why don't you make your damn kids sit on the couch and make them shut up?"

One officer asked Mr. Creighton if he owned a red and silver Buick Riviera. He said that he owned a maroon Oldsmobile. As Creighton led the officers downstairs to his garage, one of the officers punched him in the face, knock ing him to the ground and causing him to bleed from his mouth and forehead. Creighton was attempting to move past the officer to open the garage door, when the officer panicked and hit him. The officer claimed that he thought Creighton was attempting to grab his shotgun, eventhough Creighton was not a suspect in any crime and had no contraband in his house. Shaunda, the Creightons' ten-year-old daughter, witnessed her father being assaulted and screamed for her mother to help. Oneof the officers then hit her.

Sarisse Creighton telephoned her mother, but an officer kicked and grabbed the phone and told her to "hang up that damn phone." She told her children to run to their neighbor's house for safety.

The children ran out and a plainclothes officer ran after them. The officer ran into the neighbor's home and grabbed Shaunda by the shoulders and shook her violently. The neighbor told the officer, "Can't you see she's in shock? Leave her alone and get out of my house." Mrs. Creigton's mother later brought Shaunda to the emergency room at Children's Hospital for an arm injury caused by the officer's rough handling of her.

During the melee, family members and friends began arriving at the Creighton home. Sarisse Creighton asked FBI agent Russell Anderson if he had a search warrant. He replied, "I don't need a damn search warrant when I'm looking for a fugitive."

At about 3:30 in the afternoon, there was a robbery in St. Paul, which allegedly was perpetrated by Vadain Dixon, Mrs. Creighton's brother. Before searching the Creighton's home, the police had searched the homes of Dixon's mother and grandmother, also without a search warrant.

Anderson claimed that he had probable cause to search the homes of Dixon's relatives and that it would have been too difficult to get a search warrant. He believed that "exigent circumstances" justified the searches.

Violating Fourth Amendment Rights

The Creightons were badly shaken, embarrassed, and two of them were physically injured. They consulted John Sheehy, a Minneapolis lawyer across the Mississippi River from their home. Sheehy explained to them that the Fourth Amendment to the Constitution requires that police get search warrants before conducting a search of anyone's home. The only exception to the law, he explained, is when the police are in "hot pursuit" of a criminal, for example, a high-speed chase from the scene of a crime.

Attorney Sheehy filed suit on behalf of the Creightons for deprivation of their civil rights under the Constitution, for assault and battery, false arrest and false imprisonment.

In Federal Court

The government attorneys moved to dismiss the case, claiming that the police officers could not be sued because they believed that what they were doing was lawful. The District Court Judge Diana Murphy dismissed the Creighton's lawsuit.

The Creightons' attorney filed an appeal. The court of appeals reversed the lower court's ruling.[1] Judge Heaney ruled:

> A mere suspicion that a suspect might be in the home of a third party generally will not establish probable cause to search the third party's home.
>
> * * *
>
> Clearly, such speculation is not a reasonable groundjustifying the invasion of citizens' privacy.

The court of appeals also found that the district court erred by finding that the police were in "hot pursuit," and ruled that as a matter of law there was no hot pursuit because there was no chase or continuous hunt. Judge Heaney and the Court of Appeals further stated that the search was illegal and sent the case back to Judge Murphy for a trial.

The Supreme Court

The government attorneys were not at all pleased with the prospect of an FBI agent and seven police officers as defendants in a trial for damages. They attempted a long-shot: an appeal to the Supreme Court before the case went back to the district court for trial.

The Supreme Court took the unusual step of accepting a case that did not have a developed record. There had been no trial, only a decision by the district court on a motion to dismiss.

The justices voted in conference and split six to three. The case was assigned to Justice Scalia, a recent appointee to the court. He said "It is not possible to say that one 'reasonably' acted unreasonably." Since the Fourth Amendment protects citizens against "unreasonable" searches, a finding that the officer was not reasonable should mean that the search was illegal.

But Justice Scalia, although he admitted that the search was illegal, found a way to find police officers and FBI agents immune from suits even when they have violated the Fourth Amendment. He twisted the language of the Fourth Amendment, claiming that it's wording was "unfortunate." Scalia believed that the Fourth Amendment should protect citizens against "undue searches" and not "unreasonable" ones. Justice Scalia's opinion was announced on June 25,1987.

Justices Stevens, Brennan and Marshall dissented Justice Stevens asserted that the majority:

> announces a new rule of law that protects federal agents who make forcible night-time entries into the homes of innocent citizens without probable cause, without a warrant, and without any valid reason for their warrantless search. The Court stunningly restricts the constitutional accountability of the police . . . by displaying remarkably little fidelity to the countervailing principles of individual liberty and privacy that infuse the Fourth Amendment.

Epilogue

The *Creighton* case was handed down just before the first edition of this book went to press. I have used it in place of another Fourth Amendment case that was not quite as egregious. However, the Supreme Court has been undercutting the Fourth Amendment in many recent decisions. Fourth Amendment rights have been limited in trailer homes, in barns and in back yards. The Supreme Court has recently ruled that the police, without a warrant, are allowed to search your property from airplanes and helicopters.

As Justice Rehnquist stated, these cases might well: "surprise or even shock those who lived in an earlier era." His statement was made when announcing that the Bank Secrecy Act was constitutional, even though it required banks, without warrants or probable cause, to supply the IRS and other government agencies bank records of customers. In that 1974 decision, Justice Douglas dissented, opposing the "sledge-hammer approach" of the law and theunderlying assumption that every citizen is a crook.

The problem, now, is that the Supreme Court is allowing the police to act as if every citizen is a criminal. The rights of innocent citizens were trampled by the gestapo-like actions of the St. Paul Police Department and the FBIin Minnesota, on Veterans Day in 1983, and the nation's highest court has given them its seal of approval. The Fourth Amendment's requirement of a warrant, etched in the Constitution, is now as meaningless as an epitaph etched on a tombstone, with no one left to enforce it.

Endnotes

1. 766 F.2d 1269 (1985).

Chapter Thirty-Four

Indecent Exposure

"In any country there must be people who have to die. They are the sacrifices any nation has to make."

—Idi Amin (former Ugandan dictator)

This chapter includes two cases which were brought by veterans and widows to recover compensation for injuries which were suffered in the line of duty. The Veterans' Benefit Act allows veterans and their survivors to apply for benefits, if the veteran is disabled or killed while serving his country. These awards are determined by the Veterans Administration (VA). The benefits are not overly generous. Because of this, many veterans, when they are injured by the government's misconduct, seek justice in the courts.

It is ironic that the Supreme Court would deny veterans the rights that they fought to defend. While the Supreme Court has ruled that those denied welfare benefits have the right to an attorney to represent them, the Supreme Court has denied veterans this same right. The court has alsodenied veterans the right to sue the government for damages, when civilians have that right.

Radiation Victims

Albert Maxwell, an American soldier in the Pacific Theater during World War II, was captured by the Japanese. As a prisoner of war, he was held captive in Japan, and was exposed to radiation from both the Nagasaki and Hiroshima atomic bombs. He contended that this wartime exposure caused the cancer that he suffered from. In addition, Maxwell claimed that the radiation effects had caused four of his five children to die of rare congenital abnormalities in early childhood. The Veterans Administration denied his claims.

Don Cordray was exposed to radiation during atomic testing while on duty with the Navy. Mr. Cordray contracted cancer and other ailments. His claim for benefitswas denied by the Veterans Administration.

Reason Warehime served in the Pacific during World War II. He was assigned to the clean-up detail dispatched to Nagasaki after it was leveled by an atomic blast. He was also exposed to a large dose of radiation at an atomic test. His disability rating was lowered from one-hundred percent to sixty percent.

Doris Wilson is the widow of a veteran whose ship was contaminated with radiation and who died of cancer, as a result. Her claim for survivor's benefits was denied.

Top left: *Reason Warehime by Jim Lerager; top right: Don Corday by Jim Lerager; bottom left: Albert Maxell by Jim Lerager; Bottom right: James Stanley courtesy of Mr. Stanley.*

Protecting Veterans' Rights

The Veterans' law limits the amount an attorney can charge for a claim for service-related injuries to ten dollars. This fee limitation originated during the Civil War (1862) which limited attorney's fees to five dollars. In 1864, the limit was increased to ten dollars, where it has remained. In 1864, the average soldier earned about $4.50 per week. In order to protect veterans against unscrupulous lawyers, Congress limited the amount that attorneys could earn to about two weeks' salary.

Albert Maxwell, Reason Warehime, Don Cordray and Doris Wilson all sought representation by attorneys, but could not find any willing to represent them for only ten dollars. The National Association of Radiation Survivors and the Swords to Plowshares Veterans Rights Organization joined these four individuals in a federal court challenge to the ten-dollar attorney's fee limitation.

The Lower Court Ruling

In 1984, the case was heard by Judge Marilyn Hall Patel in federal court in San Francisco, California. Judge Patel ruled that the government's paternalistic interest inensuring that veterans' benefits are not depleted by attorneys' fees does not overcome the veteran's right to berepresented by counsel. The judge ruled that plaintiffsMaxwell, Warehime, Cordray and Wilson had a right to select an attorney at their expense and issued a nationwide injunction against the Veterans Administration.[1]

The court ruled, in granting a preliminary injunction,that the VA could no longer even mention the limitationon attorneys fees in any publication, form or regulation,and required the agency to post its ruling in a prominent location in every VA office in the nation.

Straight to the Supreme Court

Judge Patel's decision apparently angered the Justice Department, because it took the unusual step of appealing her order directly to the Supreme Court, sidestepping the court of appeals.

The Supreme Court decided to review the matter, even though the district court's decision was only a preliminary decision. The lower court did not rule that the limitation on attorneys' fees was unconstitutional: it ruled that after a full trial it was likely that the plaintiffs would be able to prove that the statute was unconstitutional.

The Supreme Court went beyond ruling on the appeal of the preliminary injunction and directly held that the statutory limitation on attorneys' fees was constitutional.[2] Justice O'Connor, although voting with the majority, stated that the majority should not have reached the merits of the constitutional question. Justice Sandra Day O'Connor stated that the injunction should have been dissolved, and the case returned to the lower court for considerationof the entire case.

The Supreme Court ruled that Congress had the power to regulate attorneys' fees, even if those fees were so low as to ensure that the veterans would not be represented by counsel. The court gave two reasons for its decision. First, Congress could legislate to protect veterans from attorneys and from themselves, and second, Congress could seek to minimize the cost of administering the VA's programs.

Justice John Stevens, joined by Justices William Brennan and Thurgood Marshall, wrote a brilliant dissenting opinion. He stated:

> The Court does not appreciate the value
> of individual liberty. It may well be true
> that in the vast majority of the cases a vet-
> eran does not need to employ a lawyer . . . .

* * *

Everyone agrees, however, that there are some complicated cases in which the services of a lawyer would be useful to the veteran, and indeed, would simplify the work of the agency by helping to organize the relevant facts and to identify the con-trolling issues.

* * *

The law that was enacted in 1864 to protect veterans from unscrupulous lawyers—those who charge excessive fees—effectively denied today's veteran access to all lawyers who charge reasonable fees for their services.

* * *

We are concerned with the individual's right to spend his own money to obtain the advice and assistance of independent counsel in advancing his claim against the Government.

In my view, regardless of the nature of the dispute between the sovereign [the government] and the citizen—whether it be a criminal trial, a proceeding to terminate parental rights, a claim for social security benefits, a dispute over welfare benefits, or a pension claim asserted by the widow of a soldier who was killed on the battlefield—the citizen's right to consult an independent lawyer and to retain that lawyer to speak on his behalf is an aspect of liberty that is priceless. It should not be bargained away on the notion that a totalitarian appraisal of the mass of claims processed by the Veterans' Administration does not identify an especially high probability of error.

Unfortunately, the reason for the Court's mistake today is all too obvious. It does not appreciate the value of individual liberty.

The Acid Test

In 1958, James B. Stanley was a master sergeant in the Army at Fort Knox, Kentucky, where he lived with his wife and children. He responded to a posted notice and volunteered to wear protective clothing and equipment tosee how it would work when exposed to chemical weapons. Stanley was transferred to the Army's Chemical Warfare Lab, at the Edgewood Arsenal in Aberdeen, Maryland, to take part in the testing. During his tenure at the Edgewood Arsenal, on four different occasions, Stanley was told to drink a clear liquid Like a good soldier, Master Sergeant James Stanley did what he was told and asked no questions.

During this time, Stanley suffered hallucinations, periods of incoherence, servere personality changes and loss of memory. He began to beat his wife and children. After his violent episodes, he had no memory of them.

Unbeknownst to Stanley, he was being used as a guinea pig. The clear liquid contained a heavy dose of lysergic acid diethylamide, commonly known as LSD. LSD is a strong hallucinogenic drug which was the cause of Stanley's mental disorders. Stanley was not alone: the Army subjected 1,000 others to this LSD testing between 1955 and 1958.

The University of Maryland Medical School willingly participated in these LSD tests on humans. Many believe that the CIA was behind the testing, but the intelligence agency denies that it had anything to do with it. Maryland medical interns were used to administer the hidden drugs.

Stanley stayed in the Army until he was honorably discharged in 1969. Because of the violent personality he developed after the LSD tests, his wife divorced him.

The Letter

In 1975, Stanley received a letter from the Walter Reed Army Medical Center in Washington, D.C. The letter asked Stanley if he would participate in a follow-up study concerning the LSD testing that took place in 1958. Stanley was, understandably, extremely upset. He finally understood what had happened to him, his family and his mind Because he was angry at what his government had done to him, and he sought justice in the courts.

Stanley hired an attorney who sought additional details on the LSD testing program. The attorney applied for compensation, on Stanley's behalf, with both the Army and the CIA. The government stonewalled it. They would give Stanley nothing.

Finally, in 1978, Stanley filed suit in federal court in Florida against the Army and the Central Intelligence Agency for intentionally causing him harm and subjecting him to medical experimentation without his consent, and for failing to care for him after they gave him hallucinogenic drugs.

DEPARTMENT OF THE ARMY
WALTER REED ARMY INSTITUTE OF RESEARCH
WALTER REED ARMY MEDICAL CENTER
WASHINGTON, D.C. [illegible]

SGRD-UWI-A 10 December 1975

Mr. James Bradley Stanley
345 Ponte Vedra Road
Palm Springs, Florida 33460

Dear Mr. Stanley:

According to our records, you were a participant in the chemical warfare tests with lysergic acid diethylamide (LSD) conducted by the Biomedical Laboratory, Edgewood Arsenal, Aberdeen Proving Ground, Maryland. Under the auspices of the Surgeon General, a follow-up study of volunteers who participated in these experiments will be conducted over the next two years. We earnestly solicit your cooperation and participation in this study.

The study will consist of providing all former participants with a comprehensive medical examination at an Army Medical Center. Through these examinations, we will attempt to first assess the overall health status of former participants and, second, to determine whether there have been any long-term aftereffects that might be traceable to participation in the LSD experiment.

If you have any questions, or if you would like to discuss the examination or the study, please call the Medical Follow-Up Evaluation Group at (202)427-5210 (call collect) and ask for Mrs. Sotarky. If for any reason you wish your appointment for examination in this follow-up study to be at an earlier date, do not hesitate to contact Mrs. Sotarky. She will be pleased to either discuss the examination with you or provide you access to a physician or other health professional who will be happy to answer any questions you may have.

Our thanks for your consideration and cooperation.

Sincerely,

HARRY C. HOLLOWAY, M.D.
COL, MC
Dir, Division of Neuropsychiatry

Federal Court

Stanley's case bounced around the federal courts for nearly a decade. At first, Judge Gonzalez dismissed Stanley's case against the federal government. However, Gonzalez allowed him to add individual defendants to the case, including the University of Maryland and the doctors who administered the LSD to him.[3]

Judge Gonzalez stated:

> There is a constitutional right to decide for oneself to submit to drug therapy. This court views the conduct alleged . . . as an egregious intrusion on the most precious right protected by the Constitution the right not to be deprived of life, liberty or property without due process of law.

The case was appealed to the court of appeals. The three-judge court, unanimously, ruled that Stanley could not only sue the individuals involved, but he also had the right to sue the United States government.[4] The court of appeals sent the case back for trial. However, before the case went back to the trial court, the government appealed.

At the Nation's Highest Court

The Supreme Court agreed to hear the case. On June 25, 1987, just before this book went to press, the court issued its decision by a vote of five to four.[5] Justice Antonin Scalia wrote the majority opinion in which he was joinedby Justice Harry Blackmun, William Rehnquist, Byron White and Lewis Powell.

By the slimmest of majorities, the court ruled that the government was immune from suit by those who were in the military. According to the court, lawsuits of this type would interfere with military discipline. They ruled that it would be "inappropriate for soldiers to be allowed to sue their superior officers." The court did not say what the effects of the suit would be on Army morale: our soldiers are being treated like second-class citizens and are being forced to give up their constitutional rights.

Justice O'Connor wrote a bitter dissent:

> In my view, conduct of the type alleged in this case is so far beyond the bounds of human decency that as a matter of law it simply cannot be considered a part of the military mission . . . [and we] cannot insulate defendants from liability for deliberate and calculated exposure of otherwise healthy military personnel to medical experimentation without their consent, outside of any combat, combat training, or military exigency, and for no other reason than to gather information on the effect of lysergic acid diethylamide on human beings.
>
> No judicially crafted rule should insulate from liability the involuntary and unknowing human experimentation alleged to have occurred in this case.

Justices William Brennan, Thurgood Marshall and John Stevens also vigorously dissented. Their joint dissenting opinion found that the Army had violated the Nuremburg Code, regarding medical experimentation on human beings. They concluded that the actions of the government were "serious violations of the constitutional rights of soldiers [that] must be exposed and punished."

The result of the decision is that all of the defendants were immune from suit. The Supreme Court cloaked the Army, and all persons acting under their "authority," with immunity. Had Germany won World War II, lawsuits against the Reich would have been treated in the same manner, and the Nuremburg Trials would not have occurred. As the dissent stated, "soldiers ought not be asked to defend a Constitution indifferent to their essential human dignity."

Epilogue

The dissenting opinions in these two soldiers' rights cases were joined by thecourt's liberal wing, which then included only Justices Brennan and Marshall. In the *Stanley* case, they were joined by a moderate, Justice Stevens (who later became more liberal) and by the court's relatively recently appointed conservative, Sandra Day O'Connor.

Conservative columnist James J. Kilpatrick called the *Stanley* case "indefensible" and added, "Something is sorely wrong here." Justice Stevens also authored the dissenting opinion in the radiation victims' case.

Only one of the radiation survivors, Reason Wareheim, was still alive as this book first went to press in 1987. Mr. Cordray died while the case was at the court of appeals, and Mr. Maxwell died while waiting for the Supreme Court to rule. James Stanley fared much better: he had substantially recovered from the ill-effects of LSD. From 1970 until1987, he had been a police officer with the Palm Beach County (Florida) police department. At age fifty-three, in 1987, Stanley was healthy and had resumed contact withhis ex-wife and daughters. However, he retained bitterness against the Army.

Although these cases denied remedies to members of our armed services and their families, the court arrived at its decision for different reasons. In the radiation victims' case, the court upheld the constitutionality of an actof Congress which limited attorneys' fees to ten dollars.

In the *Stanley* case, the court created its own exceptions to a federal statute. The court could have simply followed the statute and allowed Mr. Stanley to be awarded compensation. However, as in other cases, the court refused To overrule its 1950 decision in the *Feres* case, which established the doctrine that soldiers could not recover damages against the government "for injuries that arise out of their military service." The court's tendency blindly to follow earlier decisions has led to some of the nation's worst decisions.

Similarly, some of the longstanding statutes, like the one embodying the ten-dollar limitation, have survived because they have been around so long. Sunday closing laws were also approved because they had been around fora long time. But just because a law has been around for a hundred years or more does not make it good or constitutional. In fact, as Justice Stevens said concerning the ten-dollar limit, time and inflation made the law unconstitutional.

Congress has the power to change these decisions. It is up to Congress to provide justice to the men and women who are responsible for defending our country.

Endnotes

1. 589 F.Supp. 1302 (1984).
2. 105 S.Ct. 3180 (1985)
3. 549 F. Supp. 327.
4. 786 F.2d 1490 (April 21, 1986).
5. 483 US 669 (June 5, 1987).

Chapter Thirty-Five

Mother Knows Best?

"Where law ends, tyranny begins."

—William Pitt, British Prime Minister from 1783-1800

Linda Kay McFarlin dropped out of the public high school in Kendallville, Indiana, when she was sixteen. Kendallville is a town of about 8,000 people, located twenty-five miles away from Fort Wayne, and tucked into the far northeast corner of Indiana, about a half-hour drivefrom either Ohio or Michigan. Linda was an average student and was never kept behind at school. But she was bored, so she left the DeKalb County High School and found a job to support herself.

It was then that she met Leo Sparkman. They fell in love and married after a short engagement. She was only seventeen when they married, and he was barely a year older.

The Mother

Linda's mother, Ora McFarlin, was happy when her daughter got engaged and gave her consent to the marriage.

Linda had run away from home a lot when she was in her early teens. Sometimes, she had stayed out overnight, and her mother worried that she might come home pregnant one day. Mrs. McFarlin worked as a dishwasher at a nearby hospital and was relieved when Leo Sparkman married her daughter and took responsibility for her.

Leo and Linda Sparkman. Photograph by David Kurtz.

The Doctor

Linda and Leo Sparkman tried for three years to have children, without success. Disappointed, Linda asked her mother if she knew why they were infertile. Mrs. McFarlin told Linda that her fallopian tubes had been tied, but that she could have them untied if she desired to have children.

Linda could only recall having had one operation, an appendectomy five years earlier when she was fifteen-years-old. She went to see her family doctor, Dr. John Hines, who told her that he had, in fact, performed an appendectomy on her and had done nothing that would have affected her fertility.

Mrs. Sparkman and her husband didn't know whom they should believe, her mother or Dr. Hines. As far as Linda knew, Dr. Hines was the only one who had ever operated on her. And he said that he performed only an appendectomy. That is what he had told her five yearsearlier, and he told her the same thing again. But her mother told her that her tubes had been tied. One of them was lying.

The Lawyer

Linda and Leo Sparkman were determined to find out the truth. They made an appointment to see Richard Finley, one of the few lawyers in Kendallville. Mr. Finley wrote a letter to Dr. Hines, on behalf of the Sparkmans, asking him for details of the surgery that he performed on Mrs. Sparkman. In response to Mr. Finley's letter, Dr. Hines admitted the truth.

Hines admitted that he had performed a tubal ligation and that, as a result of the operation, Linda was sterile. He admitted that he never performed an appendectomy on Linda, but lied to her to conceal the true nature of the surgery. Dr. Hines stated that Ora McFarlin had received court approval for the operation and had agreed to indemnify him if there were "complications." The complications were just beginning.

Lawyer Finley drove to Auburn, Indiana, the county seat of DeKalb County, where the Circuit Court was located. He checked with the clerk's office. The clerk had no record of any lawsuit concerning either Ora or Linda McFarlin.

The attorney checked further. After an exhausttive search Finley found a document entitled "Petition to have tubal libation performed on minor and indemnity agreement." The petition read as follows:

State of Indiana
County of DeKalb:

PETITION TO HAVE TUBAL LIGATION PERFORMED ON MINOR
AND INDEMNITY AGREEMENT

Ora Spitler McFarlin, being duly sworn upon her oath states that she is the natural mother of and has custody of her daughter, Linda Spitler, age fifteen (15) being born January 24, 1956 and said daughter resides with her at 108 Iwo Street, Auburn, DeKalb County, Indiana.

Affiant states that her daughter's mentality is such that she is considered some- what retarded although sheis attending or had attended the public schools in DeKalb Central School System and has been passing along with other children in her age level even though she does not have what is considered normal mental capabilities and intelligence. Further, that said affiant has had problems in the home of said child as a result of said daughter leaving home on several occasions to association with older youth or young men and as a matter of fact having stayed overnight with said youth or men and about which incidents said affiant did not become aware of until after such incidents occurred. As a result of this behavior and the mental capabilities of said daughter, affiant believes that it is to the best interest of said child thata Tubal Ligation be performed on said minor child to prevent unfortunate circumstances to occur and since it is impossible for the affiant as mother of said child to maintain and control a continuous observation of the activities of said daughter each and every day.

Said affiant does hereby in consideration of the Court of the DeKalb Circuit Court approving the Tubal Ligation being performed upon her minor daughter hereby agree to indemnify and keep indemnified and hold Dr. John Hines, Auburn, Indiana, who said affiant is requesting to perform said operation and DeKalb Memorial Hospital, Auburn, Indiana, where said operation will be performed, harmless from and against all or any matter or causes of action that could or might arise as a result of the performing of said Tubal Ligation.

In witness whereof, said affiant, Ora Spitler Mc-Farlin, has hereunto subscribed her name this 9th day of July, 1971.

Signed
Ora Spitler McFarlin

The Judge

Mrs. McFarlin had appeared before Judge Harold Stump on the 9th of July, 1971, with her attorney. Judge Stump approved the order at once and signed his approval on the face of the petition. Linda McFarlin was neither present nor informed that her sterilization was being con- sidered. In a case like this, where a parent seeks to have her child sterilized, most judges would appoint a guardian *ad litem,* a guardian for the purpose of that case, to make sure that the interests of the child were considered. But this was not a normal case, and Judge Stump was not a very good judge. In violation of court procedures, Judge Stump didnot even have the petition filed with the clerk's office. That is why Linda McFarlin's attorney had difficulty finding it in the court's records.

Judge Stump held no hearing on the petition. He did not notify anyone that the petition was going to be considered. There was no one present to cross-examine Mrs. McFarlin. Linda McFarlin's sterilization was approved by the judge on her mother's word, alone. And because no one else knew about the judge's decision, there could be no appeal.

Daughter Versus Mother

No one told Linda McFarlin what happened in the DeKalb County Circuit Court that day. No one told her that she was going to be sterilized. Not her mother. Not her doctor. Not Judge Stump. Her mother and her doctor lied to her. They told her that she was going to have her appendix removed

On July 15, 1971, less than a week after Judge Stump's approval, Linda was admitted to DeKalb Memorial Hospital and she was irreversibly sterilized.

Understandably, the Sparkmans and their attorney were furious. Attorney Finley promptly prepared the necessary court papers, and, on November 26, 1976, Linda andLeo Sparkman filed suit against Linda's mother, Judge Stump, Dr. Hines, an assisting doctor, the anesthesiologist and the hospital. Their attorney argued, before the federal court in

Fort Wayne, that all of the defendants had conspired to deprive Linda Sparkman of her most valuablecivil right, the right to have children.

The federal judge ruled against the Sparkmans, finding that judges are absolutely immune from such suits and that Judge Stump's approval of the sterilization gave the doctors and the hospital immunity, as well.

The Sparkmans appealed The federal court of appeals for the area, that includes Indiana, is in Chicago, the United States Court of Appeals for the Seventh Circuit. Three judges are assigned to hear each federal appeal.

The court of appeals heard arguments in the case in January, 1977, and made its decision that March. Unanimously, the judges ruled that Judge Stump had had "no jurisdiction" when he ordered Linda McFarlin sterilized and that, therefore, he could be sued for damages. The court reasoned that judges were immune only from suits concerning actions taken within their authorized jurisdiction. And when judges act far beyond their authority, or outside of their jurisdiction, they are to be treated as ordinary citizens would be treated, with no immunity from lawsuits.

At last, it looked as though Linda Sparkman would receive some compensation, if only monetary, for the right that was taken away from her. But, then, Judge Harold Stump appealed the court of appeal's decision to the United States Supreme Court. The State of Indiana filed a brief in support of Judge Stump, arguing that judges must have absolute immunity, so that they will act without fear of retaliation.

A little fear would have been good for Judge Stump. Maybe he wouldn't have ordered a teenage girl to be irreversibly sterilized, without notice or a hearing, had he feared that one day he could be sued for it. Maybe Judge Stump would have asked Linda McFarlin if she objected to her sterilization, and maybe, just maybe, Judge Stump would have appointed counsel to represent the minor child.

Several mental health organizations filed briefs with the Supreme Court, in support of Leo and Linda Sparkman. The American Civil Liberties Union also filed a brief in support of the Sparkmans.

The Supreme Court

The United States Supreme Court heard oral arguments in the case in January, 1978, and issued its ruling in March. The court ruled five to three, with Justice Brennan not voting, to reverse the decision of the court of appeals. They ruled that Judge Stump could not be sued, that he was absolutely immune from lawsuits concerning his actions as a judge.[1]

Justice Byron White wrote the opinion for the majority of the court. He wrote that "because Judge Stump performed the type of act normally performed only by judges and because he did so in his capacity as a Circuit Court Judge, we find no merit to respondent's argument" that should deprive the judge of absolute immunity. Justice Potter Stewart, an Ohioan, dissented: "I think that what Judge Stump did on July 9, 1971, was beyond the pale of anything that could sensibly be called a judicial act."

The case was sent back to the court of appeals to determine whether the judge's immunity should shield the doctors and the hospital, as well as Ora McFarlin. The Court of Appeals ruled that all of the defendants wereimmune from suit and dismissed the case.

Epilogue

Linda Sparkman was still married to Leo Sparkman in 1987 when this book first went to press. They lived together in Kendallville, not far from Mrs. McFarlin. However, the mother and daughter no longer would talk to each.

Absolute immunity for judges is a court-made principle. It is not based on the Constitution of the United States, nor on a statute passed by Congress, nor by state legislation. It pure and simply is a shield made by judges, solely for judges. Federal judges have life tenure so that they can make their decisions without the fear that they will lose their judicial appointments. But, absolute judicial immunity can make judges into tyrants who cannot be questioned, except by appeal to a higher court. Absolute immunity places judges above the law. As we see from this case, they have the power to enforce, and to ignore, the law.

With ordinary cases, we do not want our judges to be sued because litigants are unhappy with the judge's decisions. In such a case, if a person disagrees with a judge's ruling, he or she can appeal it. However, with extraordinary cases, it may be in the interests of justice to seek to have a judge removed from office by complaining to a judicial review board. Federal judges can only be removed from office by Congressional impeachment proceedings, not the most effective route. Only three federal jurists have been removed by impeachment in the entire history of our republic.

Judge Stump's "order" was not an ordinary court decision. It was made *ex parte*, which means that it was made with only one side being present. This is only allowed when an emergency prevents the other side from being notified, and, in such cases, decisions can only be temporary ones, lasting no more than ten days. And when this ten-day period expires, there must be a hearing to which both sides are invited to attend.

Judge Stump made no effort to notify Linda McFarlin of the case against her, yet he ordered an irreversible operation to be performed. Judge Stump heard no testimony, allowed no examination of witnesses and depriveda young woman of due process, a fair hearing, the right to counsel, the right to cross-examine witnesses against her, theright to present witnesses on her behalf, and, worst of all, he deprived her of her natural and constitutional right to motherhood. This ruling, which gives Judge Stump,and all other judges, absolute immunity, should be changed by a constitutional amendment which gives judgesonly limited immunity. A statute along the same lines may be effective, but judges would have an opportunity to overturn such a statute. No court, not even the Supreme Court, can ignore or overturn an explicit constitutional amendment.

The Supreme Court created absolute immunity for judges out of thin air. No law or constitutional provision requires it. Similarly, the court created "qualified" immunity for police officers and prosecutors. This judge-created immunity has led to more police violence against civilians because officers believe that they won't be prosecuted. The tide may be turning against "qualified" immunity for police officers because of the omnipresence of cameras, which have captured police killings around the country.

Endnote

1. *Stump v. Sparkman,* 435 U.S. 349 (1978).

Chapter Thirty-Six

What's Bugging You?

—Benjamin Franklin

—Richard M. Nixon, 37th U.S. President

A fresh bit of *Catch 22* from the Supreme Court: Since you can never be sure if the government is secretly spying on you, you can never sue the government for spying on you. And because unless you were actually wiretapped by the government, you cannot sue to keep other citizens from being wiretapped by the government. And you can't know if your privacy was violated by the government because the government doesn't have to tell you if it read your emails.

In 2008, Congress expanded the Foreign Intelligence Surveillance Act to allow the government to initiate a wiretap on a foreign national suspected of involvement of terrorism. It was a bit belated: three years earlier the *New York Times* revealed that the Feds were already doing this. Since the surveillance occurred without a warrant, privacy groups like the ACLU and Amnesty International sued to stop the practice, fearing that U.S. citizens, protected under the Fourth Amendment from unreasonable searches and seizures, would also be caught in the government's system.

On Feburary 26, 2013, by a 5-4 vote led by its conservative members, the Court declined to hear that lawsuit. The Supreme Court sadly dismissed the ACLU's case, *Clapper v. Amnesty International*, which challenged the FISA Amendments Act (FAA)—the unconstitutional law that allows the government to wiretap without a warrant Americans communicating with people overseas. Under the FISA Amendments, the government can conduct surveillance without naming individuals and without a probable cause warrant, as the Fourth Amendment requires.

Standing to Sue

The U.S. Supreme Court has long held that plaintiffs need to have "standing," or injury in fact, in order to bring a case. This is based on the "case or controversy clause" of the constitution. The Foundation Fathers did not want the courts to issue "advisory opinions," it wanted courts only to rule on actual, not theoretical, disputes.

But the ACLU's dispute with government surveillance is not a theoretical dispute. The court didn't address the constitutionality of the law, but instead ruled that the plaintiffs—a group of lawyers, journalists, and human rights advocates who regularly communicate with likely"targets" of FAA wiretapping—couldn't prove thesurveillance was "certainly impending," so therefore didn't have the "standing" necessary to sue. In other words, since the Americans did not have definitive proof that they were being surveilled by the NSA—a fact the government nearly always keeps secret—they cannot challenge the constitutionality of the statute.

General James Clapper testifying before Congress.

The majority's reasoning was that only those affected by a law–those with legal standing–could file a complaint. And Amnesty International and the ACLU didn't know if they were affected. Nor could they. Clearly they wouldn't know if their electronic communication had been part of a government wiretap, since the practice is secret. And the fear that they *might* be included in such surveillance isn't enough. Writing for the majority, Justice Alito suggested that because the law "at most *authorizes*—but does not*mandate* or *direct*—the surveillance that respondents fear, respondents' allegations are necessarily conjectural."

And, further, even if members of either group had contact with foreign parties who might be   targeted under FISA–thereby possibly giving the organizations standing to contest the law–that, too, would bespeculation. After all, there are many other ways in which the government could wiretap those contacts besides FISA.

And *finally*, even if they *knew* the government sought to use FISA to monitor their communications, it's possible that the secret court that determined if such surveillance can go ahead might reject the government's argument. Alito summarizes: "We decline to abandon our usual reluctance to endorse standing theories that rest on speculation about the decisions of independent actors." Remove the triple negative and you get: Speculation about application of a law isn't application of a law.

Justice Stephen Breyer, writing in dissent, said that he would have allowed the lawsuit to move forward because he thinks "the government has a strong motive to listen to conversations of the kind described." Justice Breyer's dissent points out that future conduct can never be predict anything with 100% certainty, and if certainty was a requirement for standing, then virtually no cases wouldever reach conclusion. Justice Breyer runs through dozens of cases where standing has been found for plaintiffs in situations where plaintiffs had a reasonable fear of harm, and in many of those cases, the plaintiffs were much less certain than the lawyers, human rights workers andjournalist in *Clapper*. Breyer summed up the absurdity of the "certainly impending" standard by saying,

One can, of course, always imagine some special circumstance that negates a virtual likelihood, no matterhow strong. But the same is true about most, if not all, ordinary inferences about future events. Perhaps, despite pouring rain, the streets will remain dry (due to thepresence of a special chemical).

This standard is especially problematic when the harm is illegal surveillance conducted by secret government programs. Unlike physical searches of a home, electronic surveillance is by its nature hidden from the people affected, and national security surveillance is rarely made public or used in domestic criminal prosecutions. Thus, under the Supreme Court's rule, regardless of whether its surveillance was legal or constitutional, the government candeny standing to a victim of illegal surveillance just by never revealing its illegal actions to the person affected. Essentially, one can't challenge the government's surveillance unless the government agrees.

"We need only assume that the government is doing its job (to find out about, and combat terrorism) in order to conclude that there is a high probability that the government will intercept at least some electronic communication to which at least some of the plaintiffs are party," Breyer said. "The majority is wrong when it describes the harm threatened plaintiffs as "speculative," Breyer said.

ACLU Deputy Legal Director Jameel Jaffer said:

> Justice Alito's opinion for the court seems to be based on the theory that the FISA Court may one day, in some as yet unimaginedcase, subject the law to constitutional review, but that day may never come. And ifit does, the proceeding will take place in a court that meets in secret, doesn't ordinarily publish its decisions, and has limited authority to consider constitutional arguments. This theory is foreign to the Constitution and inconsistent with fundamental democratic values.

The FISC Court

Foreign Intelligence Surveillance Court was created by the FISA Amendments Act. This court operates in secret, publishing opinions that the public and Congress cannot read. Further, the judges on this court are appointed by one man, Chief Justice Roberts, without Senate confirmation. The Founding Fathers would roll over in their graves about these revelations because the FISC violates every principle of checks and balances that the Constitution created. Eleven of the twelve judges are from one political party (Republican) and worse, they are from one mindset: the government can do no wrong. This court granted 99.9% of the requests from the Justice Department for wiretapping.

It's Not Over

Four months after the Supreme Court slammed thedoor on challenges to the Foreign Intelligence Surveillance program, a little-known intelligence officer, Edward Snowden, released information about the FISA court's "secret" orders.

Snowden gave information to the *Guardian*, a leading British newspaper. The *Guardian* released an order issued by the FISC that compelled a Verizon subsidiary—Verizon Business Network Services (VBNS)—to hand over, on an "ongoing, daily basis," details for every phone call placed on its network for a prospective three-month period. Collecting those details—"metadata" that reveals who people talk to, for how long, how often, and from where— allows the government to paint an alarmingly detailed picture of Americans' private lives. The FISC order cited Section 215 of the Patriot Act as its legal basis, yet the breadth of the authority it granted to the government is simply incompatible with the text of the statute.

In the wake of Edward Snowden's revelations about the NSA's unprecedented mass surveillance of phone calls, the ACLU filed a lawsuit charging that the program violates Americans' constitutional rights of free speech,association, and privacy.

This lawsuit was file one day after the ACLUsubmitted a motion to the Foreign Intelligence Surveillance Court (FISC) seeking the release of secret court opinionson the Patriot Act's Section 215, which has been interpreted to authorize this warrantless and suspicionless collection of phone records.

The ACLU stated that it is "an organization that advocates for and litigates to defend the civil liberties of society's most vulnerable, the staff at the ACLU naturally use the phone—a lot—to talk about sensitive and confidential topics with clients, legislators, whistleblowers, and ACLU members. And since the ACLU is a VBNScus-tomer, we were immediately confronted with theharmful impact that such broad surveillance would have on our legal and advocacy work. So we're acting quickly to getinto court to challenge the government's abuse of Section 215."

The ACLU's complaint explains that the dragnet surveillance the government is carrying out under Section 215 infringes upon the ACLU's First Amendment rights, including the twin liberties of free expression and free association. The nature of the ACLU's work—in areas like access to reproductive services, racial discrimination, the that many of the people who call the ACLU wish to keep their contact with the organization confidential. Yet if the government is collecting a vast trove of ACLU phone records—and it has reportedly been doing so for as long as seven years—many people may reasonably think twice before communicating with us.

Criticism of the Clapper Decision

In addition to the ACLU and Amnesty International, many Constitutional law professors and others have criticized the *Clapper* decision. Stephen I. Vladeck, Constitutional law professor at American University said, "Absent a radical sea change from the courts, or more likely intervention from the Congress, the coffin is slamming shut on the ability of private citizens and civil liberties groups to challenge government counterterrorism policies, with the possible exception of Guantánamo."

Oregon Senator Ron Senator Wyden and other U.S. Senators are investigating how the National Security Agency spies on American citizens. Director of National Intelligence James Clapper is under fire for statements he made before Congress that suggested he had no knowledge about federal government programs that collected data on millions of Americans' phone calls and Internet activities.

In March, 2013, Intelligence Chief Clapper said at a Senate Intelligence Committee hearing that he was not aware that the National Security Agency was involved in such large-scale efforts.

The questioning of Clapper's statements followed Edward Snowden's disclosure that the NSA has been logging millions, perhaps billions, of calls and Internet activities.

Senator Wyden asked Mr. Clapper under oath, "Does the NSA collect any type of data at all on millions or hundreds of millions of Americans?"

"No, sir," Clapper responded. "It does not?" Wyden pressed.

Clapper recanted and said: "Not wittingly. There are cases where they could, inadvertently perhaps, collect -- but not wittingly."

Senator Wyden, one of the staunchest critics of government surveillance programs, said that Clapper did not give him a straight answer and called for hearings to discuss the two recently-revealed NSA programs that collect billions of telephone numbers and Internet usage daily.

Wyden was also among a group of senators who introduced legislation to force the government to declassify opinions of a secret court that authorizes the surveillance.

"The American people have the right to expect straight answers from the intelligence leadership to the questions asked by their representatives," Wyden said in a statement.

Conclusion

The American people have been injured in fact by the NSA's spying on them, and by the NSA's director lying to Congress about its extensive, abusive and unconstitutional surveillance program. The Supreme Court's ruling that the ACLU and Amnesty International don't have standing to sue to challenge NSA abuses undermines the Court's integrity and demonstrates that the "Rule of Law" is easily undermined by slamming the courthouse door and refusingto rule on the merits of a case.

Chapter Thirty-Seven

Of the Corporations,
By the Corporations and
For the Corporations

"I hope we shall crush in its birth the aristocracy of our monied corporations which dare already to challenge our government to a trial by strength, and bid defiance to the laws of our country."

—Thomas Jefferson

Vincent and Liza Concepcion responded to an advertisement for a free cellphone from AT&T Mobility. The California couple objected to a $30.22 charge for the "free" cellphone. The Concepcions had signed a two-year service agreement, a "take it or leave it" standard contract from AT&T Mobility. This agreement required the Concepcions to resolve disputes through arbitration andbarred them from banding together with others to seek class-action treatment, whether in arbitration or in traditional litigation in court.

In the District Court

The courts in California had ruled in 2005 that forced arbitration clauses in contracts, especially those that did not allow class actions, were forbidden.

The District Court for the Southern District of California consolidated the Concepcions' claim with a class action suit pending in the Court on the same issue. AT&T moved to compel arbitration. The district court denied the motion. It held that the class waiver provision of the arbitration agreement is unconscionable under California law and that California unconscionability law is not preempted by the Federal Arbitration Act. AT & T timely appealed.

AT&T Free Cell Phone Advertisement

In the Court of Appeals

The Ninth Circuit ruled against AT&T on the grounds that the arbitration provision represented an unconscionable provision and could not be enforced. The district court did not err when it held AT&T's class action waiver was unconscionable under California law, and thus unenforceable. Under 5a of the Federal Arbitration Act, arbitration agreements "shall be valid, irrevocable, and enforceable save upon such grounds as exist at law or in equity for the revocation of any contract." 9 U.S.C. § 2. The Ninth Circuit Court of Appeals ruled, "It is well-established that unconscionability is a generally applicable contract defense, which may render an arbitration provision unenforceable."

To be unenforceable under California law, a contract provision must be both procedurally and substantively unconscionable. Procedural unconscionability generally takes the form of a contract of adhesion, that is, a contract drafted by the party of superior bargaining strength and imposed on the other, without the opportunity to negotiate the terms. Substantive unconscionability focuses on overly harsh or one-sided contract terms. Both elements of unconscionability need not be present to the same degree; California courts use a sliding-scale: the more substantively unconscionable the contract term, the less procedurally unconscionable it need be to be unenforceable and vice versa.

At the High Court

The nation's High Court heard oral arguments on November 9, 2010. Justices Scalia and Sotomayor questioned Pincus (attorney for AT&T Mobility) about when unconscionability doctrines are made under state law.Pincus argued that the California law was not being applied uniformly. Scalia challenged that assertion when he asked, "Are we going to tell the State of California what it has to consider unconscionable?" Other justices questioned different issues arising from the unconscionability discussion and the scope of the rule AT&T was proposing. Deepak Gupta, representing the Concepcions, argued that the contract AT&T imposed on his clients was clearly unfair. He asserted that state law should be a guidepost in these questions. Some of his arguments drew criticism fromChief Justice John Roberts. Gupta concluded by arguing that California "has made a judgment that if you preclude class-wide relief. . . that will gut the State's substantive consumer protection laws."

The majority opinion was written by Justice Antonin Scalia, and joined by Chief Justice John Roberts and Justices Anthony Kennedy, Clarence Thomas, and Samuel Alito. "Requiring the availability of class-wide arbitration interferes with fundamental attributes of arbitration," Scalia wrote. "We find it hard to believe that defendants would bet the company with no effective means of review, and even harder to believe that Congress would have intendedto allow state courts to force such a decision."

Justice Antonin Scalia said the lower courts had failed to properly apply the Federal Arbitration Act, which overrides some state court decisions disfavoring arbitration. The dissent was written by Justice Stephen Breyer, and joined by Justices Ruth Bader Ginsburg, Sonia Sotomayor, and Elena Kagan. Breyer stated that class arbitrations are appropriate ways to resolve claims that are minor individually but significant in the aggregate. "Where does the majority get its contrary idea—that individual, rather than class, arbitration is a fundamental attribute of arbitration?" He said that without class actions, minor frauds would not be remedied. "What rational lawyer would have signed on to represent the Concepcions in litigation for the possibility of fees stemming from a $30.22 claim?"

Criticism of the Decision

The *New York Times* said: "This is the latest in the arbitration war—a battle over whether the United States will increasingly have a privatized system of justice that bars people from enforcing rights in court and, if so, what will be considered fair in that system. It would be grossly unfair for the court to let the corporation get away withwhat it wants to in *AT&T Mobility v. Concepcion*—a case that involves a small amount of money and a huge principle."

But the Supreme Court did let AT&T get away with grand theft: Theft of the consumers right to go to court, and the right to bring a class action. Both are gone, the corporations have won.

"The decision basically lets companies escape class actions, so long as they do so by means of arbitration agreements," Brian T. Fitzpatrick, a law professor at Vanderbilt University, said. "This is a game-changer for businesses. It's one of the most important and favorable cases for businesses in a very long time."

Nan Aron of the Alliance for Justice said, "Brick by brick, a wall of protection is being erected around large, powerful corporations to ensure that they never have to be held accountable for their actions or inconvenienced by the legal system that governs the rest of us. For the Roberts Supreme Court, this is the corporations' world; we just live in it."

The Court established a legal nonsequitor. You are allowed to challenge a powerful corporation through arbitration, but you have to do it on an individual basis. An individual challenge can never succeed because the cost of making the case is so high no one can afford to undertake it on their own. Voila! A process to resolve disputes has been established that effectively can never be used. How convenient for corporate America.

As Justice Elena Kagan wrote: "And here is the nutshell version of today's opinion, admirably flaunted rather than camouflaged: Too darn bad."

The *Concepcion* ruling is not an isolated event, nor was the holding mandated by the text of the Federal Arbitration Act. The conservative majority continued its trend of reaching, often beyond the bounds of reason, to grant powerful interests an ever-increasing shield against the rest of the country. What's more, this wall of immunity has been built quietly, in cases that rewrite statutory and procedural rules to make it harder for Americans to ever have their claims heard in court.

We are rapidly approaching a time when there is a private set of laws for big corporations, created and enforced by and for themselves and separate from the system that governs the rest of us. These rules, codified in the myriad contracts and agreements that govern countless everyday commercial transactions, have effectively relegated our laws and Constitutional guarantees to secondary status. By saying that the provisions of these agreements override rights well established in federal law, five justices have engaged in an astonishing abdication of their traditional role of protecting the rule of law.

States' Rights

After California outlawed bans on calls actions in 2005, at least 13 other states ruled that blanket class action bans by companies were illegal, according to a research paper by Myriam Gilles of the Cardozo School of Law and Gary Friedman, a New York attorney.

Forced arbitration clauses routinely are inserted into the fine print of contracts that people must sign to buy a product or service or get a job. Carnival Cruises uses forced arbitration – a fact that may hinder the passengers on the recent nightmare cruise the Triumph. The photo sharing service Instagram uses it–and some fear Instagram's parent company, Facebook, may be next.

Fortunately, Congress can—and must—act to restore the ability of Americans to hold powerful defendants accountable in federal court. The Arbitration Fairness Act, introduced by Rep. Hank Johnson and Sen. Al Franken, would prevent civil rights, consumer, employment, and antitrust claims from being forced into arbitration. The Alliance for Justice strongly supports this legislation, and all efforts to tear down the wall of protection and corporate privilege erected by this Court and ensure that all Americans are able to stand up for their rights.

In addition, putting class actions aside, forty state constitutions guarantee "a right of access to the courts to obtain a remedy for injury." The U.S. Supreme Court, allegedly controlled by a conservative majority, has ruled that corporations can override State rights, and the individual's constitutional right to a day in court.

Chapter Thirty-Eight

Which Side of the Border are you On?

"The very essence of civil liberty certainly consists in the right of every individual to claim the protection of the laws whenever he receives an injury."

— Chief Justice John Marshall in landmark case of
Marbury v. Madison, 5 U.S. at 163 (1803).

Sergio Adrián Hernández Güereca, a 15-year-old Mexican national, was with a group of friends in a concrete culvert that separates El Paso, Texas, from Ciudad Juarez, Mexico. The border runs through the center of the culvert, which was designed to hold the waters of the Rio Grande River but is now largely dry. Border Patrol Agent Jesus Mesa, Jr., detained one of Hernández's friends who had run onto the United States' side of the culvert. After Hernández, who was also on the United States' side, ran back across the culvert onto Mexican soil, Agent Mesa fired two shots at Hernández; one struck and killed him on the other side of the border.

Sergio Adrián Hernández Güereca

Petitioners, Hernández's parents, and Agent Mesa disagree about what Sergio Hernández and his friends were doing at the time of shooting. According to petitioners, they were simply playing a game, running across the culvert, touching the fence on the U. S. side, and then running back across the border. According to Agent Mesa, Hernández and his friends were involved in an illegal border crossing attempt, and they pelted him with rocks.

The shooting quickly became an international incident, with the United States and Mexico disagreeing about how the matter should be handled. On the United States' side, the Department of Justice conducted an investigation. When it finished, the Department, while expressing regret over Hernández's death, concluded that Agent Mesa had not violated Customs and Border Patrol policy or training, and it declined to bring charges or take other action against him. Mexico was not and is not satisfied with the U. S. investigation. It requested that Agent Mesa be extradited to face criminal charges in a Mexican court, a request that the United States has denied.

Hernández's parents were also dissatisfied and brought suit for damages in the United States District Court for the Western District of Texas. Among other claims, they sought recovery of damages alleging that Mesa violated Hernández's Fourth and Fifth Amendment rights. The District Court granted Mesa's motion to dismiss, and the Court of Appeals for the Fifth Circuit sitting en banc has twice affirmed this dismissal.

The U.S. Supreme Court ruled 5-4 that the parents had no right to sue. They did not expressly overrule *Bivens,* but they impliedly did.

Bivens

In *Bivens v. Six Unknown Fed. Narcotics Agents,* 403 U. S. 388 (1971), the U.S. Supreme Court, led by Chief Justice Earl Warren, broke new ground by holding that a person claiming to be the victim of an un-lawful arrest and search could bring a Fourth Amendment claim for damages against the responsible agents even though no federal statute authorized such a claim. The Court subsequently extended *Bivens* to cover two additional constitutional claims: in *Davis v. Passman*, 442 U. S. 228 (1979), a former congress-sional staffer's Fifth Amendment claim of dismissal based on sex, and in *Carlson v. Green,* 446 U. S. 14 (1980),a federal prisoner's Eighth Amendment claim for failure to provide adequate medical treatment.

The Dissent

Justice Ginsburg, joined by three other liberal justices, wrote in her dissent noting, "although the bullet happened to land on the Mexican side of the culvert, the United States, as in *Bivens,* unquestionably has jurisdiction to prescribe law governing a Border Patrol agent's conduct. That prescriptive jurisdiction reaches "con-duct that . . . takes place within [United States] territory." Justice Ginsburg said that the claims should be heard. She also referred to problems at the U.S. Mexico border that date back a decade: "Regrettably, the death of Hernández is not an isolated incident." She added, "One report reviewed over 800 complaints of alleged physical, verbal, or sexual abuse lodged against Border Patrol agents between 2009 and 2012; in 97% of the complaints resulting in formal decisions, no action was taken."

Ginsburg also wrote that "there is still no good reason why Hernandez's parents should face a closed courtroom door," noting that the circumstances would have been different if Hernandez had been "running up or down the United States side of the embankment."

"The Constitution does not stop at the border," ACLU attorney Lee Gelernt said after the ruling came down. The Mexican government filed a brief the case urging the justices to hear the case. Mexico's brief said that the "international human rights obligations" the U.S. has to Mexico, as well as "the fundamental right not to be arbitrarily deprived of life," require that the U.S. Supreme Court allow government agents to be sued for violation of basic human rights. It is sadly ironic that Mexico rightly is claiming the high ground on human rights

PART 8

Environmental Justice

Chapter Thirty-Nine

Global Warming

"One can see from space how the human race has changed the Earth. The polar icecaps are shrinking and the desert areas are increasing. All of this is evidence that human exploitation of the planet is reaching a critical limit. We cannot continue to pollute the atmosphere, poison the ocean and exhaust the land."

—Stephen Hawking, English theoretical physicist

"The facts are there that we have created, man has, a self-inflicted wound that man has created through global warming."

—Arnold Schwarzenegger, former California governor

"If you want to understand opposition to climate action, follow the money."

—Paul Krugman, winner of Nobel Prize in economics

The Clean Air Act of 1970 authorizes the Environmental Protection Agency to regulate power plants by setting a "standard of performance" for their emissions of pollutants into the air. That standard may be different for new and existing plants, but in each case, it must reflect the "best system of emission reduction" that the Agency has determined to be "adequately demonstrated" for the particular category. Since passage of the Act 50 years ago, EPA has exercised this authority by setting performance standards based on measures that would reduce pollution by causing plants to operate more cleanly.

In 2015 EPA issued a new rule concluding that the "best system of emission reduction" for existing coal-fired power plants included a requirement that such facilities reduce their own production of electricity, or subsidize increased generation by natural gas, wind, or solar sources. The Agency projected that it would be feasible to have coal provide 27% of national electricity generation by 2030, down from 38% in 2014. EPA explained that the Clean Power Plan, rather than setting the standard "based on the application of equipment and practices at the level of an individual facility, had instead based it on a shift in the energy generation mix at the grid level, cutting the use of coal plants."

The goal was to compel the transfer of power generating capacity from existing sources, primarily coal and natural gas, to wind and solar. The White House stated that the Clean Power Plan would "drive a[n] . . . aggressive transformation in the domestic energy industry."

West Virginia and 26 other states filed suit challenging EPA new rules. The case was filed in the Court of Appeals for the District of Columbia Circuit.   The Court of Appeals concluded that the statute could reasonably be read to encompass generation shifting and upheld EPA rulemaking.

West Virginia and the other states appealed to the U.S. Supreme Court.

Chief Justice Roberts, writing for the court, ruled:

> Capping carbon dioxide emissions at a level that will force a nationwide transition away from the use of coal to generate electricity may be a sensible "solution to the crisis of the day." But it is not plausible that Congress gave EPA the authority to adopt on its own such a regulatory scheme. A decision of such magnitude and consequence rests with Congress itself, or an agency acting pursuant to a clear delegation from that representative body.

Roberts used the freshly minted "major questions doctrine" to pass the buck to Congress and delay the regulation of power plant emissions.

Major Questions Doctrine

This case announces the arrival of the "major questions doctrine," which replaced normal text-in-context stat utory interpretation with some tougher-to-satisfy set of rules. Apparently, there is now a two-step inquiry. First,a court must decide, by looking at some panoply of factors, whether agency action presents an "extra-ordinary case." If it does, the agency "must point to clear congressional authorization for the power it claims," someplace over and above the normal statutory basis werequire. The result is statutory interpretation of an unusual kind. It is not until page 28 of a 31-page opinionthat the majority begins to seriously discuss the meaningof the Clean Air Act. And even then, it does not address directly what should be the question: Does the text of that law, when read in context and with a common-sense awareness of how Congress delegates, authorize the agency action here?

The majority claims it is just following precedent, butthat is not so. The Court has never even used the term "major questions doctrine" before. It is clearly made-up, judge-created bologna. The so-called conservative majority used this made-up doctrine to protect the coal industry, not to help clean up the air. While many conservatives have argued that liberal justices just makethings up, this is one clear instance where the con-servative justices just made up a new doctrine spun out of whole cloth.

The Dissent

Justice Kagan wrote the dissenting opinion. She was joined by justices Breyer and Sotomayor. Justice Kagan wrote,

> Today, the Court strips the Environ-mental Protection Agency (EPA) of the power Congress gave it to respond to "the most pressing environmental challenge of our time." *Massachusetts* v. *EPA*, 549 U. S.497, 505 (2007).

Congress charged EPA with addressing those potentially catastrophic harms, including through regulation of fossil-fuel-fired power plants. Section 111 of the Clean Air Act directs EPA to regulatestationary sources of any substance that "causes, or contributes significantly to, airpollution" and that "may reasonably beanticipated to endanger public health or welfare." 42 U. S. C. §7411(b)(1)(A). Carbon dioxide and other greenhouse gases fitthat description.

This Court has obstructed EPA's effort from the beginning. Right after the Obama administration issued the Clean Power Plan, the Court stayed its implementation. That action was unprecedented: Never before had the Court stayed a regulation then under review in the lower courts.

The limits the majority now puts on EPA's authority fly in the face of the statute Congress wrote. The majority saysit is simply "not plausible" that Congress enabled EPA to regulate power plants' emissions through generation shifting. But that is just what Congress did when itbroadly authorized EPA in Section 111 to select the "best system of emission reduction" for power plants. §7411(a)(1). The "best system" full stop—no ifs, ands, orbuts of any kind relevant here.

Criticism

Harvard Law Professor Lawrence Tribe wrote, the "major questions doctrine–an altogether amorphous weapon the court recently invented to strike the Center for Disease Control's eviction moratorium and the Occupational Safety and Health Administration's workplace vaccine-or-test man-date. Its premise is radical: wherever a court deems an agency's policy choice to have resolved a "major question," it must nullify that choice unless Congress, in enacting the relevant statute, anticipated the precise question and unmistakably authorized the agency's precise answer."

Professor Tribe continued, "That doctrine licenses judges to strike down whatever policy they disfavor–and invites agencies to opportunistically disclaim any regulatory authority they'd prefer not to exercise. It's also inconsistent with the fact that contemporary social problems are too complex and interwoven with changing circumstances for Congress to predict every policy answer with technical precision, requiring that it legislate in broad terms and task expert agencies with filling in the details. Routinely applying the 'major questions doctrine' might thus nihalistically nuke federal power to solve nearly any important problem."

Chapter Forty

Overturning Chevron Deference: Supreme Arrogance

"All too often arrogance accompanies strength, and we must never assume that justice is on the side of the strong. The use of power must always be accompanied by moral choice."

—Theodore Bikel, Austrian-American Composer

"Chevron deference," refers to a doctrine in which judicial deference is given to administrative action particularly within the realm of an agency's expertise. It was coined after a landmark case, *Chevron U.S.A., Inc. v. Natural Resources Defense Council, Inc.,* 468 U.S. 837 (1984). In the two-step analysis, a court first asks whether a statute is ambiguous, and if it is, whether the agency has engaged in authorized rulemaking based on a reasonable interpretation of the statute.

Loper Bright Enterprises is a commercial fishing company that sells, among other things, Atlantic herring. The Magnuson-Steven Fishery Conservation and Management Act of 1976 grants the National Marine

Services (NMFS) authority to "implement a comprehensive fishery management program." Under the Magnuson-Stevens Act, regional fishery management councils may propose to the **NMFS** the plans and amendments, including measures that are "necessary and appropriate" for conservation and management of the fishery. Among those regional fishery management councils that falls under the NMFS, the New England Fishery Management Council ("NEFMC") regulates the Atlantic herring fishery.

In 2018, the NEFMC suggested an amendment, which the NMFS approved after proper procedure in 2020. The amendment revised requirements for privately funded programs that monitor fisheries in New England. For Atlantic herring, the amendment required monitoring of 50% of herring fishing trips. The NMFS pays for a small part of the monitoring costs, while the fishing companies bear the rest. The proposed monitoring cost the Atlantic herring companies approximately $710 per day, reducing the annual income of the Atlantic herring industry by about 20%. **The fishing vessels would be required to carry observers on board their vessels to collect data about their catches and monitor for overfishing.**

In the Lower Courts

Loper, among other commercial fishing companies, filed a lawsuit against Gina Raimondo, the U.S. Secretary of Commerce, in the United States District Court for the District of Columbia. The lawsuit alleged that that the NMFS did not have authority to pass the regulation at issue because the governing statute did not provide it with that authority. The district court ruled in favor of the government, asserting that under the *Chevron* doctrine, an agency has broad latitude to act within the scope of its statutory authority. Loper appealed to the United States Court of Appeals for the District of Columbia making the same arguments, to which Raimondo responded that the statute provided the NMFS with a broad mandate to make regulations. The D.C. Circuit upheld the lower court's decision and analysis. The United States Supreme Court granted review on May 1, 2023.

At the Supreme Court

By a vote of 6-3, the justices overruled their landmark 1984 decision in the *Chevron* case. Under the Chevron doctrine, if Congress has not directly addressed the question at the center of a dispute, a court was required to uphold the agency's interpretation of the statute as long as it was reasonable. But in a 35-page ruling by Chief Justice John Roberts, the justices rejected that doctrine, calling it "fundamentally misguided." The Supreme Court could have ruled that there was no ambiguity in the law and that the district court and the Fishery Council went too far. The Supreme Court did not have to overrule a 40 year precedent.

The U.S. Supreme Court's ruling in *Loper Bright Enterprises v. Raimondo* ended the 40-year-old precedent of Chevron Deference. Judges reviewing administrative regulations and actions will no longer defer to the expertise of agencies on how to best interpret ambiguous language in the statutes that govern their responsibilities.

The fear surrounding this ruling is that politicized judges now have an easy path through which to expand their role into policymaking: interpreting arguably ambiguous statutes to their liking rather than deferring to an agency's expertise.

Justice Elena Kagan wrote in her dissent, "In one fell swoop, the majority today gives itself exclusive power over every open issue—no matter how expertise-driven or policy-laden—involving the meaning of regulatory law." 144 S. Ct. 2244, 2295 (June 28, 2024). The dissent continued, "the majority turns itself into the country's administrative czar." Id.

The implications of *Chevron* deference are clear in areas like environmental protection and health care. For example, career scientists at the Environmental Protection Agency (scientists who are long-term employees not political appointees) were traditionally given deference in interpreting "safe" amounts of mercury in the soil surrounding elementary schools.

Courts deferred to clinicians and medical doctors at the Food and Drug Administration and Centers for Disease Control and Prevention in their decisions to approve, for example, a vaccine and recommend a vaccine schedule. Without that deference, some fear that judges might overturn official agency actions based on political agendas that conflict with scientific principles and data.

The implications of *Chevron* deference in the area of patent law are far less straightforward, despite the Patent Office having a large number of implementing regulations in the Manual of Patent Examining Procedure and being uniquely situated at the forefront of scientific and technical advancement.

When the Supreme Court first issued its decision in the *Chevron* case more than 40 years ago, the decision was not necessarily regarded as a particularly consequential one. But in the years since then, it became one of the most important rulings on federal administrative law, cited by federal courts more than 18,000 times.

Although the *Chevron* decision–which upheld the Reagan-era Environmental Protection Agency's interpretation of the Clean Air Act that eased regulation of emissions–was generally hailed by conservatives at the time, the ruling eventually became a target for those seeking to curtail the administrative state, who argued that courts, rather than federal agencies, should say what the law means. The justices had rebuffed earlier (including by one of the same lawyers who argued one of the cases here) to consider overruling *Chevron* before they agreed last year to take up a pair of challenges to a rule issued by the National Marine Fisheries Service.

The agency stopped the monitoring in 2023 because of a lack of funding. While the program was in effect, the agency reimbursed fishermen for the costs of the observers.

After two federal courts of appeals rebuffed challenges to the rules, two sets of commercial fishing companies came to the Supreme Court, asking the justices to weigh in.

Chevron deference, Justice Roberts explained in his opinion for the court is inconsistent with the Administrative Procedure Act, a federal law that sets out the procedures that federal agencies must follow as well as instructions for courts to review actions by those agencies. The APA, Roberts noted, directs courts to "decide legal questions by applying their own judgment" and therefore "makes clear that agency interpretations of statutes—like agency interpretations of the Constitution—are *not* entitled to deference. Under the APA," Roberts concluded, "it thus remains the responsibility of the court to decide whether the law means what the agency says."

Roberts rejected any suggestion that agencies, rather

than courts, are better suited to determine what ambiguities in a federal law might mean. Even when those ambiguities involve technical or scientific questions that fall within an agency's area of expertise, Roberts emphasized, "Congress expects courts to handle technical statutory questions"– and courts also have the benefit of briefing from the parties and "friends of the court."

Moreover, Roberts observed, even if courts should not defer to an agency's interpretation of an ambiguous statute that it administers, it can consider that interpretation when it falls within the agency's purview, a doctrine known as *Skidmore* deference.

Stare decisis–the principle that courts should generally adhere to their past cases–does not provide a reason to uphold the *Chevron* doctrine, Roberts continued. Roberts characterized the doctrine as "unworkable," one of the criteria for overruling prior precedent, because it is so difficult to determine whether a statute is indeed ambiguous.

And because of the Supreme Court's "constant tinkering with" the doctrine, along with its failure to rely on the doctrine in eight years, there is no reason for anyone to rely on *Chevron*. To the contrary, Roberts suggested, the *Chevron* doctrine "allows agencies to change course even when Congress has given them no power to do so."

Roberts indicated that the court's decision would not require earlier cases that relied on *Chevron* to be overturned. "Mere reliance on *Chevron* cannot constitute a 'special justification' for overruling" a decision upholding agency action, "because to say a precedent relied on *Chevron* is, at best, just an argument that the precedent was wrongly decided"–which is not enough, standing along, to overrule the case.

Justice Clarence Thomas penned a brief concurring opinion in which he emphasized that the *Chevron* doctrine was inconsistent with the Constitution's division of power among the three branches of government.

The *Chevron* doctrine, he argued, requires judges to give up their constitutional power to exercise their independent judgment, and it allows the executive branch to "exercise powers not given to it."

Justice Neil Gorsuch filed a long (33-page) concurring opinion in which he emphasized that "[t]oday, the Court places a tombstone on *Chevron* no one can miss. In doing so, the Court returns judges to interpretative rules that have guided federal courts since the Nation's founding." He sought to downplay the impact of the ruling, contending that "all today's decision means is that, going forward, federal courts will do exactly as this Court has since 2016, exactly as it did before the mid-1980s, and exactly as it had done since the founding: resolve cases and controversies without any systemic bias in the government's favor."

Justice Kagan, who read a summary of her dissent from the bench, was sharply critical of the decision to overrule the *Chevron* doctrine. Congress often enacts regulatory laws that contain ambiguities and gaps, she observed, which agencies must then interpret. The question, as she framed it, is "[w]ho decides which of the possible readings" of those laws should prevail?

For 40 years, she stressed, the answer to that question has generally been "the agency's," with good reason: Agencies are more likely to have the technical and scientific expertise to make such decisions. She emphasized the deep roots that *Chevron* has had in the U.S. legal system for decades. "It has been applied in thousands of judicial decisions. It has become part of the warp and woof of mod-

modern government, supporting regulatory efforts of all kinds — to name a few, keeping air and water clean, food and drugs safe, and financial markets honest."

By overruling the *Chevron* doctrine, Kagan concluded, the court has created a "jolt to the legal system."

Kagan also pushed back against the majority's suggestion that overruling the *Chevron* doctrine would introduce clarity into judicial review of agency interpretations. Noting the majority's assurances that agency interpretations may be entitled to "respect" going forward, she observed that "[i]f the majority thinks that the same judges who argue today about where 'ambiguity' resides are not going to argue tomorrow about what 'respect' requires, I fear it will be gravely disappointed."

"Courts motivated to overrule an old *Chevron*-based decision can always come up with something to label a 'special justification,'" she posited. "All a court need do is look to today's opinion to see how it is done."

But more broadly, Kagan rebuked her colleagues in the majority for what she characterized as a judicial power grab. She lamented that, by overruling *Chevron*, the court had, in "one fell swoop," given "itself exclusive power over every open issue — no matter how expertise-driven or policy-laden — involving the meaning of regulatory law."

The Public Reaction

Roman Martinez, who argued the case on behalf of one of the fishing companies, applauded the decision. "By ending *Chevron* deference," he said in a statement, "the Court has taken a major step to preserve the separation of powers and shut down unlawful agency overreach. Going forward, judges will be charged with interpreting the law faithfully, impartially, and independently, without deference to the government. This is a win for individual liberty and the Constitution,"

But Kym Meyer, the litigation director for the Southern Environmental Law Center, decried the ruling in a statement. "[T]he Supreme Court today says individual judges around the country should decide the best reading of a statute. That is a recipe for chaos, as hundreds of federal judges — who lack the expertise of agency personnel — are certain to reach inconsistent results on the meaning of federal laws as applied to complex, technical issues."

Every law student for the past four decades knows *Chevron*'s familiar interpretive rubric, as it has been the anchor of administrative law in the United States for decades. One class of students I taught gave me a Chevron trucker hat as an end-of-semester gift to commemorate our time together and the case's central importance. Now the hat symbolizes little more than a time when judges recognized the limits of their own abilities.

Chevron's central point is that when a statute leaves a particular question unanswered or ambiguous and an agency is assigned responsibility for administering that statute, the agency is better positioned to resolve the ambiguity than a court, and a court should defer to the agency's interpretation if it is reasonable. This is a sensible rule for allocating interpretive responsibility that "reflect[s] what Congress would want," as Justice Elena Kagan noted in her dissent in *Loper Bright*. Congress, she wrote, "knows that it does not — in fact cannot — write perfectly complete regulatory statutes" and would prefer to have the inevitable ambiguities and gaps to be resolved by an agency. The agency has the relevant subject-matter expertise and political accountability because agency heads report to the president.

Judge Laurence Silberman is a conservative Republican judge on the United States Court of Appeals for the District of Columbia Circuit, the court that hears most challenges to administrative agency decisions. As Silberman put it in a speech to the American Bar Association in 1989, "*Chevron*'s rule—that the federal judiciary must defer to an agency's reasonable construction of a statute it is charged with enforcing, if Congress has not directly addressed the question at issue—is simply a sound recognition that a political branch, the executive, has a greater claim to make policy choices than the judiciary." As he noted, "The agencies—even the independent ones — have superior political standing to the life-tenured federal judiciary in performing that policy making function."

This was not just an abstract principle for Judge Silberman. The judge deferred to agencies during Republican and Democratic presidential administrations, to policies he undoubtedly agreed and disagreed with. It was one of the things that gave me faith in the judicial process and convinced me that courts are doing something other than politics.

The Roberts Court's rejection of this principle shows how far conservatives have come. They are no longer the advocates of judicial restraint they previously claimed to be. Far from it, they are decimating settled law at every turn. While Justice Gorsuch can claim in his concurrence that the Court's reconsideration of precedent is an act of "judicial humility" because it is an acknowledgment that judges do not always get things right the first time, it is hardly humble to overturn the decisions other people made with which you personally disagree. That is not modesty but a power grab.

Chief Justice John Roberts wrote the majority opinion

and he argued that this new framework of no deference makes sense because statutes "have a single, best meaning" and "agencies have no special competence in resolving statutory ambiguities. Courts do." So, under the new interpretive framework he has established, where agencies get no deference, Chief Justice Roberts will now be the one deciding whether a new product on the market that is designed to promote healthy cholesterol levels is a "dietary supplement" or a "drug" under the relevant statute. It will not matter what the Food and Drug Administration thinks. Or, to take another example from Justice Kagan's dissent, courts and not the Fish and Wildlife Service will now decide whether the Washington State population of gray squirrels is "distinct" for purpose of the Endangered Species Act. Want to know how much noise is acceptable for purposes of a statute that requires aircraft flying over the Grand Canyon National Park to "provide for substantial restoration of the natural quiet"? According to *Loper Bright*, John Roberts is the expert in that one, not the Department of the Interior or the Federal Aviation Administration.

At his confirmation hearing, Chief Justice Roberts said it was the job of the judge "to call balls and strikes, and not to pitch or bat." The *Loper Bright* decision, however, has taken agencies out of the lineup and replaced them entirely with federal judges.

The six-justice conservative majority on the Court now stands at the ready to reverse any agency decision it does not like, unfettered by any sense of deference of the agency view. It does not take a fortune teller to predict they will favor the conservative outcomes and reject the liberal ones, for that has been the pattern of this Court. Lower-court judges will certainly keep this in mind as they review agency decisions, and conservative judges will know the Court will have their back.

It is no wonder the Supreme Court has its lowest approval ratings on record, with 58 percent of the country disapproving of the way the Court is handling its job. Decisions like this undermine faith in the judicial process because people can see through the Court's rhetoric of just giving statutes their one true meaning. Anyone who speaks the language knows it is not that simple. Ambiguities and gaps will give the Court license to do whatever it wants, and it is usurping authority from people who know better—people in the fields of medicine, science, finance, and all the other areas where agencies set policies for good reason.

Justice Kagan's dissent notes that the majority decision replaces "a rule of judicial humility" with one of "judicial hubris." And because doing so requires overruling a 40-year-old precedent, she quipped that a good title for the majority opinion might be "Hubris Squared." If you consider not just *Loper Bright* but the entire term, it is clear the Roberts Court's hubris is growing exponentially, and there is no end in sight."

The U.S. Supreme Court's ruling today in *Loper Bright Enterprises v. Raimondo* dealt a severe blow to the ability of federal agencies to do their jobs by ending the 40-year-old precedent of "Chevron deference." Instead of deferring to the expertise of agencies on how to interpret ambiguous language in laws pertaining to their work, federal judges now have the power to decide what a law means for themselves. As a result, despite not being accountable to the people, judges will now be able to expand their role into the realm of policymaking.

Justice Elena Kagan wrote in her dissent, "As if it did not have enough on its plate, the majority turns itself into the country's administrative czar."

The decision has profound consequences, not only for the country's rule of law but also for how agencies—such as those protecting the public against everything from pollution and contaminated food to workplace hazards and rising drug prices—are able to function. Here's what you need to know.

The Balance of Power

We were taught in school about how the U.S. government's separation of powers is supposed to work: Congress writes the laws, the executive branch carries them out, and the judiciary—including the Supreme Court—resolves arguments about what these laws mean and evaluates whether they're being enforced properly. In reality, these powers overlap at times between the branches of government, and overall, the system relies on a certain degree of trust.

For instance, as society, technology and the economy have grown more complex, so, too, has the task of governance. Because Congress is not equipped to micromanage the day-to-day administration of the legislation that it passes, it must rely on federal agencies—under the supervision of the president—to carry out laws and policies according to their best good-faith interpretations. Likewise, federal judges have a role in determining the meaning of Congress's laws in order to settle disputes. But the act of policymaking has always belonged to the two elected branches.

The Supreme Court seized for both itself and lower-court judges a policymaking role that the Constitution did not intend for them to have. The court stripped many federal agencies tasked with protecting public health, public safety, and the environment—including the U.S. Environmental Protection Agency (EPA) and the U.S. Food & Drug Administration, to name just two—of their power to interpret the laws they carry out. Instead, federal judges now get to call the shots.

Chevron deference's detractors argue that the doctrine gives agencies a rubber stamp to impose onerous restrictions and rules. But as noted by the Brennan Center for Justice, a nonpartisan law and policy institute started by Supreme Court Justice William Brennan, federal agencies face legal challenges to their rules all the time—and only prevail in about 70 percent of these challenges, even with the Chevron doctrine on their side. In other words, their powers are far from unchecked.

An even more obvious problem with giving judges this unrestrained interpretive authority? The federal court system is huge—and the roughly 850 judges who sit on the lower courts are a philosophically and ideologically diverse group. And as the judicial appointments process has become increasingly partisan, the range of these judges' views has gotten even wider. Ending Chevron deference is tantamount to throwing a dart at a lower-court dartboard...and hoping for the best.

The Supreme Court in the *Loper* case gave the Supreme Court more power. As it did in *Bush v. Gore,* the Supreme Court is no longer calling balls and strikes: It is now calling all of the shots. Concerning the separation of powers, the Supreme Court's ruling is an arrogant seizure of power and a determination that the Court is better at making decisions than experts, scientists and those who spend their lives evaluated drugs, chemicals and environmental harm.

Afterword

I wrote the first edition of *Black Mondays* in 1987, thirty-seven years ago. The court was quite different then. Even though seven of the nine justices in 1987 were appointed by Republican presidents, the court was still quite moderate. Thurgood Marshall, appointed by Lyndon Johnson, and Byron White appointed by John F. Kennedy, were the only justices appointed by Democratic presidents on the court in 1987. William Brennan and John Paul Stevens, appointed by presidents Eisenhower and Ford, respectively, turned out to be very liberal. Sandra Day O'Connor, appointed by President Reagan, was moderate, as was Anthony Kennedy, also appointed by President Reagan.

Now the court is packed with far-right extremists, three appointed by disgraced, twice-impeached, one-term President Donald Trump. Many commentators have claimed that the *Dobbs* case overturning *Roe v. Wade* was the only time the Supreme Court took away citizen's rights. This is not true. The court took away consumer's rights when it ruled that the Federal Arbitration Act allowed corporations to take away the right to bring a civil case and have a jury trial. The court has also taken away the right of citizens in mostly Southern states to have access to the ballot box when it ruled that the Voting Rights Act was no longer valid. It also took away the right to breathe clean air when it ruled that the Environmental Protection Agency did not have the authority to regulate carbon dioxide emissions. The court has undermined the principal of "one man, one vote" by effectively overturning cases that had allowed citizens to challenge redistricting.

During the past two years I have been researching the Israeli Supreme Court. Israel gives its citizens broad access to the judicial system that our Supreme Court does not. The U.S. Supreme Court has exceptionally strict standing rules therefore closing the courthouse door on many litigants. It also has ruled that citizens cannot challenge gerrymandering in federal court (but allows challenges to gerrymandering in state court.) This makes no sense. In addition, the court has allowed badly gerrymandered districts to stay that way, tilting elections and depriving citizens of "one man, one vote."

Israel requires all judges to retire at age 70. This provides for more turnover on the bench and effectively setsterm limits. Life expectancy was about 40 years of age whenthe U.S. Constitution was written life more than 200 years ago. Now with life tenure, we may be stuck with Justice Amy Coney Barrett for 30 or more years. We have been burdened with Justice Clarence Thomas for more than 30 years. It is time to implement constitutional changes to the court. We could fix the term of judges at 12 years, and also impose a mandatory retirement age of 75. This would prevent judges appointed by rogue presidents like Donald Trump from having an outsized influence on the judiciary.

We now have the worst Supreme Court in my lifetime. Fifty years in the future historians will look back at the gun control cases, gerrymandering, abortion, *Bush v. Gore* and *Citizens United* cases as aberrations, mistakes and worse. *Bush v. Gore* was a judicial coup d'etat where the Supreme Court, on a purely political basis, overturned the Florida Supreme Court and installed George W. Bush as president, even though all the votes had not yet been counted, and George W. Bush did not win a majority of the popular vote.

The Supreme Court never should have taken that case and should have allowed Florida to finish counting its ballots.

In the last term alone, the High Court overturned *Roe v. Wade,* overruled a New York law that restricting carrying weapons without a permit and ruled that the Environmental Protection Agency was not allowed to implement regulations limiting power plant emissions. We have an exceptionally activist and regressive court that has no respect for *stare decisis,* forCongress or for the states.

By overturning *Roe v. Wade*, the Supreme Court overruled nearly 50 years of precedents. The three Trump-appointed justices, who all promised in their confirmation hearings, to respect *stare decisis,* reneged on their promises. They lied. Under oath. *Stare decisis* is a legal principle by which judges are bound by precedents. In Latin *stare decisis* means "to stand with the-things-that-have-been-decided."

The New York gun control law was in effect for more than 100 years. The court's timing was ironic as the murder rate nationwide from guns has spiraled out of control. I must add that the court, in an earlier term, overturned a California law that limited the sale of violent video games to children. Only an idiot would consider that violent video games are harmless. Many of the mass murderers of the past decade were young men addicted to violent video games. Similarly, global warming is a scientific fact of life, and the Supreme Court's overturning of EPA's reasonable regulation of coal-fueled power plants mocks those who believe that man has created global warming.

Constitution of the

United States

We the people of the United States, in order to form a more perfect union, establish justice, insure domestic tranquility, provide for the common defense, promote the general welfare, and secure the blessingsof liberty to ourselves and our posterity, do ordain and establish this Constitution for the United States of America.
[The Legislative Branch]

Article I

Section 1. All legislative powers herein granted shall be vested in a Congress of the United States, which shall consist of a Senate and House of Representatives.

Section 2. The House of Representatives shall be composed of members chosen every second year by the people of the several states,and the electors in each state shall have the qualifications requisite for electors of the most numerous branch of the state legislature.
No person shall be a Representative who shall not have attained to the age of twenty five years, and been seven years a citizen of the United States, and who shall not, when elected, be an inhabitant of that state in which he shall be chosen.

[Representatives and direct taxes shall be apportioned among the several states which may be included within this union, according to their respective numbers, which shall be determined by adding to the whole number of free persons, including those bound to service for a term of years, and excluding Indians not taxed, three fifths of all other Persons.][1] The actual Enumeration shall be made within three years after the first meeting of the Congress of the United States, and within every subsequent term of ten years, in such manner as they shall by law direct. The number of Representatives shall not exceed one for every thirty thousand, but each state shall have at least one Representative; and until such enumeration shall be made, the state of New Hampshire shall be entitled to chuse three, Massachusetts eight, Rhode Island and Providence Plantations one, Connecticut five, New York six, New Jersey four, Pennsylvania eight, Delaware one, Maryland six, Virginiaten, North Carolina five, South Carolina five, and Georgia three.

When vacancies happen in the Representation from any state, the executive authority thereof shall issue writs of election to fill such vacancies.

The House of Representatives shall choose their speaker and other officers; and shall have the sole power of impeachment.

Section 3. The Senate of the United States shall be composed of two Senators from each state, [chosen by the legislature thereof,][2] for six years; and each Senator shall have one vote. Immediately after they shall be assembled in consequence of the first election, they shall be divided as equally as may be into three classes. The seats of the Senators of the first class shall be vacated at the expiration of the second year, of the second class at the expiration of the fourth year, andthe third class at the expiration of the sixth year, so that one third maybe chosen every second year; [and if vacancies happen by resignation, or otherwise, during the recess of the legislature of any state, the executive thereof may make temporary appointments until the next meeting of the legislature, which shall then fill such vacancies]. [3]

No person shall be a Senator who shall not have attained to the age of thirty years, and been nine years a citizen of the United States and who shall not, when elected, be an inhabitant of that state for which he shallbe chosen.

The Vice President of the United States shall be President of the Senate, but shall have no vote, unless they be equally divided.

The Senate shall choose their other officers, and also a President protempore, in the absence of the Vice President, or when he shall exercisethe office of President of the United States.

The Senate shall have the sole power to try all impeachments. When sitting for that purpose, they shall be on oath or affirmation. When the President of the United States is tried, the Chief Justice shall preside:

And no person shall be convicted without the concurrence of two thirds of the members present.

Judgment in cases of impeachment shall not extend further than to removal from office, and disqualification to hold and enjoy any officeof honor, trust or profit under the United States: but the party convicted shall nevertheless be liable and subject to indictment, trial, judgment and punishment, according to law.

Section 4. The times, places and manner of holding elections for Senators and Representatives, shall be prescribed in each state by the legislature thereof; but the Congress may at any time by law make or alter such regulations, except as to the places of choosing Senators.
The Congress shall assemble at least once in every year, and such meeting shall be [on the first Monday in December,][4] unless they shallby law appoint a different day.

Section 5. Each House shall be the judge of the elections, returns and qualifications of its own members, and a majority of each shallconstitute a quorum to do business; but a smaller number may adjourn from day to day, and may be authorized to compel the attendance ofabsent members, in such manner, and under such penalties as each House may provide.

Each House may determine the rules of its proceedings, punish its members for disorderly behavior, and, with the concurrence of two thirds, expel a member.

Each House shall keep a journal of its proceedings, and from time to time publish the same, excepting such parts as may in their judgment require secrecy; and the yeas and nays of the members of either House on any question shall, at the desire of one fifth of those present, be entered on the journal.

Neither House, during the session of Congress, shall, without the consent of the other, adjourn for more than three days, nor to any other place than that in which the two Houses shall be sitting.

Section 6. The Senators and Representatives shall receive a compensation for their services, to be ascertained by law, and paid out of the treasury of the United States. They shall in all cases, except treason, felony and breach of the peace, be privileged from arrest during their attendance at the session of their respective Houses, and in going to and returning from the same; and for any speech or debate in either House, they shall not be questioned in any other place.

No Senator or Representative shall, during the time for which he was elected, be appointed to any civil office under the authority of the United States, which shall have been created, or the emoluments whereof shall have been increased during such time: and no person holding any office under the United States, shall be a member of either House during his continuance in office.

Section 7. All bills for raising revenue shall originate in the House of Representatives; but the Senate may propose or concur with amendments as on other Bills.

Every bill which shall have passed the House of Representatives and the Senate, shall, before it become a law, be presented to the President of the United States; if he approve he shall sign it, but if not he shall return it, with his objections to that House in which it shall have originated, who shall enter the objections at large on their journal, and proceed to reconsider it. If after such reconsideration two thirds of that House shall agree to pass the bill, it shall be sent, together with the objections, to the other House, by which it shall likewise be reconsidered, and if approved by two thirds of that House, it shall become a law. But in all such cases the votes of both Houses shall be determined by yeas and nays, and the names of the persons voting for and against the bill shall be entered on the journal of each House respectively. If any bill shall not be returned by the President within ten days (Sundays excepted) after it shall have been presented to him, the same shall be a law, in like manner as if he had signed it, unless the Congress by their adjournment prevent its return, in which case it shall not be a law.

Every order, resolution, or vote to which the concurrence of the Senate and House of Representatives may be necessary (except on a question of adjournment) shall be presented to the President of the United States; and before the same shall take effect, shall be approved by him, or being disapproved by him, shall be repassed by two thirds of the Senate and House of Representatives, according to the rules and limitations prescribed in the case of a bill.

Section 8. The Congress shall have power to lay and collect taxes, duties, imposts and excises, to pay the debts and provide for the common defense and general welfare of the United States; but all duties, imposts and excises shall be uniform throughout the United States; To borrow money on the credit of the United States;

To regulate commerce with foreign nations, and among the several states, and with the Indian tribes;

To establish a uniform rule of naturalization, and uniform laws on the subject of bankruptcies throughout the United States;

To coin money, regulate the value thereof, and of foreign coin, and fix the standard of weights and measures;

To provide for the punishment of counterfeiting the securities and current coin of the United States;

To establish post offices and post roads;

To promote the progress of science and useful arts, by securing for limited times to authors and inventors the exclusive right to their respective writings and discoveries;

To constitute tribunals inferior to the Supreme Court;

To define and punish piracies and felonies committed on the high seas, and offenses against the law of nations;

To declare war, grant letters of marque and reprisal, and make rules concerning captures on land and water;

To raise and support armies, but no appropriation of money to that use shall be for a longer term than two years;

To provide and maintain a navy;

To make rules for the government and regulation of the land and naval forces;

To provide for calling forth the militia to execute the laws of the union, suppress insurrections and repel invasions;

To provide for organizing, arming, and disciplining, the militia, and for governing such part of them as may be employed in the service of the United States, reserving to the states respectively, the appointment of the officers, and the authority of training the militia according to the discipline prescribed by Congress;

To exercise exclusive legislation in all cases whatsoever, over such District (not exceeding ten miles square) as may, by cession ofparticular states, and the acceptance of Congress, become the seat of the government of the United States, and to exercise like authority overall places purchased by the consent of the legislature of the state in which the same shall be, for the erection of forts, magazines, arsenals, dockyards, and other needful buildings;--And

To make all laws which shall be necessary and proper for carrying into execution the foregoing powers, and all other powers vested by this Constitution in the government of the United States, or in any department or officer thereof.

Section 9. The migration or importation of such persons as any of the states now existing shall think proper to admit, shall not be prohibited by the Congress prior to the year one thousand eight hundred and eight, but a tax or duty may be imposed on such importation, not exceedingten dollars for each person.

The privilege of the writ of habeas corpus shall not be suspended, unless when in cases of rebellion or invasion the public safety may require it.

No bill of attainder or ex post facto Law shall be passed.

No capitation, or other direct, tax shall be laid, unless in proportion to the census or enumeration herein before directed to be taken.

No tax or duty shall be laid on articles exported from any state.

No preference shall be given by any regulation of commerce or revenue to the ports of one state over those of another: nor shall vessels bound to, or from, one state, be obliged to enter, clear or pay duties in another.No money shall be drawn from the treasury, but in consequence of appropriations made by law; and a regular statement and account of receipts and expenditures of all public money shall be published from time to time.

No title of nobility shall be granted by the United States: and no person holding any office of profit or trust under them, shall, without the consent of the Congress, accept of any present, emolument, office, ortitle, of any kind whatever, from any king, prince, or foreign state.

Section 10. No state shall enter into any treaty, alliance, or confederation; grant letters of marque and reprisal; coin money; emit bills of credit; make anything but gold and silver coin a tender in payment of debts; pass any bill of attainder, ex post facto law, or law impairing the obligation of contracts, or grant any title of nobility.
No state shall, without the consent of the Congress, lay any imposts or duties on imports or exports, except what may be absolutely necessary for executing it's inspection laws: and the net produce of all duties and imposts, laid by any state on imports or exports, shall be for the use of the treasury of the United States; and all such laws shall be subject tothe revision and control of the Congress.

No state shall, without the consent of Congress, lay any duty of tonnage, keep troops, or ships of war in time of peace, enter into any agreement or compact with another state, or with a foreign power, or engage in war, unless actually invaded, or in such imminent danger as will not admit of delay.

Article II

Section 1. The executive power shall be vested in a President of the United States of America. He shall hold his office during the term offour years, and, together with the Vice President, chosen for the
same term, be elected, as follows:

Each state shall appoint, in such manner as the Legislature thereof may direct, a number of electors, equal to the whole number of Senators and Representatives to which the State may be entitled in the Congress: but no Senator or Representative, or person holding an office of trust or profit under the United States, shall be appointed an elector.
[The electors shall meet in their respective states, and vote by ballot for two persons, of whom one at least shall not be an inhabitant of the same state with themselves. And they shall make a list of all the persons voted for, and of the number of votes for each; which list they shallsign and certify, and transmit sealed to the seat of the government ofthe United States, directed to the President of the Senate. The President of the Senate shall, in the presence of the Senate and House of Representatives, open all the certificates, and the votes shall then be counted. The person having the greatest number of votes shall be thePresident, if such number be a majority of the whole number of electors appointed; and if there be more than one who have such majority, and have an equal number of votes, then the House of Representatives shall immediately choose by ballot one of them for President; and if no person have a majority, then from the five highest on the list the said House shall in like manner choose the President. But in choosing the President, the votes shall be taken by States, the representation from each state having one vote; A quorum for this purpose shall consist of a member or members from two thirds of the states, and a majority of allthe states shall be necessary to a choice. In every case, after the choiceof the President, the person having the greatest number of votes of the electors shall be the Vice President. But if there should remain two or more who have equal votes, the Senate shall choose from them
by ballot the Vice President.][5]

The Congress may determine the time of choosing the electors, and the day on which they shall give their votes; which day shall be the same throughout the United States.

No person except a natural born citizen, or a citizen of the United States, at the time of the adoption of this Constitution, shall be eligibleto the office of President; neither shall any person be eligible to thatoffice who shall not have attained to the age of thirty five years, andbeen fourteen Years a resident within the United States.
[In case of the removal of the President from office, or of his death,

resignation, or inability to discharge the powers and duties of the said office, the same shall devolve on the Vice President, and the Congressmay by law provide for the case of removal, death, resignation or inability, both of the President and Vice President, declaring what officer shall then act as President, and such officer shall act accordingly, until the disability be removed, or a President shall be elected.][6]

The President shall, at stated times, receive for his services, a compensation, which shall neither be increased nor diminished during the period for which he shall have been elected, and he shall not receive within that period any other emolument from the United States, or anyof them.
Before he enter on the execution of his office, he shall take the following oath or affirmation:—"I do solemnly swear (or affirm) that I will faithfully execute the office of President of the United States, and will to the best of my ability, preserve, protect and defend theConstitution of the United States."

Section 2. The President shall be commander in chief of the Army and Navy of the United States, and of the militia of the several states, when called into the actual service of the United States; he may require the opinion, in writing, of the principal officer in each of the executive departments, upon any subject relating to the duties of their respective offices, and he shall have power to grant reprieves and pardons for offenses against the United States, except in cases of impeachment.
He shall have power, by and with the advice and consent of the Senate, to make treaties, provided two thirds of the Senators present concur; and he shall nominate, and by and with the advice and consent of the Senate, shall appoint ambassadors, other public ministers and consuls,judges of the Supreme Court, and all other officers of the United States, whose appointments are not herein otherwise provided for, and whichshall be established by law: but the Congress may by law vest the appointment of such inferior officers, as they think proper, in the President alone, in the courts of law, or in the heads of departments.
The President shall have power to fill up all vacancies that may happen during the recess of the Senate, by granting commissions which shallexpire at the end of their next session.
Section 3. He shall from time to time give to the Congress information of the state of the union, and recommend to their consideration such measures as he shall judge necessary and expedient; he may, on extraordinary occasions, convene both Houses, or either of them, and in case of disagreement between them, with respect to the time ofadjournment, he may adjourn them to such time as he shall think proper; he shall receive ambassadors and other public ministers; he shall take care that the laws be faithfully executed, and shall commission all the officers of the United States.

Section 4. The President, Vice President and all civil officers of the United States, shall be removed from office on impeachment for, andconviction of, treason, bribery, or other high crimes and misdemeanors.

Article III

Section 1. The judicial power of the United States, shall be vested in one Supreme Court, and in such inferior courts as the Congress may from time to time ordain and establish. The judges, both of the supreme and inferior courts, shall hold their offices during good behaviour, and shall, at stated times, receive for their services, a compensation, which shall not be diminished during their continuance in office.

Section 2. The judicial power shall extend to all cases, in law and equity, arising under this Constitution, the laws of the United States, and treaties made, or which shall be made, under their authority;--to all cases affecting ambassadors, other public ministers and consuls;--to all cases of admiralty and maritime jurisdiction;--to controversies to which the United States shall be a party;--to controversies between two or more states;--between a state and citizens of another state--between citizens of different states;--between citizens of the same state claiming lands under grants of different states, and between a state, or the citizens thereof, and foreign states, citizens or subjects.

In all cases affecting ambassadors, other public ministers and consuls, and those in which a state shall be party, the Supreme Court shall have original jurisdiction. In all the other cases before mentioned, theSupreme Court shall have appellate jurisdiction, both as to law and fact, with such exceptions, and under such regulations as the Congress shall make.

The trial of all crimes, except in cases of impeachment, shall be by jury; and such trial shall be held in the state where the said crimes shall have been committed; but when not committed within any state, the trial shall be at such place or places as the Congress may by law have directed.

Section 3. Treason against the United States, shall consist only in levying war against them, or in adhering to their enemies, giving themaid and comfort. No person shall be convicted of treason unless on the testimony of two witnesses to the same overt act, or on confession inopen court.

The Congress shall have power to declare the punishment of treason, but no attainder of treason shall work corruption of blood, or forfeiture except during the life of the person attainted.

Article IV

Section 1. Full faith and credit shall be given in each state to the public acts, records, and judicial proceedings of every other state. And the Congress may by general laws prescribe the manner in which such acts, records, and proceedings shall be proved, and the effect thereof.

Section 2. The citizens of each state shall be entitled to all privilegesand immunities of citizens in the several states.
A person charged in any state with treason, felony, or other crime, who shall flee from justice, and be found in another state, shall on demand of the executive authority of the state from which he fled, be delivered up, to be removed to the state having jurisdiction of the crime.
[No person held to service or labor in one state, under the laws thereof, escaping into another, shall, in consequence of any law or regulation therein, be discharged from such service or labor, but shall be delivered up on claim of the party to whom such service or labor may be due.][7]

Section 3. New states may be admitted by the Congress into this union; but no new states shall be formed or erected within the jurisdiction of any other state; nor any state be formed by the junction of two or more states, or parts of states, without the consent of the legislatures of the states concerned as well as of the Congress.

The Congress shall have power to dispose of and make all needful rules and regulations respecting the territory or other property belonging to the United States; and nothing in this Constitution shall be so construedas to prejudice any claims of the United States, or of any particular state.

Section 4. The United States shall guarantee to every state in this union a republican form of government, and shall protect each of them against invasion; and on application of the legislature, or of theexecutive (when the legislature cannot be convened) against domestic violence.

Article V

The Congress, whenever two thirds of both houses shall deem it necessary, shall propose amendments to this Constitution, or, on the application of the legislatures of two thirds of the several states, shallcall a convention for proposing amendments, which, in either case, shall be valid to all intents and purposes, as part of this Constitution, when ratified by the legislatures of three fourths of the several states, or by conventions in three fourths thereof, as the one or the other mode of ratification may be proposed by the Congress; provided that no amendment which may be made prior to the year one thousand eight hundred and eight shall in any manner affect the first and fourth clauses in the ninth section of the first article; and that no state, without its consent, shall be deprived of its equal suffrage in the Senate.

Article VI

All debts contracted and engagements entered into, before the adoption of this Constitution, shall be as valid against the United States under this Constitution, as under the Confederation.
This Constitution, and the laws of the United States which shall be made in pursuance thereof; and all treaties made, or which shall be made, under the authority of the United States, shall be the supreme law of the land; and the judges in every state shall be bound thereby, anything in the Constitution or laws of any Stateto the contrary notwithstanding.
The Senators and Representatives before mentioned, and the members of the several state legislatures, and all executive and judicial officers, both of the United States and of the several states, shall be bound by oath or affirmation, to support this Constitution; but no religious test shall ever be required as a qualification to any office or public trust under the United States.

Article VII

The ratification of the conventions of nine states, shall be sufficientfor the establishment of this Constitution between the states so ratifying the same.

Amendment I

Congress shall make no law respecting an establishment of religion, or prohibiting the free exercise thereof; or abridging the freedomof speech, or of the press; or the right of the people peaceably to assemble, and to petition the government for a redress of grievances.[8]

Amendment II

A well regulated militia, being necessary to the security of a free state, the right of the people to keep and bear arms, shall not be infringed.

Amendment III

No soldier shall, in time of peace be quartered in any house, without the consent of the owner, nor in time of war, but in a manner to be prescribed by law.

Amendment IV

The right of the people to be secure in their persons, houses, papers,and effects, against unreasonable searches and seizures, shall not be violated, and no warrants shall issue, but upon probable cause, supported by oath or affirmation, and particularly describing the placeto be searched, and the persons or things to be seized.

Amendment V

No person shall be held to answer for a capital, or otherwise infamous crime, unless on a presentment or indictment of a grand jury, except in cases arising in the land or naval forces, or in the militia, when in actual service in time of war or public danger; nor shall any person be subjectfor the same offense to be twice put in jeopardy of life or limb; norshall be compelled in any criminal case to be a witness against himself, nor be deprived of life, liberty, or property, without due process of law;nor shall private property be taken for public use, without just compensation.

Amendment VI

In all criminal prosecutions, the accused shall enjoy the right to a speedy and public trial, by an impartial jury of the state and district wherein the crime shall have been committed, which district shall have been previously ascertained by law, and to be informed of the natureand cause of the accusation; to be confronted with the witnesses against him; to have compulsory process for obtaining witnesses in his favor, and to have the assistance of counsel for his defense.

Amendment VII

In suits at common law, where the value in controversy shall exceed twenty dollars, the right of trial by jury shall be preserved, and no fact tried by a jury, shall be otherwise reexamined in any court of the United States, than according to the rules of the common law.

Amendment VIII

Excessive bail shall not be required, nor excessive fines imposed, nor cruel and unusual punishments inflicted.

Amendment IX

The enumeration in the Constitution, of certain rights, shall not be construed to deny or disparage others retained by the people.

Amendment X

The powers not delegated to the United States by the Constitution, nor prohibited by it to the states, are reserved to the states respectively, or to the people.

Amendment XI

The judicial power of the United States shall not be construed to extend to any suit in law or equity, commenced or prosecuted against one of the United States by citizens of another state, or by citizens or subjects of any foreign state.[9]

Amendment XII

The electors shall meet in their respective states and vote by ballot for President and Vice-President, one of whom, at least, shall not be an inhabitant of the same state with themselves; they shall name in their ballots the person voted for as President, and in distinct ballots the person voted for as Vice-President, and they shall make distinct lists of all persons voted for as President, and of all persons voted for as Vice-President, and of the number of votes for each, which lists they shall sign and certify, and transmit sealed to the seat of the government of the United States, directed to the President of the Senate;—The President of the Senate shall, in the presence of the Senate and House of Representatives, open all the certificates and the votes shall then be counted;—the person having the greatest number of votes for President, shall be the President, if such number be a majority of the whole number of electors appointed; and if no person have such majority, then from the persons having the highest numbers not exceeding three on the list of those voted for as President, the House of Representatives shall choose immediately, by ballot, the President. But in choosing the President, the votes shall be taken by states, the representation from each state having one vote; a quorum for this purpose shall consist of a member or members from two-thirds of the states, and a majority of all the states shall be necessary to a choice. [And if the House of Representatives shall not choose a President whenever the right of

Choice shall devolve upon them, before the fourth day of March next following, then the Vice-President shall act as President, as in the case of the death or other constitutional disability of the President.][10] The person having the greatest number of votes as Vice-President, shall be the Vice-President, if such number be a majority of the whole number of electors appointed, and if no person have a majority, then from thetwo highest numbers on the list, the Senate shall choose the Vice- President; a quorum for the purpose shall consist of two-thirds of the whole number of Senators, and a majority of the whole number shall be necessary to a choice. But no person constitutionally ineligible to theoffice of President shall be eligible to that of Vice-President ofthe United States.[10, 11]

Amendment XIII

Section 1. Neither slavery nor involuntary servitude, except as apunishment for crime whereof the party shall have been duly convicted, shall exist within the United States, or any place subject to their jurisdiction.

Section 2. Congress shall have power to enforce this article by appropriate legislation.[12]

Amendment XIV

Section 1. All persons born or naturalized in the United States, and subject to the jurisdiction thereof, are citizens of the United States and of the state wherein they reside. No state shall make or enforce any law which shall abridge the privileges or immunities of citizens of the United States; nor shall any state deprive any person of life, liberty, or property, without due process of law; nor deny to any person within its jurisdiction the equal protection of the laws.

Section 2. Representatives shall be apportioned among the several states according to their respective numbers, counting the whole number of persons in each state, excluding Indians not taxed. But whenthe right to vote at any election for the choice of electors for President and Vice President of the United States, Representatives in Congress, the executive and judicial officers of a state, or the members of the legislature thereof, is denied to any of the male inhabitants of such state, being twenty-one years of age, and citizens of the United States, or in any way abridged, except for participation in rebellion, or other crime, the basis of representation therein shall be reduced in the proportion which the number of such male citizens shall bear to the whole number of male citizens twenty-one years of age in such state.

Section 3. No person shall be a Senator or Representative in Congress, or elector of President and Vice President, or hold any office, civil or military, under the United States, or under any state, who, having previously taken an oath, as a member of Congress, or as an officer ofthe United States, or as a member of any state legislature, or as an executive or judicial officer of any state, to support the Constitution ofthe United States, shall have engaged in insurrection or rebellion against the same, or given aid or comfort to the enemies thereof. But Congress may by a vote of two-thirds of each House, remove such disability.

Section 4. The validity of the public debt of the United States,authorized by law, including debts incurred for payment of pensions and bounties for services in suppressing insurrection or rebellion, shall not be questioned. But neither the United States nor any state shall assume or pay any debt or obligation incurred in aid of insurrection or rebellion against the United States, or any claim for the loss or emancipation of any slave; but all such debts, obligations and claimsshall be held illegal and void.

Section 5. The Congress shall have power to enforce, by appropriate legislation, the provisions of this article.[13]

Amendment XV

Section 1. The right of citizens of the United States to vote shall not be denied or abridged by the United States or by any state on account of race, color, or previous condition of servitude.

Section 2. The Congress shall have power to enforce this article by appropriate legislation.[14]

Amendment XVI

The Congress shall have power to lay and collect taxes on incomes, from whatever source derived, without apportionment among the several states, and without regard to any census or enumeration.[15]

Amendment XVII

The Senate of the United States shall be composed of two Senators from each state, elected by the people thereof, for six years; and each Senator shall have one vote. The electors in each state shall have the qualifications requisite for electors of the most numerous branch of the state legislatures.

When vacancies happen in the representation of any state in the Senate, the executive authority of such state shall issue writs of election to fill such vacancies: Provided, that the legislature of any state may empowerthe executive thereof to make temporary appointments until the peoplefill the vacancies by election as the legislature may direct.

This amendment shall not be so construed as to affect the election or term of any Senator chosen before it becomes valid as part of the Constitution.[16]

Amendment XVIII

Section 1. After one year from the ratification of this article the manufacture, sale, or transportation of intoxicating liquors within, the importation thereof into, or the exportation thereof from the United States and all territory subject to the jurisdiction thereof for beverage purposes is hereby prohibited.

Section 2. The Congress and the several states shall have concurrent power to enforce this article by appropriate legislation.

Section 3. This article shall be inoperative unless it shall have been ratified as an amendment to the Constitution by the legislatures of the several states, as provided in the Constitution, within seven years fromthe date of the submission hereof to the states by the Congress. [17]

Amendment XIX

The right of citizens of the United States to vote shall not be denied or abridged by the United States or by any state on account of sex. Congress shall have power to enforce this article by appropriate legislation.[18]

Amendment XX

Section 1. The terms of the President and Vice President shall end at noon on the 20th day of January, and the terms of Senators and Representatives at noon on the 3d day of January, of the years in which such terms would have ended if this article had not been ratified; and the terms of their successors shall then begin.

Section 2. The Congress shall assemble at least once in every year, and such meeting shall begin at noon on the 3d day of January, unless they shall by law appoint a different day.

Section 3. If, at the time fixed for the beginning of the term of the President, the President elect shall have died, the Vice President electshall become President. If a President shall not have been chosen before the time fixed for the beginning of his term, or if the Presidentelect shall have failed to qualify, then the Vice President elect shall actas President until a President shall have qualified; and the Congress may by law provide for the case wherein neither a President elect nor aVice President elect shall have qualified, declaring who shall then act as President, or the manner in which one who is to act shall be selected, and such person shall act accordingly until a President or Vice President shall have qualified.

Section 4. The Congress may by law provide for the case of the deathof any of the persons from whom the House of Representatives may choose a President whenever the right of choice shall have devolved upon them, and for the case of the death of any of the persons fromwhom the Senate may choose a Vice President whenever the right of choice shall have devolved upon them.

Section 5. Sections 1 and 2 shall take effect on the 15th day of October following the ratification of this article.

Section 6. This article shall be inoperative unless it shall have been ratified as an amendment to the Constitution by the legislatures of three-fourths of the several states within seven years from the date of its submission.[19]

Amendment XXI

Section 1. The eighteenth article of amendment to the Constitution of the United States is hereby repealed.

Section 2. The transportation or importation into any state, territory, or possession of the United States for delivery or use therein of intoxicating liquors, in violation of the laws thereof, is hereby prohibited.

Section 3. This article shall be inoperative unless it shall have been ratified as an amendment to the Constitution by conventions in the several states, as provided in the Constitution, within seven years from the date of the submission hereof to the states by the Congress.[20]

Amendment XXII

Section 1. No person shall be elected to the office of the Presidentmore than twice, and no person who has held the office of President,or acted as President, for more than two years of a term to which some other person was elected President shall be elected to the office of the President more than once. But this article shall not apply to any person holding the office of President when this article was proposed by the Congress, and shall not prevent any person who may be holding the office of President, or acting as President, during the term within which this article becomes operative from holding the office of President or acting as President during the remainder of such term.

Section 2. This article shall be inoperative unless it shall have been ratified as an amendment to the Constitution by the legislatures of three-fourths of the several states within seven years from the date of its submission to the states by the Congress. [21]

Amendment XXIII

Section 1. The District constituting the seat of government of the United States shall appoint in such manner as the Congress may direct:A number of electors of President and Vice President equal to the whole number of Senators and Representatives in Congress to which the District would be entitled if it were a state, but in no event more than the least populous state; they shall be in addition to thoseappointed by the states, but they shall be considered, for the purposes of the election of President and Vice President, to be electors appointedby a state; and they shall meet in the District and perform such duties as provided by the twelfth article of amendment.

Section 2. The Congress shall have power to enforce this article by appropriate legislation.[22]

Amendment XXIV

Section 1. The right of citizens of the United States to vote in any primary or other election for President or Vice President, for electorsfor President or Vice President, or for Senator or Representative in Congress, shall not be denied or abridged by the United States or anystate by reason of failure to pay any poll tax or other tax.

Section 2. The Congress shall have power to enforce this article by appropriate legislation.[23]

Amendment XXV

Section 1. In case of the removal of the President from office or of his death or resignation, the Vice President shall become President.

Section 2. Whenever there is a vacancy in the office of the Vice President, the President shall nominate a Vice President who shall take office upon confirmation by a majority vote of both Houses of Congress.

Section 3. Whenever the President transmits to the President pro tempore of the Senate and the Speaker of the House of Representatives his written declaration that he is unable to discharge the powers and duties of his office, and until he transmits to them a written declaration to the contrary, such powers and duties shall be discharged by the Vice President as Acting President.

Section 4. Whenever the Vice President and a majority of either the principal officers of the executive departments or of such other body as Congress may by law provide, transmit to the President pro tempore of the Senate and the Speaker of the House of Representatives their written declaration that the President is unable to discharge the powers and duties of his office, the Vice President shall immediately assume the powers and duties of the office as Acting President.

Thereafter, when the President transmits to the President pro tempore of the Senate and the Speaker of the House of Representatives his written declaration that no inability exists, he shall resume the powers and duties of his office unless the Vice President and a majority of either the principal officers of the executive department or of such other body as Congress may by law provide, transmit within four days to the President pro tempore of the Senate and the Speaker of the House of Representatives their written declaration that the President is unable to discharge the powers and duties of his office. Thereupon Congress shall decide the issue, assembling within forty-eight hours for that purpose if not in session. If the Congress, within twenty-one days after receipt of the latter written declaration, or, if Congress is not in session, within twenty-one days after Congress is required to assemble, determines by two-thirds vote of both Houses that the President is unable to discharge the powers and duties of his office, the Vice President shall continue to discharge the same as Acting President; otherwise, the President shall resume the powers and duties of his office.[24]

Amendment XXVI

Section 1. The right of citizens of the United States, who are 18 years of age or older, to vote, shall not be denied or abridged by the UnitedStates or any state on account of age.

Section 2. The Congress shall have the power to enforce this article by appropriate legislation.[25]

Amendment XXVII

No law, varying the compensation for the services of the Senators and Representatives, shall take effect, until an election of Representatives shall have intervened. [26]

1. Changes by the 14th Amendment.
2. Changed by the 17th Amendment.
3. Changed by the 17th Amendment.
4. Changes by the 20th Amendment.
5. Superseded by the 12th Amendment.
6. Modified by the 25th Amendment.
7. Superseded by the 13th Amendment.
8. The first ten amendments (Bill of Rights) were ratified December 15, 1791.
9. The 11th Amendment was ratified February 7, 1795.
10. The 12th Amendment was ratified June 15, 1804.
11. Superseded by the 20th Amendment.
12. The 13th Amendment was ratified December 6, 1865.
13. The 14th Amendment was ratified July 9, 1868.
14. The 15th Amendment was ratified February 3, 1870.
15. The 16th Amendment was ratified February 3, 1913.
16. The 17th Amendment was ratified April 8, 1913.
17. The 18th Amendment was ratified January 16, 1919. It was repealed by the 21st Amendment.
18. The 19th Amendment was ratified August 18, 1920.
19. The 20th Amendment was ratified January 23, 1933.
20. The 21st Amendment was ratified December 5, 1933.
21. The 22nd Amendment was ratified February 27, 1951.
22. The 23rd Amendment was ratified March 29, 1961.
23. The 24th Amendment was ratified January 23, 1964.
24. The 25th Amendment was ratified February 10, 1967.
25. The 26th Amendment was ratified July 1, 1971.
26. The 27th Amendment was ratified May 7, 1992.

About the Author

Joel D. Joseph is the author of eighteen books, most about law. A graduate of Georgetown University Law Center, Mr. Joseph earned his economics degree at Northwestern University.

Mr. Joseph's constitutional law professor at Georgetown was Chester Antieau. It was during Prof. Antieau's constitutional law class that the germination of this book began.

Mr. Joseph has presented many cases to the Supreme Court, representing a diverse client base. His clients included more than sixty members of Congress, among them Senators Eugene McCarthy, Howard Metzenbaum and Trent Lott. He also represented Madeline Murray O'Hair, the director of the American Atheists.

In one case where he represented Ms. O'Hair, Joseph challenged the constitutionality of a federal statute authorizing the salary for a Senate chaplain. In that case Judge Ruth Bader Ginsburg, who became Justice Ginsburg, wrote the opinion for the court, ruling that the law authorizing the salary for a chaplain for the United States Senate was unconstitutional. *Murray v. Buchanan,* 674 F.2d 14 (D.C.Cir., 1982). The full D.C. Circuit reheard the case *en banc* and overturned Justice Ginsburg's decision.

Joseph has also represented many trade unions including the United Steelworkers Union, the Teamsters, the American Federation of State, County and Municipal Employees, the Screen Actors Guild and Laborers International Union. In one of these cases, Joseph challenged the constitutionality of the North American Free Trade Agreement. He argued that NAFTA was a treaty under the constitution, and that as such required two-third senate approval, which it did not receive. The district court ruled that NAFTA was indeed a treaty but ruled that the constitution nonetheless allowed international agreements like NAFTA to be passed by both houses of Congress by simple majorities. The Eleventh Circuit reversed, ruling that the case presented a non-justiciable political question. The Supreme Court denied certiorari.

Joseph also served as publisher at National Press Books for ten years. At National he worked with Senator Paul Simon on three books including *Advice and Consent: Clarence Thomas, Robert Bork and the Intriguing History of the Supreme Court's Nomination Battles*. Harvard Professor Laurence Tribe wrote the foreword.

Joseph was the Chairman of the Made in the USA Foundation for thirty years. He now is the CEO of California Association for Recycling All Trash (CARAT), www.calrecycles.com. He resides in California.